PRINCIPLES OF
HEALTH AND DISABILITY INSURANCE

THIRD EDITION

Dearborn
R&R Newkirk
a division of Dearborn Financial Publishing, Inc.

This publication is designed to provide accurate and authoritative information in regard to the subject matter covered. It is sold with the understanding that the publisher is not engaged in rendering legal, accounting or other professional service. If legal advice or other expert assistance is required, the services of a competent professional person should be sought.

This text is updated periodically to reflect changes in laws and regulations. To verify that you have the most recent update, you may call Dearborn at 1-800-423-4723.

Library of Congress Cataloging-in-Publication Data

Principles of health & disability insurance selling.

1. Insurance, Health—United States.   2. Insurance,
Disability—United States. 3. Insurance, Health—
Agents I. R&R Newkirk. II. Title: Principles
of health and disability insurance selling. [DNLM:
1. Insurance, Health—economics—United States.
2. Marketing of Health Services—methods—United States.
W 275 AA1 Pk5]
HG9396.P75   1987   368.3'8'00688   87–16281
ISBN 0-79310-585-4

Foreword

Health insurance today demands a significant role in financial planning for the client. Adequate protection against the ever-present threat of heavy medical expenses and loss of income due to disability must be a prime consideration, if a person's financial future is to be assured against the unexpected.

Most of us depend on earned income. Earned income is the compensation we receive for what we do in the workplace. Our most important asset, therefore, is our ability to earn income.

This course never loses sight of that fact. It constantly stresses the losses that may and do arise from illness or accident—those twin evils, which, in a flash, can cause an individual's earning power to evaporate into thin air. The course also emphasizes the obligation and responsibility that you, the agent, assume when you set out to protect a person's earning power against disability and the heavy collateral costs involved in serious illnesses and injuries. In this capacity, you are dealing with the very foundations of the individual's and the family's existence. You cannot meet this obligation unless you have a thorough grasp of what is at stake and know how to cope with the problems involved.

Throughout this course you will find techniques for assuring your competence in the health insurance market. Some of them are things for you to know, some are things for you to do and say, others are for your clients to see. Use these techniques and they will make you succeed.

The purpose of this course, therefore, is to help you gain a sound, thorough knowledge in the principles of health and disability insurance selling and thereby to become better equipped to discharge your professional obligation to present and future clients.

Acknowledgments

The publisher wishes to acknowledge the work of Arlene Foreman, CLU, ChFC, and thank her for her contribution to this third edition of *Principles of Health and Disability Insurance Selling*.

Table of Contents

Chapter 1
Selling Health Insurance Is Good Business

LESSON TEXT—Agent Advantages . . . Your Health Insurance Income . . . If You Sell Life Insurance . . . You in Action . . . Provides Flexible Interview Opportunities . . . The Rainy-Day Fund Delusion . . . Do You Want a Raise?

Today people are becoming acutely aware of the critical need for health insurance (both medical-expense and disability-income coverage). Newspaper headlines and news telecasts daily provide convincing evidence of the need for such protection. Stories of persons injured in accidents or stricken by disease, soaring health-care costs, cutbacks in Medicare payments—all underscore the important role of the health insurance agent in helping persons obtain adequate financial protection against heavy medical expenses and lost income due to disability.

Without such protection, many families easily can become financially devastated. Health-care spending more than tripled in a recent ten-year period. In one year alone, nearly 14 percent of all Americans (34 million people) were disabled, the largest percentage being afflicted with respiratory conditions and injuries.[1] The rising average age of Americans virtually guarantees an increased demand for medical care. Also, increased life expectancy means a longer risk of disability.

Even so, many agents sell life insurance and don't bother with health insurance. They are passing up a golden opportunity. The insurance products, of course, are strikingly different, but the prospects (and buyers) are the same. Certainly how much and what type of insurance coverage a person needs depend upon changing individual circumstances as they unfold in an unpredictable future. But there is no doubt that nearly every adult needs *both* health insurance and life insurance.

The field underwriter who is prepared to serve prospects and clients in both areas will open up many more sales opportunities than the agent who works only with life insurance and ignores the health insurance need.

[1]1990 Source Book of Health Insurance Data

AGENT ADVANTAGES

Your opportunities in the health insurance market are unlimited. Your success will be determined directly by the extent to which you capitalize on the market's potential and sales advantages.

Basic, Wide Appeal

The market for health insurance is growing, with no saturation point in sight. The need is everywhere and people recognize that need when they are made aware of the possibilities. People often feel secure and say, "I have health insurance." What they mean is that they have a *policy.* They may have a hospital policy or a surgical policy, but it may not provide adequate coverage. It is wonderful to have hospital or surgical coverage when one goes to the hospital or has an operation; however, not all disabling accidents or sicknesses require prolonged hospitalization or an operation.

In addition, when they say they have health insurance, they rarely mean *disability* insurance. Yet if there is no income, what happens to the mortgage payments? To the car payments? To life insurance premiums? And to other everyday needs?

Some people have disability income insurance purchased 15 or 20 years ago when $200 or $300 a month income may have been a fair measure of protection. Today, these individuals need considerably more disability insurance.

Disability insurance, in fact, is of personal interest to almost every working person because it appeals to every prospect's self interest. Disability insurance talks about cash for the insured's benefit. It counteracts the have-to-die-to-win attitude some still feel about life insurance. Its benefits are paid to the insured, not to some beneficiary. While no one would want to be ill or injured in order to collect on health insurance, the insured knows that when disability strikes and there is no other income, there will be many times the premiums paid—and more—returned as benefits. In terms of consumer need and appeal, there is probably no product in this country today which has greater market potential than disability insurance.

An Easy Market to Enter

Your prospects and clients need education and guidance in obtaining protection against risks which should not be left uninsured. They need the services of the well-informed, well-equipped and well-trained agent who talks their language, who can understand their individual situations and who can solve their problems on a personalized basis.

In some lines of business, experience is often obtained and knowledge available only on a trial-and-error basis. This is a slow, costly procedure. It is characteristic of the health insurance business, on the other hand, that the new agent can benefit from the successful experiences of others. He or she can avoid tedious experimentation and sidestep discouraging mistakes by applying field-tested, proven methods. A wealth of material for attaining success is readily available to give you a knowledge of the business and techniques for using that knowledge to your best advantage.

Quality Products

An essential requisite for success in health insurance selling is a quality product that delivers all its promises. Your products—the health insurance contracts you sell—are quality products. They will deliver everything they promise. A thorough understanding of your products will enable you to give sound presentations and answer questions raised by your prospects. There is a wide variety of contracts available to buyers today, and some policies fit certain situations better than others. The consumer is looking to you for the details he or she needs to make an informed decision. The information and products you have can drastically affect a client's standard of living if catastrophe strikes.

Always in Season

Selling health insurance—disability or medical expense coverage— is always in season. It is not like the resort or fuel oil business. For example, in the spring, physical resistance is often at low ebb. There is the constant threat of illnesses such as flu or sore throats leading to pneumonia or other serious ailments. In the summer, traveling is at its height. Vacations usually are taken and accidents are an ever-present possibility. In the fall, hunting and fishing are at their peaks. Harvesting is done on the farm. The home is being prepared for winter. Days grow shorter, so there is increasing traffic after dusk. And, with colder weather, illnesses and accidents are on the increase. In the winter, fresh air and sunshine are at the minimum. Hazardous streets are at their worst. Illnesses and accidents are frequent. Health insurance is needed in all seasons.

Health insurance selling is usually a simple sale. It is easier to get in to talk to a prospect. It is particularly adapted to telephone appointments and cold canvassing. Your sales presentation, built around your prospect's plans and a continuing income, is an attention-getter. The sales interview itself often requires less than an hour to complete from the approach to the completion of the application.

Once a contract has been placed, there is a minimum of detailed service work involved. Policy changes are rare, unless it is to increase the amount of monthly income provided or to broaden the coverage. You will find, however, that contact with your insureds at regular intervals, as discussed more fully later, improves persistency and leads to additional sales.

Selling health insurance can help many agents survive in today's highly competitive marketplace. Health insurance selling offers a quick road to income. For the new agent, it provides the opportunity to get under way rapidly, to start selling early in his or her career, and to start making money almost immediately. As the agent makes sales, a feeling of satisfaction and a sense of accomplishment is gained. The agent picks up sales momentum and with it increasing self-confidence. Health insurance selling helps an agent to become quickly and soundly established in the personal insurance business.

Successful agents will tell you that the greatest thrill they find in this business is making a sale. When an insured is laid up and receiving important benefits, the agent—whose wise and persistent sales efforts are responsible for the policy being in force—has a deep inner glow of relief and satisfaction. All of this starts with the sale. Each sale recharges the agent, gives renewed vigor, builds enthusiasm. "The best time to make a sale is right after making a sale."

More Frequent Sales

In the health insurance business, sales are frequent. Some agents sell at least an application a day for long periods of time. Three sales a week for many months in a row for some agents is not unusual. If an agent is also in the life insurance business, one or two health insurance sales a week (without interfering with regular life sales) is a reasonable beginning goal.

Prospects who don't want to *discuss* life insurance often readily *purchase* health insurance. Every interview provides you with the opportunity to go into collateral sales discussions. Regardless of what other personal insurance products you have in your sales kit, when you are in the health insurance business, you *know* you can sell. You feel self-confident.

YOUR HEALTH INSURANCE INCOME

Your health insurance income depends on skillful field work, your knowledge of contracts and your skill in the sales presentation and closing. It depends on sufficient field work, your activity in the field, and frequency of interviews. It depends on selective field work, the kind of prospects you talk to and your average premium per sale.

Your agency head or supervisor will be glad to help you set up a reasonable sales quota and forecast the commission earnings you may expect to receive over the years ahead by maintaining your quota. Keep in mind as you study the figures: if you write more business than the results are based on, you will earn proportionately more income! In this business the amount of money you earn depends on you.

This is a creative business. With the stroke of a pen you create something, which a minute ago did not exist. You create security to protect against modern times' most threatening problems—the problems of poor health or disability. Yet these are not problems you bring to your prospect. They are problems which already exist. You simply illustrate the easiest method of solving them.

You have the security of employment which comes from acquiring skills which one one can take away from you. You also have the added security for yourself and your family which comes from renewal commissions.

IF YOU SELL LIFE INSURANCE

Selling health insurance can help the well established life insurance agent to increase life insurance production, prestige, income and service.

A POOR BET

"Saving enough money for time or medical needs is feasible only for those who are lucky or those with considerable wealth. It is not feasible for even the moderately well-to-do, if they are not lucky . . . trying to save for medical and hospital costs isn't a good gamble. It isn't an Irish Sweepstakes. You don't risk a little in hope of winning a lot. Rather, you risk financial ruin in the hope of gaining a little.''

—Dr. Joseph G. Molner

Health insurance is a full-fledged partner to life insurance. It is personal insurance just like life insurance. It is a natural companion to life insurance. Adding disability and medical-expense insurance to your sales kit equipment is like adding more arrows to your quiver.

Life insurance protects against the actual death of dying too soon, or the retirement death of living too long. Health insurance protects against the worst of the three forms of death, the *living death.*

A potential, prolonged illness or disabling injury is of constant concern to almost everyone who works for a living. It is not as remote as death, nor as far in the future as retirement. Almost everyone knows of a case of a prolonged, expensive disability happening to a relative, or to a close friend, or to a business associate, or to a neighbor, or to someone. We hear of it happening almost every day.

The Need for Total Protection

Suppose John Walker is one of your clients. He is a good citizen in your community. When you first approached him several years ago, you found that he was a conscientious, loving father working hard to provide a comfortable living for his family. Like most men, he sought security for himself and his family. He had some savings, some bonds, some life insurance. But like many people he had a poor concept of what life insurance could do and the services you could render. You helped him to visualize his situation. You helped him to uncover some pressing needs. And you demonstrated to him how life insurance was the one, sure certain solution . . . how life insurance would step into his shoes, if he died too soon, and provide for his family while the children were growing up.

John Walker is grateful for the help you gave him. He is a close friend and a valuable center of influence. You are rightfully proud of the peace of mind you were able to provide by substituting your certain method for his uncertain method of building security. You are proud of the thorough, complete job you performed for John Walker—to the best of your knowledge and belief at that time.

Now, with a shock, it comes to you that this wall of protection around the Walker family is complete. A serious disabling sickness or accident can tear down this wall of protection around the Walker family so completely that it can never be rebuilt. As John Walker's insurance adviser, you have a serious responsibility to discuss his health insurance needs with him.

Conserving Life Business

Your present clients—regardless of their position in the business world, regardless of the size of their earned income, regardless of their family or personal responsibilities already covered by life insurance—need their incomes insured against interruption by sickness or accident. Who is going to make this needed protection available to your clients? Will it be you or your competitor?

Your insureds have confidence in you. They have demonstrated this confidence by buying life insurance from you. You have in your insureds' files information about them, about their families, about their incomes. You know they are the kind of people you can do business with because you have already done business with them. They will listen to you and seriously weigh your recommendations. You have a natural market for health insurance—a gold mine—in your files of life insurance policyowners.

And you have a grave responsibility to these insureds. A major cause of the lapsation of life insurance is the high cost of disability coupled with loss of income. With continuing income, and insurance covering medical expenses, people can pay their premiums; they can avoid borrowing against their life insurance cash values. Your insureds expect you to recommend the personal protection they should have: life, medical and disability insurance.

A Prestige Builder

By constantly keeping health insurance in mind and constantly making it a part of your selling activities as an adjunct to life insurance, you will impress your client and prospects with your comprehensive understanding of their insurance problems. You will win their admiration for your knowledge of personal insurance and its functions. You will further build prestige among many clients.

When you sell life insurance, you promise the delivery of dollars at a future date. That date may be decades away. Your insured may never see those life insurance dollars. Your other life insurance services often are to update existing policies, arrange for the repayment of policy loans or to help reinstate needed protection. These services are vitally important to your insureds. But because of their nature they differ from your services in providing protection against accident and sickness.

YOU IN ACTION

Through health insurance you deliver benefits directly to the eligible insured who may be worried, anxious and deeply disturbed about the many financial troubles which can follow illness or injury. This money for the insured is the result of your services. Your promises that money will be paid—to the insured for medical expenses or when he or she is unable to work—come to life and are manifest. They see you in action. Prestige cannot be built on a firmer, more lasting foundation.

Another remarkable feature about the health insurance business is that a claim is often the beginning of many new clients, a constantly widening circle of prospects on whom you can call with high recommendations and convincing evidence of the need for disability protection. Your client, who is happily receiving the benefits of the protection you made available, is ready for you to talk to his or her friends. This client feels, and rightly so, that he or she is doing friends a favor by introducing you to them. You have gained new stature and added respect in the eyes of such clients. You gain prestige as you build a permanent, satisfied, growing clientele. So another advantage you win in selling health insurance is an ever-expanding market.

PROVIDES FLEXIBLE INTERVIEW OPPORTUNITIES

One of the greatest agent advantages of health insurance as an additional sales tool is the opportunity to switch from one kind of sale to another. The life underwriter can easily pivot from a life insurance approach to a health insurance presentation, or vice versa.

Life to Health

It is not always possible to make a sale on the first life insurance interview. When there is strong buyer resistance, it may be advisable to switch to a health insurance presentation. You may salvage a sale out of what appears to be a hopeless situation. The conversation might go something like this:

"All right, (Prospect), you say you are not interested in this life insurance plan at the moment. We can talk about it again later on. But there is something I would like to discuss with you. That is your income in the event of a long disability.

"You may not realize that the average person is disabled several times during a lifetime. We don't know when it will happen. We don't know how long each disability will last. But we must be prepared to replace our earned income when it is cut off by illness or an accident.

"My company has a plan which is de- *signed for just that purpose. It could very well be a godsend to you. This is the way it works."*

To make this transition successfully, you must be sold completely on the concept that health insurance is *vital* protection. Believe wholeheartedly that the human life value is jeopardized by illness and injury as well as by death. Feel strongly that income is as essential to the person facing *living death* as it is to the family of the person who is no longer here or who is too old to work.

You must overcome buyer resistance and at the same time arouse interest. You may already have an organized life insurance sales presentation. This text furnishes you with the necessary

---

PIVOT PRESENTATIONS

When the Prospect Has Bought Health Insurance from You—

"(Insured), in order to complete my service to you, there is one thing I must call to your attention.

"I have been thinking about your family—your spouse and your children. If you need $1,000 a month—over and above whatever else you'd get from all sources—to keep your home running when you are disabled, could your family get by on any less than that if you should not recover?

"I notice on your application that you own $25,000 of life insurance. That is a fine start but at least $5,000 of that would go for bills and last expenses. That would leave $20,000.

"At the rate of about $1,000 a month—over and above what your family would get from all other sources—it isn't hard to figure that $20,000 won't last very long.

"When it's gone, what will your spouse do? With little or no money coming in—two children still to support and educate—there would be a serious problem, wouldn't there?

"How much can you set aside each month to guarantee that the income will be continued until your children are educated and grown?

When the Prospect Has Bought Life Insurance from You—

"(Insured), in order to complete my service to you, there is one thing I must call to your attention.

"You have done a fine job of providing for your family if death comes too soon. By the same purchase, you have increased the pension for yourself, if you live.

"But there is a third hazard to which we have not given sufficient consideration. That is the hazard of disability due to serious illness or accident.

"Statistics show that for everyone who dies this year, there will be at least a couple of people who will become totally disabled.

"Neither you nor I know when it may happen to us—or how long a period of disability we may be in for. But whether you are laid up for one year—or five—or ten—income must continue.

"You have made it possible for life to go on for your family if you die. Don't you think you should permit life to go on for all of you if you are sick or injured and unable to work?"

tools for equal success in health insurance. You need to make a smooth transition from one type of insurance to another with a well-organized sales talk on each. To save time, get into the meat of your subject quickly.

Your third requirement is skill in making the shift. This will come only with practice and you should have daily opportunities to try it. The more frequently you use this two-edged sword of personal insurance, the more proficient you will become.

Health to Life

The other technique used by many agents is to lead with a health insurance sale, and from the information obtained for the health insurance application (which is often more than the life agent uncovers in a fact-finding interview), develop life insurance business.

As one nationally recognized sales authority states: "You have to win your prospect's attention with your first ten words if you expect him or her to hear the next ten hundred words." Health insurance ideally is suited to the approach. And, as we discuss more fully in another chapter, the purpose of the approach is no more than to win agreement from your prospect to listen to the ideas you wish to present.

THE RAINY-DAY FUND DELUSION

People in the United States and Canada have long considered thrift a virtue. They try to save for the rainy day. They will tell you that they wish to build a cash fund they can call on in an emergency. The major emergency they instinctively dread is the cost of a serious sickness or an accident. Unexpected bills for doctors, hospital, an emergency operation, or prolonged disability all loom as a constant threat to their financial security. But, the trouble is, they dip into their savings from time to time. They use the money for a vacation, a down payment on an automobile, needed household furnishings or appliances, or for something else they feel they must have.

Any banker will tell you that most people, in spite of their best intentions, do not carry through their plans for saving money.

As a result, when the emergency of a sickness or accident arises, the rainy-day fund usually is already dissipated.

Releases Dollars for Life Insurance

When you sell a person health insurance, in effect, you sell a rainy-day fund. You guarantee by contract to set aside the amount your prospect agrees is required and which will be delivered as needed. The entire fund is created with the very first premium. For example, the amount of money may total $9,600 to be paid at the rate of $800 a month while the insured cannot earn an income—or $18,000 payable at the rate of $1,500 a month when the insured is laid up by either sickness or accident.

How long would it take your prospect to save those amounts of money? With put-and-take savings habits, it is unlikely that he or she could ever accumulate that much. But you can guarantee that the total amount will be available for just a few cents on the dollar. *And the individual can buy this sum of money with convenient installments.* In this way, *the rainy-day fund is immediately created.* This, in turn, releases extra dollars for additional life insurance needs.

Profitable Cold-Canvass Activity

Some days your careful planning pays off handsomely in saved hours and sales. You have arranged your calls in a concentrated area. And all day your planned sales calls go along smoothly. Your appointments go according to schedule. Even your luncheon date with a center of influence produces excellent leads.

By the time you complete your day's planned work, there are still several good working hours to spare. That is a time you might polish up your health insurance sales presentation by making some cold-canvass calls—approaching people you do not yet know, who work for a living in the area where you are at or others on your way back to the office.

Other days your careful planning is unavoidably upset. You are left stranded in your prospect's outer office. The person is very sorry, but he or she has been called into an important business meeting and cannot see you on time. But if you would care to wait about an hour, the person will be glad to see you then. What will you do? Kill time by reading magazines in the reception room?

It would be better for your morale, more interesting and more profitable to employ your time with health insurance cold-canvassing. No additional travel is involved. There is no extra cost. You will be smoothing your approach techniques, sharpening your sales ingenuity, and putting yourself in a positive frame of mind for the interview to follow. Some agents do very well making cold calls. You will not sell all to whom you talk during these spare hours, but the law of averages usually works in your favor to make such calls well worth the effort.

DO YOU WANT A RAISE?

If you are already selling life insurance, do you want an increase in income this year—this very month? Would you like to earn several thousand dollars more during the next 12 months? You can have this raise, if you wish. And you can have this increase in income without interfering with your regular life insurance sales. You can have this extra money simply by selling health insurance contracts *in addition* to life insurance.

Because you already have a nest of prospects in your existing policyowners, your ratio of preapproach calls to interviews should be excellent. Because these prospects already know you and have confidence in you, your ratio of sales to interviews should be high. You hold within your grasp the means for earning the extra income. Renewal commissions from one or more sales a week, 50 weeks a year, will swell your income as each year passes. Health insurance business, once it renews into the second year, shows remarkable persistency. **Thus you can build a stable, dependable income and broaden the foundation for your successful future.**

Many agents in the personal insurance business today will tell you that a substantial part of their income is from health insurance business written over the years. It should be obvious that here is a tremendous opportunity for well-trained and well-equipped field underwriters.

Selling health insurance fits naturally into your activities in many ways. It rounds out the services you perform. It strengthens your relations with insureds. It helps conserve life business which is already in force, and often results in additional life sales to insureds. When a health insurance claim arises, you can perform valued services for the insured which leads to new contacts, frequently with personal introductions. The advantages of including health insurance in the life agent's sales kits are numerous and profitable. About the only investment required is an investment in your training and in knowledge.

Moreover, this is more than well-paid work. It is socially beneficial and nationally important. People today more than ever before want the protection that health insurance provides. They need your services. If you do the job well, there can be no more beneficial or honorable and satisfying career in the world.

THOSE UNPREDICTABLE COSTS

"If personal health services could be purchased like any other goods or services— when desired and in the quantity and of the quality to fit one's purse—perhaps the problem of medical debt could be dismissed as of no more concern than the balance owed by a family on its automobile or television set. The cost of these items is known in advance.

". . . The cost of personal health services is not so known and when they are needed the consumer usually has no choice but to seek the necessary service, regardless of cost, even if it means going into debt.

"Systematic savings is not a solution, since families would not know how much should be saved annually.

"An effective and accepted mechanism today is an adequate insurance plan to meet the unpredictable costs of personal health services. . . such a plan is, in effect, a program of many people pooling their money and their risks."

—Health Information Foundation

Chapter 2
Sales Opportunities

While routine illnesses and injuries can drain our energy and resources, there is one major risk we all face which can rob us of almost everything. It can demolish our physical health and affect our minds, sideline us from society, and even bankrupt our homes.

That risk is prolonged disability—the living death.

LIVING DEATH

When a prolonged disability strikes, it throws us into one of the most crucial periods of our lives. It robs us of the ability to work and often creates catastrophic medical expenses. We find ourselves *physically alive*, but *emotionally* and *economically dead*. In the twinkling of an eye, our role is changed from income earner to asset spender. We become dependent on those who once depended on us. We are thrust outside the normal pattern of living and find ourselves stripped of the identity we had spent years developing.

All at once, the plans a person has made are jeopardized. Even the most carefully arranged financial plan can be wrecked by disability. What had been a plan for the future suddenly may be transformed into a *plan for survival*. Providing for economic necessities—food, clothing, shelter—usually becomes a serious problem. Providing for anything else—family recreation or children's education—becomes an impossibility. Even taking care of medical expenses and costs of rehabilitation strain or eliminate a lifetime's savings.

TIMES HAVE CHANGED

Disability wasn't always so dreadful from a financial standpoint. Years ago, families lived on farms and ranches. They built their own homes, grew their own food, provided their own fuel and made their own clothes. Each family was a tightly knit unit, entirely self-sufficient. When the head of the family was disabled, it was certainly shocking, painful and emotionally upsetting. But there generally were still plenty of ready, willing and able hands available to sow the crops, reap the harvest, tend the cattle. There was also little the family could do for the disabled person, aside from giving love and care. There were few hospitals or clinics. The disabled person was destined to stay home, attended only infrequently by the local doctor.

Today this picture has changed completely. We no longer live as closely knit families. Our relatives are often scattered far and wide. Each separate family unit, while related to other units, maintains its own home. Each stands on its own feet, independent and generally unaided by other family members.

Furthermore, few of us today can be completely self-sufficient. We depend heavily on exchanging our special talents for earned income. We use the dollars we earn to buy the services we need. The cost of availing ourselves of those outside services, especially those of doctors and hospitals, has skyrocketed, and continues to rise.

So, our primary concern is not *what* to get, nor *where* to get it, but *how* to obtain the money to pay for what we need and want.

To pay for what we need and want, all of us must have income regularly—and in sufficient amounts.

REGULAR INCOME

Over our working lifetime, each of us probably works somewhere between 75,000 and 80,000 hours. Our total earnings can amount to $500,000, $1,000,000 or $1,500,000 or more over our working life. This is important only as it determines how many of our needs and wants we can satisfy. However, what is most important is that we receive our earnings in *regular installments*—weekly, semimonthly, monthly.

Early in life, most of us see the wisdom of obtaining *regular income*. We cajole our parents into giving us a regular allowance. We try to earn money regularly by delivering newspapers, babysitting, mowing laws, etc. When we enter the business world, we seek a job that will keep us occupied regularly, full-time.

The size of the income we earn determines our standard of living. But, to provide even the barest necessities of life, we must have a regular income. The knowledge that we have a steady job that produces a regular income is really what makes it possible for us to plan ahead and dream our dreams!

The loss of regular income when disability strikes is, therefore, a basic problem we all face.

THE ODDS

The odds that we will face the problems brought on by disability are not as small as we might think.

There's little anyone can do about preventing most disabilities. They occur suddenly, and when least expected. They happen to millions of persons daily, forcing them to stay away from work. Fortunately, most of us who become sick or have an accident can return to our jobs fairly soon. However, the older we are the more chance for disability. This is borne out by statistics.

In 1988, for example, 9.6 percent of the country's population from ages 17 to 44 suffered limitation of activity due to illness or injury compared to 25 percent for such persons in the 45 to 64 age group.[1]

It seems ironic that most people have at least some life insurance coverage and many businesses are insured against the deaths of key employees—but the odds of a person suffering a long-term disability are more than four times greater than death for certain ages. This is revealed in Figure 2–1 which follows:

Figure 2–1
PROBABILITY OF BEING DISABLED
90 DAYS OR LONGER
MUCH MORE LIKELY THAN DEATH*

Age at Disability	Chance of Disability Compared to Death
22	3.5 to 1
32	4.3 to 1
42	3.5 to 1
52	2.8 to 1
62	2.3 to 1

1980 C.S.D. Mortality Table and 1964 Commissioners Disability Table

[1] 1990 Statistical Abstract of the United States

It now seems clear that an economic loss with disability can be even greater than with death because a disabled income producer continues in the role of a consumer. The disabled person becomes another dependent added to the family. In addition, the mobility of other family members usually is decreased, since many of their activities will be restricted for economic reasons or because of time spent in caring for the disabled individual.

Experience through the years also has shown what average number of persons will be disabled at various ages and how long such disabilities may last. Note the following in Figure 2–2.

FIGURE 2–2
HOW MANY PERSONS OUT OF 100
WILL BE DISABLED BEFORE AGE 65
AT VARIOUS AGES FOR THE PERIODS SHOWN

Age	For 6 Months	For 1 Year	For 2 Years	For 5 Years
25	22	14	12	8
30	22	14	12	8
35	21	14	11	8
40	21	13	11	8
45	20	13	11	8
50	18	12	9	7

Source:
1964 Commissioners Disability Table combined with 1958 Commissioners Standard Ordinary Mortality Table.

For persons who become disabled, what sources can they tap for the money needed to live on? Basically, there are only two sources of income and those are *people-at-work* and *dollars-at-work*. Let us consider those sources next.

PEOPLE-AT-WORK

For most of us, the primary source of the money we need is earned income. This is born out by a report which indicated that: Most people between the ages of 21 and 65 depend 100 percent on earned income to meet their daily cash needs.

Also, there are two kinds of earned income—*past* and *future*.

Past income has maintained our family's standard of living. It has provided us with food, clothing, shelter and whatever luxuries of life we have enjoyed. It has brought us and our families up to the present moment of our lives. But past income has done its work. It is gone. From here on, we must depend on *future* earned income.

Future Earned Income

Most people can make no plan or promise for the future which does not depend for completion upon the certainty of earned income. Parents promise their sons and daughters a good education. They promise a musically talented child that he or she will have the opportunity to attend a fine music school. A husband and wife plan someday to take a trip abroad. For these are the plans and promises out of which life is built. And for most people they are contingent upon the ability to continue to work, to continually earn income.

It has been said that when a young person is successful at 30, he or she will be increasingly successful during the years to come.

But the fact that people have a lifetime in which they have the right to expect to earn bigger dollars presents the big problem!

The plans made depend on those future dollars. Those are the dollars that someday will make possible a larger home. Those are the dollars that will send the children to college. Those are the dollars that are going to pay for trips the family hopes to enjoy. Those are the most important dollars because everything in the future depends on them.

And people normally depend on being able to work and earn income!

A temporary gap of a week or two in earned income, or an unexpected minor expense—these are not the uncertainties of the future which we fear. We know we can make up such losses—just as long as we can work and earn income, month after month, and year after year. But what if disability robs us of our ability to earn income next month, next year, and perhaps, even for the rest of our working lifetime!

What Is the Future Worth?

Have you ever stopped to calculate just how much an individual's future earned income totals? The accompanying chart shows that it's quite a fortune! For example, if you are 40 years old and earn $3,000 a month for the next 25 years, you will earn a total of nearly a million dollars! This money can be yours—provided you live and continue to work.

This fortune is yours—if a disabling sickness or injury doesn't rob you of the chance to earn it. But people become disabled every day.

So, while everyone depends heavily on future earned income, it may be lost—and often is—in the twinkling of an eye. Let a person's temperature vary a few degrees and he or she is too sick to work. Let timing be off a few seconds as a person drives along or crosses the street in heavy traffic, and he or she may be injured too seriously to work. In either case, a person's most valuable asset—future earning ability—is wrecked! (See Figure 2–3 on future earning power.)

FIGURE 2–3
FUTURE EARNING POWER

Age	Months to Age 65	$1,000	$1,500	$2,000	$3,000	$4,000	$5,000
			Total Future Earnings Based on Monthly Income of:				
20	540	$540,000	$810,000	$1,080,000	$1,620,000	$2,160,000	$2,700,000
22	516	516,000	774,000	1,032,000	1,548,000	2,064,000	2,580,000
24	492	492,000	738,000	984,000	1,476,000	1,968,000	2,460,000
26	468	468,000	702,000	936,000	1,404,000	1,872,000	2,340,000
28	444	444,000	666,000	888,000	1,332,000	1,776,000	2,220,000
30	420	420,000	630,000	840,000	1,260,000	1,680,000	2,100,000
32	396	396,000	594,000	792,000	1,188,000	1,584,000	1,980,000
34	372	372,000	558,000	744,000	1,116,000	1,488,000	1,860,000
36	348	348,000	522,000	696,000	1,044,000	1,392,000	1,740,000
38	324	324,000	486,000	648,000	972,000	1,296,000	1,620,000
40	300	300,000	450,000	600,000	900,000	1,200,000	1,500,000
42	276	276,000	414,000	552,000	828,000	1,104,000	1,380,000
44	252	252,000	378,000	504,000	756,000	1,008,000	1,260,000
46	228	228,000	342,000	456,000	684,000	912,000	1,140,000
48	204	204,000	306,000	408,000	612,000	816,000	1,020,000
50	180	180,000	270,000	360,000	540,000	720,000	900,000
52	156	156,000	234,000	312,000	468,000	624,000	780,000
54	132	132,000	198,000	264,000	396,000	528,000	660,000
56	108	108,000	162,000	216,000	324,000	432,000	540,000
58	84	84,000	126,000	168,000	252,000	336,000	420,000
60	60	60,000	90,000	120,000	180,000	240,000	300,000

DOLLARS-AT-WORK

Another way we can earn income is through investments. Properly invested, dollars-at-work can produce dividends, interest, royalties, value growth, etc.

However, large sums are usually required to obtain much income from this source. As Figure 2–4 shows, $100,000 invested at 6 percent is needed to obtain a modest income of $500 a month. At 7 percent interest, $85,714 is needed.

How many people have such amounts available? Most people do not have sufficient liquid assets to provide enough income to see them through a period of disability, even a short-term disability.

FIGURE 2–4
AMOUNT OF CAPITAL
REQUIRED TO PRODUCE
VARIOUS AVERAGE MONTHLY INCOMES

	At 6% Interest	At 7% Interest	At 8% Interest
$ 400 per month	$ 80,000	$ 68,571	$ 60,000
500 per month	100,000	85,714	75,000
750 per month	150,000	128,571	112,500
1,000 per month	200,000	171,429	150,000

This is a fairly good indication that most of us are in no position to depend on dollars-at-work in the event disability strikes.

An Alternative

If disability does strike and we have neither people-at-work nor dollars-at-work, what can we do? Our normal reaction would be to use up whatever savings we have in an attempt to meet our continuing financial needs. Usually, in a very short time we would find that our savings are gone.

Fortunately, human ingenuity has invented a system under which we can put a few dollars to work today, while we are well, which will yield big benefits tomorrow, if we become disabled. This system is called health insurance, a general term which covers both medical-expense and disability insurance. Health insurance provides the insured with benefits if he or she becomes sick or hurt. However, it might more accurately be called *benefits by contract*, since it guarantees—by contract—that if a stipulated amount is put to work by the insured, certain benefits will be paid for any of the following, alone or in combination:

- Loss of Income
- Medical Expenses
- Hospital Bills
- Business Overhead Expense

In the pages that follow we shall explore how each of these types of coverage works.

HISTORY OF HEALTH INSURANCE

Satisfactory income by contract and protection against high medical expenses haven't always been available. Early attempts to protect ourselves against the hazards of disability were inept and unsuccessful.

The early Greek sailors were protected by their laws against sickness while on the sea. The 17th century soldiers of the Netherland Republic were insured by the government against loss of eye or eyes, hands, arms, feet or legs. In 1757, the British Parliament compelled those employing stevedores to protect them against sickness. However, it wasn't until 1848 that the first real attempt was made to protect the general public against accidents. In that year, the Railway Passengers Assurance Company was formed in London to write *ticket insurance.* This protection was offered to railway passengers and paid benefits if they suffered accidental death or severe injury while riding the railways. This proved so popular that the company expanded its protection to all kinds of accident insurance. Thus was born the health insurance business.

Inspired by the success of the Railway Passengers Assurance Company, the Travelers Insurance Company of Hartford was formed in 1859 to offer accident insurance in America. Other groups were quickly formed for the same purpose. By 1866 there were 60 such companies in America. However, without adequate statistics and experience, all but one of these insurers floundered and failed. By 1871, the Travelers was the sole survivor.

At the turn of the century, numerous companies that had discontinued selling accident insurance were back in the field, however, joined by many new ones. They offered many types of accident insurance, and even ventured into sickness insurance. But most were not successful for very long.

Improper underwriting, inadequate premiums and the lack of scientifically constructed morbidity tables, with which to predict the probability of accident and sickness, aggravated by a bad business climate—all these things converted the 1930s into one of the most trying times in the history of health insurance. As a result, some insurance companies closed their doors forever. Others withdrew from the health insurance field entirely and concentrated on selling other forms of protection.

It wasn't until after World War II that the health insurance industry recovered from the staggering blows dealt it by the rough 1930s. Since then, many new companies have come into the field, and others that had dropped out have reentered it. However, guided by the costly lessons learned during the thirties, most companies today base their coverage and rates on the scientific morbidity studies constantly being made by actuaries. They also have learned the wisdom of underwriting risks at the time policies are issued, rather than at the time of claim.

Despite the high degree of caution that now pervades the health insurance industry, companies are constantly experimenting with both new coverages and new methods of improving old coverages.

WORKING KNOWLEDGE NEEDED

To be able to operate capably and confidently in the health insurance market, you must have a good working knowledge of the various types of health insurance contracts, policy provisions, government regulations and how health insurance is underwritten. While these subjects may appear somewhat technical, keep in mind that they are the very heart of the health insurance business. Without them, there could be no such business.

The more you know, the more effective you

will be. The more you know, the more sales you are certain to make. Your knowledge of health insurance and health-care services will make you more enthusiastic about your career and features of the policies you have to offer.

You will often find that your prospects are confused about the full extent of the protection afforded them by a health insurance policy they presently own, or by new health insurance you may recommend. Thus, it is important that you are able to interpret for them the provisions of their old policies and explain clearly how the policy you propose they buy will be valuable protection against injury and sickness.

The easiest way to analyze a prospect's existing health insurance policy—or to present a newly recommended policy—is to discuss its benefits. Policies may be divided into different categories, each of which gives a clue as to the type of benefits. The major categories of health insurance and health-care services include the following:

1. Disability Insurance
   a. Loss of Income
   b. Business Overhead Expense
2. Medical-Expense Insurance
   a. Hospital Expense
   b. Surgical Expense
   c. Major Medical
   d. Comprehensive Medical Expense
   e. Dental-Care and Vision-Care Coverage
   f. Hospital Indemnity Policies
3. Other Health Insurance Contracts
   a. Accidental Death & Dismemberment (AD&D)
   b. Credit Accident and Health
   c. Limited and Special Risk Contracts
   d. Industrial Policies
   e. Health Maintenance Organizations (HMOs)
   f. Preferred Provider Organizations (PPOs)
   g. Medicare
   h. Medicare Supplements
   i. Medicaid

This course will discuss each category of coverages in a separate unit. In presenting each type of health insurance, we'll be referring to individual policies, except where specific reference is made to group insurance.

MOTIVATION IS VITAL

Armed with product knowledge, you will have the challenge of motivating prospects to take action. You will draw on the skills you've used up till now, and the ones you will learn in this course, to encourage prospects to buy medical-expense or disability insurance.

People insure their homes and furniture against fire even though the odds of household fires occurring are about one in 100. They wouldn't dream of driving their new cars out of the showrooms without insurance, even though the odds of their being in an auto accident are about one in 50. They don't hesitate insuring their lives against death, although the chances of their dying this year are about one in 400 (at age 35).

Why then shouldn't they insure their capacity to earn income against disability when their chances of losing that ability through accident alone are much greater than the odds shown above? And these odds are magnified more when disability through sickness is included! Finally, why shouldn't they protect themselves against the medical expenses which always accompany injury or sickness?

HEALTH INSURANCE IS BASIC

Today, health insurance is basic. It is a necessity for a stable, happy home. In no other way can people make sure that when they can no longer earn a living, they will not become total consumers, entirely dependent on others for support. If income earners are laid up and unable to work, there is no other way they can avoid eating up limited savings and going into debt, or keep away from bankruptcy.

Only through health insurance can a person make sure of continuing to take care of his or her responsibilities. Only with health insurance can one live and work with peace of mind.

And yet, in spite of health insurance being so essential, most people will not go out on their own and purchase the protection they need. Instead, for them to obtain the protection they need requires the urging and health of you—the health insurance field representative.

They need you to help them acknowledge their exposure to risk, recognize the need for protection and do what they can to insure against everyday hazards. They need you to bring them the knowledge and products that will solve their dilemma. They need you to explain coverages and to motivate them to take action. They need you!

Chapter 3
Key Features of Disability Insurance Contracts

LESSON TEXT—Types of Policies...Maximum Benefits...Disability Provisions...Exclusions and Limitations...Key Words and Phrases...Nondisabling Injury Provisions...Renewable Provisions...Noncan Underwriting...Business Overhead Insurance

As long as a person has a job and can return to it within a reasonable time, he or she usually can overcome the financial burdens imposed by sickness or an accident. However, what an individual generally cannot cope with are sustained periods of disability after his or her income is cut off. Income protection against such disabilities is important. And that is the role of disability insurance.

Disability insurance is seen in various forms: individual policies, riders on life insurance policies (especially older policies), group insurance, employers' sick pay plans and union administered plans. There are even disability programs set up by government bodies.

In businesses, disability policies are used to protect business owners and key employees, to assure business continuation, and/or to fund buy-sell agreements. In addition, businesses establish group disability plans to provide employee benefits—short-term or long-term, or both. Our discussion in this text, however, will center primarily on individual policies that provide personal protection.

Disability may devastate the financial planning of any individual. Thus, disability insurance should be a part of every well-constructed financial plan. The specific kind of disability protection also is an important consideration.

Some policies pay income in the event the covered individual is disabled by either sickness or accidental injury. Others pay only if the insured is disabled by accident. If all factors were equal, applicants naturally would choose the broader coverage for disability caused by either accident or sickness. After all, when a person is disabled—regardless of the cause—there is need for income to replace the earnings lost. The disabled person usually needs to receive his or her disability benefits as soon as possible, because it doesn't take long for the average person's savings to be depleted.

The ways in which different health plans provide protection vary widely. To understand a specific plan, you must analyze it carefully. In particular, you must check:

- Accident vs. sickness
- Total amount of benefits and how determined
- Rate and time of payment
- When benefits start and when they stop
- Limitations and exclusions
- Premium guarantees

Last, you must closely examine:

- Key words, phrases, clauses and provisions that determine the limit of liability assumed under the plan
- Conditions under which benefits will be paid
- Insured's rights to renew the contract

As you can see, analyzing disability insurance is not a simple task. However, this checklist gives you a convenient track to run on.

TYPES OF POLICIES

Disability insurance policies can be categorized by the way in which it is determined if a person is disabled.

Social Security

The Social Security definition of disability stipulates that to be eligible for benefits a covered worker's disability must be expected to last at least 12 months or result in earlier death. This definition is so restrictive that the results are not surprising: more than half of the people who file claims are denied benefits by Social Security.

Occupation

One type of disability insurance is designed specifically to replace a specific amount of an insured's earned income, providing he or she is totally and permanently disabled by injury or sickness. Coverage frequently is based on a disabled insured's occupational status.

Any Occupation

Some policies stipulate that insured individuals, in order to collect benefits, must be disabled to the extent that they are unable to work at *any* occupation. This is a narrow definition and restricts benefits to insureds who cannot work in any gainful employment.

A slightly broader definition allows benefits for disabled insureds who are unable to work in any occupation *for which they are reasonably suited by reason of their education, training or experience.*

Other policies use an "own occupation" definition and pay benefits if the insureds are unable to work at their own occupations because of disability resulting from bodily injury or sickness. Thus, the disabled insured, who remains under a physician's care for a disability, would collect benefits even though he or she were able to—or actually did—work in another occupation.

There are several variations on the "own occupation" definition. Some apply the "own occ" definition to only the first few years, after which an "any occupation" provision applies. Some apply the "own occ" definition to age 65, or for life. Still others apply the "own occ" definition only so long as the insured does not actually go to work in another occupation.

"Own occupation" policies have the advantage that full benefits will be paid even though an insured has incurred no loss of income: the person may well be earning the same or more in another occupation and still collect benefits. However, it

---

WILL YOU QUALIFY? AND FOR WHAT?

"Social Security rejects more than half of the claims it receives each year for disability benefits. In spite of this, more than 2.5 million people collect Social Security benefits for one year or more.

"The median length of disability for Social Security beneficiaries is 5 years. And a large percentage of them can be expected to last more than 15 years.

"Will you become one of the nearly 3 million disabled people who do not qualify for Social Security? And if you do qualify, will what Social Security pays be enough for you to live on—for one year, 5 years, or a lifetime?"

is possible that an insured would receive no benefits because he or she was qualified to work at the "own occ" on a part-time basis.

Income Replacement

Another type of disability insurance ignores the occupational question and bases the eligibility for benefits on whether or not an insured has suffered a loss of income. Such a policy ties the benefit payments directly to the proportion of actual earnings lost. A full benefit would be paid for total loss of income. Or, if the insured experiences a 40 percent of the specified maximum benefit, the percentage might be refigured monthly as the disabled insured's income varies. Generally, no benefits are paid under a "residual" policy if the loss of income is less than 20 percent or 25 percent.

Jargon vs. Meaning

Historically, the term "disability income" referred to all policies that provided income benefits to an insured for a disability. As the distinctions referred to above have developed, the companies have sought a way to differentiate between the approaches.

What has resulted are two terms: *disability income* which purports to include all policies that pay a stated benefit, and *income replacement* which claims benefits are payable as a function of the actual amount of income lost. In reading industry literature, therefore, you will have to pay close attention to the terms of a particular contract, because neither of the names truly describes the policy's scope. In this text, we use "disability insurance" to reference both types.

To your prospects, "disability income" and "income replacement" are one and the same: you're providing income if disability occurs, and you're replacing income that has been lost. Whatever type policy you propose, don't confuse your prospect by trying to differentiate between names. Make sure they understand the substance of the contract and what must happen in order for them to collect benefits. Don't let a "tempest in a teapot" cloud the real issue—if your prospect is disabled, you can provide cash.

MAXIMUM BENEFITS

With disability insurance, benefits are defined and controlled by companies according to: (1) the amount of benefit payable weekly or monthly; (2) an elimination period (discussed later); and (3) a stated benefit period. An applicant normally is limited in the amount of disability income protection a company will write, based on a maximum percentage of the person's salary or wages. For example, a person earning $2,000 a month may be limited by Company A to a monthly benefit of $1,200, representing 60 percent of regular income. If that person also has an existing disability policy from Company B providing $400 monthly income, Company A would issue no more than $800 in monthly benefits. Some companies now provide maximum monthly income protection up to $6,000 or more.

One company at this writing now offers up to a $25,000 monthly benefit with its group long-term disability insurance for professional groups. This particular coverage also has a zero day (no waiting period) residual benefit (explained later) for partial disability—even if not preceded by total disability. Thus, it will replace a portion of earnings lost when the insured is not able to work full time at his or her own occupation due to sickness or injury, but is able to work part time.

Companies have not found it feasible to sell

FIGURE 2–5
PROBABILITY THAT A PERSON OF A GIVEN AGE WILL BECOME DISABLED FOR MORE THAN 90 DAYS BEFORE AGE 65

At Age	Chance of Becoming Disabled Before Age 65
30	28.9%
35	28.4%
40	27.8%
45	26.7%
50	25.0%
55	22.5%
60	15.8%

Source:
1971 Experience Modification To The 1964 Commissioners Disability Table

policies that pay income for disability caused by sickness alone because of the high morbidity rate (the rate at which disability occurs) of sickness disability.

ACCIDENT-ONLY POLICIES

Some policies attractively combine benefits for accidental death, accidental dismemberment, accidental medical expense and accidental disability income. Limited policies usually restrict payments to accidents that occur on a common carrier (e.g., airplane, bus, railroad). Broader policies cover nonoccupational accidents. Broad form accident policies offer protection against any and all accidents, regardless of where and when they occur, day or night, at home, abroad, at work or at play.

The premium for accident-only disability insurance—whether it's issued alone or as part of a package—is nominal, especially in view of the large benefits such plans usually pay. However, these premiums are small because the accident morbidity rate is low, compared to the rate for sickness.

SICKNESS AND ACCIDENT POLICIES

Policies that pay income when the insured becomes disabled from sickness or accident naturally require higher premiums than do accident-only contracts. However, the protection they offer is much more comprehensive since statistics show that disability through illness is several times more prevalent than illness through injury.

Therefore, the chances that an insured will collect some benefits under an accident or sickness loss of time contract are much greater.

TOTAL AMOUNT OF BENEFITS

Due to the size of claims that may be incurred, insurance companies are extremely cautious as to the amount of disability insurance they will underwrite on any individual. They know that if

it is profitable, or even convenient, for a person to stay at home when well enough to go to work, the person may be tempted to malinger (feign disability). Putting this temptation far out of the minds of its insureds is an objective for which all insurance companies strive.

The amount of disability insurance that a company will issue to an individual is affected by such underwriting factors as the applicant's sex, health, age, occupation, income (both present and past) and the amount of such benefits currently owned by the individual in the same and other companies.

Another factor in underwriting disability insurance is a person's net earned income. First, a distinction is drawn between "earned" income (what a person is paid for work performed in the workplace) and "unearned income" (what is generated by investment dollars, such as interest, dividends, etc.) Insurance companies will allow a person to purchase disability insurance based on earned income, because that is what will stop if a person becomes disabled, whereas unearned income continues as long as dollars are invested.

A second distinction is drawn between "gross" earned income (the total amount a person receives for work performed in the workplace, such as salary, fees, etc.) and "net" earned income (what is left after deducting business expenses and taxes). If a person is disabled, most business expenses will cease. In addition, since a healthy, working person spends those dollars on business purposes, they are not available and not needed for personal uses. Therefore, in case of disability, the person won't need those dollars to be replaced by disability insurance. (If your prospect does in fact have business expenses which will continue beyond a disability, you can provide Business Overhead Expense Insurance, discussed later in this unit.)

Along the same lines, taxes are deducted from the gross earned income of a healthy person. Those dollars, thus, were not available to the person for personal uses and do not need to be replaced by insurance if the person is disabled. In addition, disability insurance benefits paid on individually owned policies are not taxable, so no provision needs to be made to replace those dollars.

The purpose of disability insurance is to provide a standard of living for disabled insureds that is comparable to what it was before they became disabled (assuming the person purchases the maximum available disability coverage). Therefore, most companies will not knowingly provide disability benefits beyond a reasonable portion of a person's income after business expenses and taxes.

Limits

In seeking to avoid malingering, most companies follow three rules to limit the amount of disability insurance a company will issue to an individual.

Rule 1. The amount issued to any individual by the company shall not exceed its stated maximum. In addition, individuals within specified occupational categories may be limited to specific maximum benefits. The duration for which benefits are to be paid and the insured's rights to renew the contract (discussed later) also influence the amount most companies will accept.

Rule 2. The total amount of disability protection already owned by the insured within the company and out, plus the new insurance, shall not exceed a fixed limit set by the company.

Rule 3 The insured's total disability income shall not exceed a fixed percent of the insured's income. This relationship between the insured's total disability benefits and income is an overriding consideration in determining how much new disability insurance a company will issue to an individual. In evaluating the maximum benefit a person may purchase, the company will look at the person's net worth and total unearned income. A large net worth indicates assets that may be liquid enough to provide the proposed-insured with additional cash for living expenses. In this case, the company may limit the benefit amount and/or the benefit duration. If unearned income represents a significant portion of the proposed-insured's total income, the fixed percent the company normally uses may be reduced in underwriting this case.

In addition to these three considerations in limiting the amount of disability insurance they will issue, companies may incorporate other provisions in their contracts to prevent an insured from finding malingering profitable. Every company publishes its own underwriting rules and conditions. You should be thoroughly familiar with your company's specific guidelines. Some of these provisions will be discussed shortly.

Rate and Time of Payment

The rate at which benefits are paid and the time they will be paid are important to the insured. Most plans pay benefits weekly or monthly. Generally, if the insured becomes eligible for benefits, he or she receives a settlement for an initial period of loss. If the person remains disabled, he or she must submit additional proof of continuing disability.

Benefits—Start and Stop

Ideally, disability income benefits should start when the insured becomes disabled, and stop when the person either recovers or dies. Generally, this objective can be met when a disability is caused by accident. Many policies provide that benefits start on the first day of injury and continue for life, or until the insured ceases to be disabled.

If a claim is certain to run for a long period, the company will set payments on a schedule basis and only require proofs of loss periodically. This is done in order to avoid undue administration and paperwork for the insured, the physician and the company.

However, to attempt to provide lifetime income when disability is caused by illness could be—has been—financially disastrous to the insuring company. Many companies used to offer lifetime protection in the event of disability whether caused by accident or sickness. Unfortunately, many people found ways and means of converting these policies into retirement plans for themselves. This caused the companies to suffer great financial losses because they had not anticipated this turn of events and had not built sufficient reserves into their premium structures to counter the effects.

As a result, most insurance policies that offer disability income for sickness rigidly fix the starting and stopping periods. Usually, disability benefits for illness start on the 15th day (or later), and stop at a certain age (e.g., 65). In fact, most companies will allow lifetime sickness benefits only for insureds who are in low-risk occupations. Naturally, the premium charged depends heavily on when sick benefits start and when they stop. The sooner they start and the longer they run, the higher the premium.

ELIMINATION (OR WAITING) PERIOD

Disability contracts often state that the insured must be disabled for a period of time (7, 14, 30, 90 days or even a year) before benefits begin. This is known as the elimination or waiting period. Since the insured assumes personal responsiblity for any loss of income suffered during this period, the company can afford to charge a lower premium than if it were required to pay benefits from the first day. Furthermore, since many small claims, which are expensive to administer, are screened out, the company can afford to apply the premium toward the purchase of the largest possible amount of benefits for the longest period of time.

In many disability policies, the waiting period is shorter for accident disability than it is for sickness disability. For instance, it may be 0 days for accident but 15 days for sickness, or 7 days for accident but 30 days for sickness, etc. The reasoning behind this is that the premium for early accident disability protection is much lower than it is for early sickness disability insurance. Furthermore, accidents usually cause additional expenses which make immediate or early payment desirable.

Another point is that the insured can buy more income with what is known as coterminist periods (e.g., 7–7, 14–14, 30–30, instead of 0–7; 0–14; 0–30). Here, the beginning day for benefits is the same, whether the cause was accident or sickness. A 30–30 elimination period is very common. Some plans are written with 180–180 elimination periods so that benefits begin when an employer-sponsored short-term disability plan ends.

When you sell disability insurance, you should coordinate the waiting period in the new policy (especially for sickness benefits) with the client's existing benefits from such sources as

group insurance, the employer's formal sick pay plans, etc. You thereby avoid duplicate protection and can apply premium dollars to the greatest advantage.

PROBATIONARY (INCUBATION) PERIOD

In addition to an elimination or waiting period, some disability policies provide for a probationary (or incubation) period applicable to benefits payable in the event of illness. This provision is designed primarily to prevent adverse selection against the company. It does this by stipulating that any disabling illnesses that occur within a specified period (e.g., 15 or 30 days from the date of application or of policy issue) will not be covered. Thus, if the insured has been exposed to any communicable disease just prior to buying the policy, or has a health condition which needs immediate attention (tonsils, appendicitis, etc.), the company will not pay benefits for disability from illness within the probationary period.

EXCLUSIONS AND LIMITATIONS

The exclusions and limitations are clearly stated in disability contracts.

Accident Exclusions

Generally, the most common exclusions and limitations found in an individual accidental disability policy or the policy section dealing with accidental loss are:

1. Suicide, or attempted suicide, while sane or insane;
2. Hernia of any type;
3. Any loss caused by or contributed to by disease or medical treatment. (This exclusion usually excepts any bacterial infections which arise as a result of accidental cuts or wounds);
4. Aircraft accidents, except if the insured was riding as a fare-paying passenger on a scheduled airline;
5. War or any act of war;
6. Accidents suffered while the insured is in

the armed forces of any country at war; and

7. Losses caused during extensive travel or residence outside the United States or Canada.

Keep in mind that the wording of these exclusions differs in most policies and not all of them are found in every policy. If the policy is a limited form, the coverage may be further restricted to a specific type of accident (e.g., commercial airplane, public conveyance).

Sickness Exclusions and Limitations

Some of the exclusions and limitations usually found in an individual sickness disability contract or the policy section dealing with it are:

1. Preexisting conditions, such as illness or disease which was contracted before the policy goes into effect (The probationary period helps protect the company against these conditions to some extent);
2. Disease contracted while in the armed forces of a country at war;
3. Accidental bodily injury;
4. Pregnancy, childbirth or miscarriage;
5. Sickness or disease contracted or sustained outside the Dominion of Canada or the United States; and
6. Cost of treatment covered under Workers' Compensation.

Again, remember that these are only representative exclusions and limitations. Not all of them will necessarily be found in any one policy,

and others not listed may be included. Also, if the policy is a limited one, payments may be further restricted to a specific type of illness or disease (e.g., cancer).

Some agents look upon exclusion provisions as barriers to the sale, and omit explaining them to prospects or newly acquired clients, or quickly gloss over them. This can lead to trouble and embarrassment when claims come up that are not covered because of contractual exclusions, but which claimants mistakenly believe are covered.

To avoid putting yourself in this unhappy situation, don't fail to explain the exceptions and exclusions to each prospect and client. However, when explaining the exclusions, accentuate the positive. For instance, in talking about the exclusion of suicide or attempted suicide, point out that the premium for the policy is predicted on the number of unexpected illnesses and accidents which occur annually. For the company to include the number of claims which might also arise when people intentionally inflict injury on themselves would mean increased premiums. Therefore, by excluding benefits for those who attempt to end it all, your client's premiums are minimized.

DISCLOSING CRITICAL STIPULATIONS

"(Prospect), in order to provide a broad range of benefits to the widest portion of our clients, the company has designed the policy with certain stipulations of items that either will not be covered or will be covered on a limited basis.

"Let me take a moment to go over these with you, so that there won't be any surprises for you, or for us, later on. It is to your benefit to be sure that you know exactly what coverage you have, and what coverage you do not have."

EXPLAINING AN EXCLUSION

"For example, (Prospect), the policy will not pay any benefits for suicide or attempted suicide. The premium for the policy is predicated on the number of unexpected illnesses and accidents which occur annually.

"For the company to include the number of claims which might also arise when people intentionally inflict injury on themselves would mean increased premiums. Therefore, by excluding benefits for those who attempt to end it all, your premiums are minimized."

Use this same line of reasoning with other limitations—that they serve to save the insured money by protecting against the few who might cause the rates to go up if the exclusions or limitations were not included.

It is essential that your prospect understand the protection under the health insurance policies they now own. The better you understand policy provisions, the better you will be able to serve the needs of your clients. Only by thorough mastery of these contracts can you appreciate the unique benefits they provide. Only then can you bring that motivating power into your sales interview.

Interpreting contracts is the main root from which much of the permanent success of the career agent stems. It is your responsibility to understand the health insurance business so thoroughly that you can clearly transfer this knowledge to your prospects and clients.

KEY WORDS, PHRASES, CLAUSES, PROVISIONS

People buy fire insurance to protect against the financial losses that would occur if their home were destroyed by fire. They apply to the fire insurance company for a policy and pay a premium for a given period. If there is not fire, the company pays no money. And the transaction is absolutely fair. Protection was provided.

Disability insurance also provides a form of protection. When people buy disability policies, their understanding of what disability means, or what sickness or accident means may be clouded with preconceived notions. What they think they are buying is a source of continuing income to keep them and their families going if they become disabled. Whether there is actually such protection in the policies they now have and those you may sell is up to you. Whether these contracts satisfy your prospects' needs is something you should determine.

The following pages are devoted to a careful analysis of key words, phrases, provisions and clauses that are commonly found in disability contracts. Study them carefully. You will find great satisfaction in knowing precisely what each means and how its inclusion or absence in a policy affects the insured's rights and benefits.

Type of Disability Important

"When is a person disabled?" A good answer might be, "When a person is physically unable to work, due to sickness or accident." However, this question is more complex and can't readily be answered without studying each particular case. For instance, a crushed hand may not disable a salesperson, but it will most certainly disable a surgeon who depends 100 percent on his or her skillful fingers.

Disability is not as clear-cut and as final as death. It varies from the individual who is occasionally incapacitated by asthma to the one who is totally disabled by blindness.

The difficulty of defining disability is seen in the different definitions given to it by government plans, Workers' Compensation, disability insurance policies, etc. There is no standardization in any of these, and to determine what each means when it refers to disability can only be ascertained by careful study.

This inability to give disability a standard definition has led to countless court cases. In these cases, the claimants thought they had legitimate claims, while the defendants felt the interpretation of disability under their policies absolved them of any liability. The courts have often dealt more liberally with the claimants in these cases than the facts seemed to warrant, because they felt that the defendants' interpretations of disability were too rigid under the circumstances.

Partial Disability

If an accident prevents the insured from performing one or more important daily duties of his or her occupation, some contracts will consider the insured as partially disabled and will pay limited benefits. These usually amount to one-half of the amount (50 percent) of weekly or monthly indemnity that would be payable if the insured were totally disabled. Partial disability benefits are also paid for a shorter time (e.g., six weeks, one year).

Some policies will pay for a partial disability only if it commences within a stipulated period after an accident (e.g., 30 days after). Other policies will pay for partial disability only if it immediately follows a period of total disability caused by sickness.

Residual Disability

A more liberal approach to partial disability is the concept of *residual* disability: if a person returns to work on a part-time basis, he or she will receive benefits from the policy for the full benefit period. The amount of benefit will be based on the percentage of earnings a person receives working part-time as compared with what he or she had been earning when working fulltime. The purpose of a residual approach to disability is to encourage people to return to work.

There are many varieties of residual provisions. Some require a period of total disability before residual benefits will be paid. Some residual benefits begin a full month after the elimination period has been satisfied. Some pay residual benefits only to age 65. And so on. It is vital that you—and your prospect—understand the specific provisions of your policy.

A person who is disabled may recover, and then weeks or months later the disability will reoccur. Thus, policy provisions having to do with recurrent disabilities are important, because they determine how and when benefits are payable under certain circumstances.

If a recurrent or second disability qualifies in the same benefit period as the first disability, a new waiting period or deductible is not required. However, if the recurrent disability begins a new benefit period, a new waiting period or deductible will have to be fulfilled by the insured before benefits will be payable again.

As an example, suppose Tracey P. has a policy which stipulates that a new benefit period begins if the insured is disabled, recovers and returns to work for at least six months, and then becomes disabled again. The maximum benefit period is five years. Tracey is totally disabled and off work from January 15 to April 15, then returns to work. Later Tracey is stricken again the same year and is off work from September 1 to November 10.

In that case, Tracey's policy would resume paying benefits, up to the maximum amount, in the same benefit period and a new waiting period would not be required.

When Disability is Delayed

There are cases when total disability does not occur immediately after an accident, but develops some days or weeks later. Most policies have a provision allowing a certain amount of time during which total disability may result from an accident and the insured will still be eligible for benefits. Depending on how the policy is written, the amount of time allowed for a delayed disability, for example, may be 30, 60 or 90 days.

Nondisabling Injury Benefit

Frequently, a person may have a disability policy and suffer an injury which does not qualify the insured for income benefits. Many such policies do include a provision for a medical-expense benefit that pays the actual cost of medical treatment for nondisabling injuries which result from an accident.

This benefit is generally limited to a percentage of the weekly or monthly income benefit provided in the policy. It is payable to eligible insureds in lieu of other benefits under the policy.

Presumptive Disability

Most disability contracts today presume that total disability has occurred if the insured suffers certain losses: speech, two limbs, sight or hearing. The insured will receive full-policy benefits for the full-benefit period regardless of whether or not he or she is under a physician's care or is able to earn an income.

Starter Plans

As discussed earlier, companies have specific limits on the amount of disability coverage a client can purchase. This is a function of many factors, including occupation and current income. For many young professionals, just starting out and earning relatively low salaries, the normal limits belie their substantial earning potential. In addition, they are often self-employed and in debt for substantial education loans.

Some companies allow these prospects to purchase more disability insurance than their current earnings would justify. Lawyers, doctors and dentists in their first year of practice are eligible for these plans. Also, medical, dental and law students sometimes are allowed to purchase these higher limits. These plans enable you to discuss substantial amounts of disability coverage with prospects who are highly qualified and generally able to afford the low premiums inherent in their younger ages.

Step-Rate Plans

To help young professionals even further, some companies allow them to purchase disability coverage at lower-than-normal premiums for the first few years, with increases later on that remain level for the life of the contract. At the time the premium increase occurs, these insureds usually are in a better financial position to afford the new premium level.

TYPICAL POLICY RIDERS

Additional benefits and provisions often are added to a disability contract by an insured. The most common of these are explained below.

Cost-of-Living Adjustment (COLA) Riders

Persons on fixed incomes, including those receiving disability benefits, have been hard pressed with inflation in recent years. Facing this reality, companies offering disability insurance developed Cost-of-Living Adjustment (COLA) provisions or riders to help protect insureds against inflation.

Such provisions or riders allow maximum benefit increases annually from 5 percent to 10 percent based on similar increases in the Consumer Price Index (CPI). This is how it works: After an insured has been disabled for at least one year, his or her monthly benefits are increased in line with increases in the CPI. After a second year of disability, benefits can be increased again up to a maximum of 5 percent or 10 percent depending on the CPI. An overall maximum total of COLA increases also is specified. Of course, if the CPI goes down, the insured's benefits also may be ad-

justed downward—but never to less than the original benefit.

Cost-of-living protection is valuable protection for your clients to have, even though it is not effective for the first year or two of disability. Persons afflicted with long-term disability can testify to the damage of inflation.

Once a disability ends, the benefit level reverts back to the original benefit amount. A new disability would then start a new series of benefit adjustments.

Buy-Back Options

An insured who has recovered from a disability may want the policy benefit to be adjusted to the level it had grown to during a disability under a COLA. That way, if a new disability occurs, the beginning benefit level will be the higher rate, rather than the original lower rate. Some companies allow the insured to "buy back" the additional benefit.

For example, an insured has a policy with a $2,000 original benefit plus a COLA rider. The insured becomes disabled. During the disability, the benefits rise to $2,600. When the disability ends, the benefit would normally revert back to the $2,000 level. Instead, the insured can buy back the $600—without qualifying medically or financially—for a premium based on the insured's present age. Thus, if a new disability occurs, the beginning benefit will be $2,600.

Social Insurance Riders

Many disability insurance carriers now offer Social Insurance riders, which provide *divided* coverage. One part of the benefit is paid regardless of other benefits, while the second part is paid only if the client is *not* collecting government-sponsored benefits such as Social Security.

Since the Social Security definition is so restrictive, and since more than half the people who file for Social Security disability benefits are denied them, it is important that insureds be certain that they will receive benefits if they do not qualify for Social Security. Premiums for the Social Insurance Rider are reasonable, and in most cases it will pay for your client to have this type of protection.

Guaranteed Insurability Riders

Many companies offer a Guaranteed Insurability rider with disability policies for those applicants who show promise for increased future earnings or for continued high earnings. These riders give insureds the opportunity to purchase additional coverage in the future at certain ages *without evidence of insurability.*

The options to purchase usually may be exercised before the insured reaches a specific age, such as age 50—providing an earnings test is met prior to each purchase. The company requires the earnings test as a means of avoiding overinsurance with an individual. Generally, such riders are available for applicants up to age 40 or 45. This is important extra protection for applicants who qualify.

Rehabilitation Benefit

The benefit helps a disabled insured get back to work and self-sufficiency as soon as possible. The insured meets with a claims representative, doctors and the employer to plot a path of rehabilitation. This may involve retraining, job placement services or a myriad of other options.

Benefits under this rider are paid in various ways, sometimes as an additional monthly benefit or as lump-sum cash payments for certain aspects of the rehabilitation. The key is to find creative ways for insureds to return to being productive members of society.

Waiver of Premium

The waiver of premium benefit in disability insurance is similar to that in life insurance. After a period—usually 90 days—from the commencement of disability, all future premiums are waived. Some carriers refund all premiums that were paid during the original period (the 90 days, for example); others prorate a refund.

Return-of-Premium Rider

Some companies offer a rider that refunds part or all of the premiums paid for a policy if claims experience has been good during a specified period of time. This is done either periodically or at some specified date (e.g., at age 65), depending on the company.

In-Hospital Elimination Period Reduction

If an insured is hospitalized during a disability, this rider eliminates the normal elimination period required before benefits would otherwise begin. The effect of this is that a waiting period could be reduced to zero if the insured were disabled and hospitalized on the same day.

PROVISIONS FOR POLICY RENEWAL

One of the most important provisions in any health insurance policy is the one which usually appears prominently on the policy and describes the renewability of the contract. By carefully studying this provision, you can determine to what extent the insured has the right to continue the contract.

There are six major types of renewable provisions used in health insurance contracts today. The reason companies draw the distinction is simple: with disability insurance, the exposure to more than one claim is great. Therefore, the company decides up-front how it is going to underwrite that exposure: accept a risk for only a limited period of time or for only certain circumstances, or accept a risk for an extended period of time for a broad spectrum of circumstances or something in between.

1. Single Term (Nonrenewable)
A health insurance contract that is commonly used for flight insurance, automobile trips, vacation trips, etc., offers protection for a *single term only.* It does not contain any provisions for renewal. Therefore, immediately after the trip is completed, or the term of the policy has expired, there is no longer any right of continuance on the part of the insured. The policy is automatically canceled.

2. Optionally Renewable (Cancelable)
This type of health insurance is renewable only at the option of the company. This is often referred to as *renewable at company's option* or *guaranteed term.*

A typical provision in this policy might read:

"This Policy is renewable at the option of the Company only...."

Another paragraph in the policy states:

"Subject to the consent of the Company, this Policy may be renewed from term to term by payment of the premium, prior to the expiration of the grace period hereinafter provided, at the company's premium rate in force at the time of such renewal"

3. Conditionally Renewable

This type of policy will be automatically renewed at the anniversary date or premium due dates *if* specific conditions outlined in the policy continue to be met by the insured. The conditions specified in the contract vary amongst insurers (being a full-time employee is a typical condition), but deteriorating health may not be one of them.

4. Collectively Renewable

Under this type of provision, a group of contracts may be cancelled. Examples are: all policies of a certain class, or a class of policies in a certain state or all policies in a certain state. Individual cancellation is not permitted.

5. Guaranteed Renewable

Under this clause, the company does not have the right to cancel the contract, nor does it have the option to refuse to renew at the end of the term. The insured is guaranteed the right to continue the contract up to the age stipulated (e.g., age 65).

However, under this type of contract, the company reserves the right to increase the premiums for broad classes of insureds.

A safeguard that is built into guaranteed renewable insurance for the insured is that before the company can increase the premium rates under existing policies it must obtain the approval of the insurance commissioner in the state in which it is domiciled. If the increase is approved, the increase will be permitted.

The guaranteed renewable disability policy gives insureds more rights and more security than the previously mentioned types of policies.

At the same time, this policy makes it possible for the companies to readjust their premium structures to more equitable ones if the experiences of any classes of insureds become extremely unsatisfactory.

6. Guaranteed Renewable and Noncancelable (True "Noncan")

This type of renewable clause is truly noncancelable (noncan). Under it, the insured is truly the policyowner. He or she has contractual right to keep the policy in force up to a specific age (e.g., 65) simply by paying the premiums. If the insured meets this one obligation, the company has no alternative but to keep the policy in force until its terminal date. It can't cancel the protection for any reason. It can't alter the protection in any way. It can't increase the premium. It can't alter the rights of the insured. It can't change any provision of the policy from the way it was originally issued.

Noncan Underwriting

Under the terms of the strictly noncan contract, the company has no opportunity to correct errors in its original selection. Therefore, in underwriting noncan health insurance applications, the insurer recognizes that it is accepting responsibilities which are extraordinary when compared with those under other types of policies. The power to terminate a policy, or at least to amend its provisions or premium structure, is denied the company issuing noncan insurance. It is reasonable, then, that noncan insurance be issued only to the best risks and in limited amounts which will not encourage malingering.

Noncan generally is issued only after a complete and satisfactory medical checkup and inspection reports have been obtained. The individual whose business life, associates and habits point to a tendency to turn a quick dollar is not a good noncan risk. There are numerous factors the insurance company evaluates in underwriting a proposed insured:

- employment stability
- vocational motivation and job satisfaction
- occupational risk
- moral risk

- age
- health
- avocations
- benefits (amount/duration) applied for
- type contract (renewability)

Considering all the elements of risk, it is surprising that noncancelable disability insurance is even available!

Underwriting Decisions
Because the underwriters must make a once-and-forever decision when evaluating a risk for noncan disability insurance, they have devised six alternatives for expressing that decision. They can decline the policy. Or they can issue it (1) as applied for; (2) with certain conditions waived for coverage; (3) with an additional premium (a rating), (4) with modified benefits; or (5) with a combination of any of these.

The range of alternatives gives underwriters a lot of flexibility, and few policies are outright declined.

Distinctive Noncan Features
Noncan policies contain some provisions which are unique. These are designed primarily to protect the company issuing such insurance against the few unscrupulous and dishonest insureds it might inadvertently insure. Another purpose of these provisions is to limit the company's risk to some extent.

Under most noncan policies, lifetime benefits are usually made available for disability resulting from accidents. However, benefits payable for long-term disability resulting from illness are often limited to a period of years (e.g., five, ten) or to a specified age (e.g., 65, 70).

A distinctive feature of many noncan contracts is the transition which occurs in the definition of disability. This definition usually changes from an *own occupation* to *any gainful occupation* after a stipulated period of disability, such as two or five years.

Naturally, for those policies that base benefits on the amount of income reduction an insured will experience, this change in definition has no effect.

Another safeguard introduced in some noncan policies is the *aggregate limit* clause. Under this, the company promises to pay up to a total of months or years (e.g., 15 months, two years, five years, ten years), for an aggregate of all disabilities. If the insured under a five-year aggregate contract becomes disabled for two years and then recovers, there are three years of disability pretection left. When the total of all disabilities benefits equals the aggregate limit (e.g., five years), the policy expires.

What makes this clause so very important is that if the insured returns to the job on a full-time basis for a continuous period of six months or more, any disability occurring thereafter is considered as a completely new period of indemnity. In this case, the waiting period and new benefit limits apply.

Prorating Benefits
A major problem faced by health insurance companies is overinsurance. This is particularly severe problem in noncan disability insurance since, once a policy is issued, the company has no recourse except to keep it in effect as long as its premiums are paid.

When a noncan policy is applied for, the company usually carefully checks for any disability insurance the applicant already owns. It then determines whether to issue the insurance applied for, based on such considerations as the company's limit, and the principle of not exceeding a certain percentage of the insured's earnings. However, overinsurance often arises after a company's policy has been issued. To combat this, some companies have used one or more methods of prorating benefits. Among these are the optional provisions which cover *other insurance* and *averaging of earnings*.

Other Insurance Clause
This provision stipulates that if one or more of the policies issued by the insuring company to the insured result in a total benefit due that exceeds a specified maximum, the excess shall be void and premiums paid for it refunded.

Along the same line, another provision states that if the insured has duplicate coverage with other companies of which the company hasn't been notified in writing, benefits will be prorated. The company will only pay the pro rata portion that its benefits bear to the total benefits guaranteed under all policies.

Average Earnings Clause (Relations of Earnings to Insurance)

This provision stipulates that if at the time the disability commences the total benefit payable under all coverage owned by the insured exceeds the average earnings of the insured over the preceding two years, the benefits well be reduced pro rata to such amount, however, in no event to less than $200 per month or the monthly indemnity of the policy, if less. If the company exercises this provision, it must refund the premium paid for any insurance that is invalidated for two years preceding disability.

From a practical standpoint, these prorating clauses have not proved very effective in overcoming the problem of overinsurance with individual disability policies, and apply more to group health insurance. The other insurance clauses aren't appropriate for use in noncan or guaranteed renewable insurance because to some extent they refute the promise made in these contracts that the insured is guaranteed the benefits promised.

Best Type of Insurance

Health insurance policies today generally are issued as one of the six types we have reviewed.

Which of these plans is best? The answer depends on the individual's financial position, needs, feelings, etc. Actually, each individual must work out the answer with the help of the agent.

Matching benefit for benefit, the *premium* for guaranteed renewable insurance is less than it is for noncan. Companies that issue noncan insurance require extra premium dollars to pay for the additional claims they face, for the physical examinations they give, for the complete inspection reports they obtain, for the more intense underwriting they give each application received, for the closer supervision they give their claims, and for the more thorough analysis they make of actual policy experience. Insureds who have noncan policies and who develop physical impairments are careful to keep their policies in force because they realize they are probably uninsurable and that claims may be imminent.

If anyone knew he or she would never become an impaired risk the person could buy a *cancelable* or guaranteed renewable policy and enjoy the lower cost. However, no one can guarantee that he or she won't become an impaired risk. Nor can anyone guarantee that group protection will not be lost. Therefore, the only way a person can be absolutely sure of not losing all or part of their health insurance protection is by buying noncan insurance.

In essence, the additional cost of noncan over other types of health insurance is the price the insured pays to make sure that the policy will be kept in force up to its terminal point, at his or her discretion, rather than at the company's. Furthermore, noncan insurance also guarantees that the premium will not increase beyond the stipulated amount, such as might occur in either cancelable or guaranteed renewable policies.

In summary, all disability insurance policies are good. Some offer more advantages or benefits, but the insured must be able to afford them. However, even if one has the money to buy noncan health insurance, one may not be able to obtain it! It takes more than money to buy it. The company must insist that the applicant meet some very rigid health standards because it will be on the risk for many years into the future.

BUSINESS OVERHEAD EXPENSE INSURANCE

Business Overhead Expense policies are a unique type of health insurance sold on an individual basis to professional persons in private practice, some self-employed business persons, partners, and sometimes to small close corporations.

It is not uncommon for self-employed persons to anticipate that any disability that might happen to them will be short-term. They think they'll be back on the job within a few days or possibly within a week and their initial impulse is to keep their offices, stores or shops open for business.

Even if the disability does last only a short time, business overhead expenses—such as rent or mortgage payments, electricity, heat, water, laundry, telephone, employees' salaries, leased equipment, installment purchases, etc.—continue.

Such expenses continue and must be paid. The answer is Business Overhead Expense insurance. The primary purpose of Business Overhead Expense insurance is to reimburse insured professionals and eligible business owners for actual overhead expenses with benefits payable in the event they become disabled.

How Benefits Are Paid

The benefits paid will be either the covered expenses actually incurred or the maximum benefits payable under the policy, whichever is less.

For example, assume that Dr. Hill is the insured in a Business Overhead Expense policy that pays maximum benefits of $5,000. If the doctor became disabled and had actual covered monthly expenses of $3,950, the monthly benefits paid would be $3,950. And if Dr. Hill's actual covered expenses were $5,700, benefits payable would be $5,000.

A key point is that benefits do not include any compensation for the insured professional person or business owner or a replacement for that person—but salaries for his or her employees may be covered in the benefits. The maximum benefit period is one or two years with an elimination (waiting) period of 14, 30, 60 or 90 days generally to be observed following the onset of disability before benefits become payable.

Issue limits vary from company to company, but the maximum monthly benefits may range up to $15,000 or higher. Since the premium for this type of insurance is a legitimate business expense, the premiums are tax deductible. The benefits, however, when paid would be treated as taxable income.

Chapter 4
Key Features of Medical Insurance Contracts

LESSON TEXT—Major Types of Medical Insurance...Hospital Surgical Expense...Major Medical...How Benefits Are Paid...Comprehensive Medical Expense...Dental and Vision Care...Hospital Indemnity...Controlling Costs

INTRODUCTION

Everyday, each one of us is exposed to the risk of illness or injury. Everyone of us has had a cold or been to a doctor. Most of us have had multiple ailments over the years. While they seemed debilitating at the time, they generally passed and left us no worse off—except for the cost.

We spend approximately 11.1 percent of our Gross National Product[1] each year on medical and health-care services. We use doctors, hospitals, clinics, pharmacies, laboratories, etc. to diagnose, treat and rehabilitate. Some costs for services are financed in the U.S. and Canada by the government. In both countries, however, there remain many costs which must be borne by the individual patient.

In this chapter we will explore the major types of insurance contracts which provide cash to meet healthcare expenses.

HOSPITAL EXPENSE

One of the most widely owned types of basic health insurance is *Hospital Expense*. In the United States, it's sold through insurance companies and Blue Cross associations. Since 1958, it has also been available in the United States, under Medicare, to persons over 65 or disabled individuals who qualify. About the same time, hospital insurance was made available in Canada under a plan also supported by taxes and administered by the government.

This type of policy pays benefits for two categories of hospital expense—(1) daily room and board and (2) miscellaneous expenses. The expression "first dollar" often is used to describe basic Hospital Expense insurance. That means that basic coverages are payable right from the time the "first dollar" of medical expense is incurred in a hospital.

[1]1990 Statistical Abstract of The United States

How Benefits Are Paid

Although hospitalization policies differ in some respects, most of them pay benefits on a *reimbursement* basis. Thus, the insured is reimbursed for actual covered expenditures up to a stated limit.

Another type of Hospital Expense insurance (discussed later as Hospital Indemnity coverage) pays a flat daily hospital benefit for room and board, *regardless of the actual rate charged* by the hospital. Benefits are paid on an *indemnity basis*, meaning that a specified benefit is paid to the insured for a loss which is insured under the policy. The payment may be the full stated amount, or something less (depending on the terms of the policy) if actual expenses are less—but never more, even if the actual expenses are more.

Some policies pay benefits on a *service basis*, rather than a reimbursement or indemnity basis. The principal service organizations are Blue Cross and Blue Shield. Both are voluntary, nonprofit organizations. Typically, under a Blue Cross plan, the insured is billed only for services not covered by the particular policy, while the member hospital providing the covered services is paid directly by Blue Cross. Blue Shield plans provide benefits to cover medical and surgical expenses and generally are closely coordinated with Blue Cross plans.

Hospital Expense policies vary, not only as to the daily amount paid for room and board, but also as to the length of time the benefits are payable. Some policies will pay an in-hospital benefit for as long as 365 days, others for 90 days or 30 days. Of course, the longer the benefit period the larger the premium.

Miscellaneous Expense Benefit

Another type of benefit included in Hospital Expense policies is the miscellaneous expense benefit. This covers hospital extras up to a specified limit. Many policies limit these benefits to "reasonable and customary charges" for such items as dressings, drugs, X-rays, anesthesia, use of the operating room, laboratory fees and supplies.

Generally, the maximum miscellaneous expense benefit is expressed as a multiple of the daily room and board benefit, but may be a maximum dollar amount. For example, the maximum may be 10 times or 20 times the daily room and board benefit. Some policies specify individual maximums within the maximum miscellaneous benefit. In effect, the policy will pay only up to stipulated amounts for certain miscellaneous expenses. Thus, if the overall maximum for miscellaneous expenses is said to be $1,000, the maximum payable for use of the operating room might be $150, for anesthesia, $125, and so on, but the total miscellaneous benefit would be limited to $1,000.

Conditions of Payment

To collect under an individual Hospital Expense policy, the insured must be confined to a hospital at the request of a legally qualified physician or surgeon. Furthermore, the stay in the hospital must be for a stipulated, minimum period (e.g., 24 hours) before it is considered confinement. Exceptions to this requirement are often made if the insured is admitted for a surgical operation, or as an emergency case due to an accident. The insured may enter the hospital as an outpatient without being admitted as a patient. Such treatment generally is excluded or limited to a fixed dollar amount.

If the insured requires successive periods of hospital confinement, they generally are considered as one continuous confinement unless he or she has completely recovered, or has returned to normal duties for a stipulated period.

Exclusions

Hospital Expense policies exclude certain specific types of confinement. Usually excluded are hospital confinement due to war, mental illness, injury or sickness covered by Workers' Compensation, etc. Some contracts also exclude or limit coverage for venereal disease, alcoholism, drug addiction, quarantinable disease and charges for cosmetic surgery. Not all hospital policies exclude every one of these types of confinement, and some contain additional exclusions not listed above.

Maternity Benefits

Pregnancy sometimes causes unexpected and unusual expenses to the family. Accordingly, individual hospital policies may contain a maternity benefit provision either as a part of the contract or as a supplement benefit.

Most policies impose some sort of limits on maternity benefits. These may be expressed either in fixed dollar amounts, or as a multiple of the daily hospital benefit (e.g., ten times the daily room and board).

Most insurers (including Blue Cross), include a waiting period in their maternity provisions. This requires that before any maternity benefits will be paid, the individual's policy must be in force for at least a stipulated number of months. When available for individual policies, the maternity benefit usually is included only as an added benefit for an additional premium.

Many group hospital plans cover maternity immediately, even if the insured is pregnant at the time the policy is issued. Also, in group health insurance plans prior to 1979, maternity coverage was strictly limited. It usually provided a benefit for up to a flat dollar total amount or allowed separate maximums for the hospital and the obstetrician.

That was changed as a result of U.S. Public Law 95–555, which became effective in 1979, establishing that there could be no discrimination against women on the basis of sex. The law did not mandate insurance coverage for pregnancy, but did require that health-care benefits provided by employers be the same for pregnancy cases as for any illness. Most employers, therefore, elect to have maternity provisions included in their group medical-expense policies in order to treat pregnancy routinely like any sickness. The law had no direct effect on individual medical-expense policies.

SURGICAL EXPENSE

Many individual health insurance policies include a Surgical Expense benefit that pays for operations according to a surgical schedule. The schedule lists maximum amounts payable for all the professional fees incurred in an operation (e.g., surgeon, anesthetist and post-operative care). A surgical schedule typically lists a hundred or more operations and those not listed are paid for on a basis consistent with the schedule.

Some policies, however, pay the surgeon's fee up to the "reasonable and customary" charge for the procedure in a given area. No surgical schedule is included in such a policy.

Other insurance companies use a "relative value schedule" in which unit values—and not dollar amounts—are assigned to listed surgical procedures. These policies specify a *conversion factor*, in a dollar amount, e.g., a factor of perhaps $2.50 to $20. The unit value multiplied by the conversion factor equals the benefit to be paid for a particular operation. For example, the unit value for a hysterectomy might be shown as 45 in a particular schedule. If the conversion factor given were $10, the maximum surgical benefit for that kind of operation would be $450 (45 × 10). The unit value approach allows flexibility in establishing the dollar value of any schedule, which can be easily adapted to different geographic locations or prospect's needs.

The maximum Surgical Expense benefit payable is intended generally to cover all the professional fees involved, including those of any surgeons who assist the chief surgeon, as well as the cost of any post-operative care.

The Surgical Expense schedule sets out what the maximum benefits payable for each operation listed will be. If two, three or more operations are performed during a single period of disability, the maximum payable depends on the provisions contained in the contract. Some contracts provide only for payment for the most expensive of the operations. Others provide for payment for each of the operations actually performed.

Blue Shield plans insure their members for surgical expense. Like Blue Cross, these plans make payments directly to the doctor rendering the service, rather than reimbursing the insured. The benefits they pay vary from locality to locality. Therefore, to understand properly Blue Shield benefits (or Blue Cross), you should check to see what they are in your community.

Surgical Expense and Hospital Expense benefits may be combined with one or more additional benefits in a single policy or issued separately. The additional benefits that may or may not be included include maternity benefits, physicians' expense benefits, nursing expense benefits or convalescent home-care benefits.

MAJOR MEDICAL INSURANCE

Major Medical insurance in both individual and group policies has made it possible for many people to achieve substantial protection against the high costs of medical care. This is broad coverage. It typically pays benefits for hospital room and board, hospital extras, nursing services in-hospital or at home, blood, oxygen, prosthetic devices (artificial limbs and eyes), surgery, physicians' fees, ambulance and more. While some companies no longer issue individual Major Medical policies, it is generally available. Major Medical insurance usually picks up where basic medical-expense insurance leaves off.

As indicated, such insurance pays for a wide assortment of covered services and supplies, as long as these are performed or prescribed by a licensed physician and necessary for the treatment of an insured's illness or injury. The benefit period may be on a calendar-year basis, or may be specified as a two - to five-year period. Individual Major Medical policies provide total maximum benefits to individual insureds from about $20,000 to $250,000 or more.

To avoid small claims and abuses, Major Medical coverage includes two important features— the *deductible* and *coinsurance.* These features make it possible for companies to offer broad coverage at reasonable premiums.

The Deductible

A deductible is that portion of medical expenses which must be paid by the insured before the policy starts paying benefits. Deductible provisions may be described as any of three kinds: *flat, corridor* or *integrated.*

If a Major Medical policy includes a *flat deductible,* (Figure 4–1) the entire deductible amount is paid by the insured before policy benefits become payable. Suppose the insured incurs

FIGURE 4–1

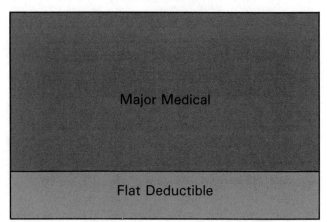

$2,000 of covered expenses and has a policy with a $500 deductible. The insured must pay the $500 deductible, after the the policy pays its share of the remaining $1,500.

The corridor deductible works in conjunction with a basic Hospital Expense policy. (Figure 4–2). The first covered expenses incurred are paid by the basic Hospital Expense policy. After the basic policy benefits are exhausted, the insured pays the full deductible amount, after which the Major Medical benefits are payable.

The integrated deductible is "integrated" with a basic Hospital Expense policy. (Figure 4–3). All or part of the deductible is absorbed by the basic policy; then Major Medical benefits are payable. If the basic policy benefits do not cover the entire deductible amount specified in the Major Medi-

FIGURE 4–2

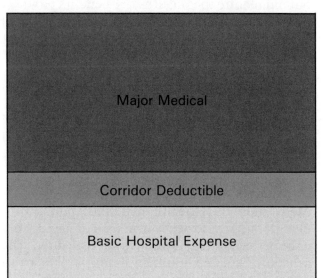

cal policy, the insured is compelled to make up the difference. For example, if a Major Medical policy has a $10,000 deductible, the first $10,000 of expenses must be paid before Major Medical benefits will begin. Whatever amount of the $10,000 that is not covered by the basic Hospital Expenses policy must be paid by the insured.

Coinsurance

Coinsurance, or percentage participation, is simply a sharing of expenses by the insured and the company. After the deductible amount of a Major Medical policy is satisfied, the company pays a large percentage of the additional covered expenses—usually 75 percent or 80 percent—and the insured pays the remaining 25 percent or 20 percent, respectively. The company, of course, will pay benefits only up to the maximum total limit of the policy.

Stop Loss Feature

Some Major Medical policies have a "stop loss" provision, which provides that the company pays 100 percent of covered expenses after the insured's out-of-pocket payments for eligible expenses reach a specified level, such as $1,000 or $2,000. That is valuable protection for the insured.

Figure 4–3

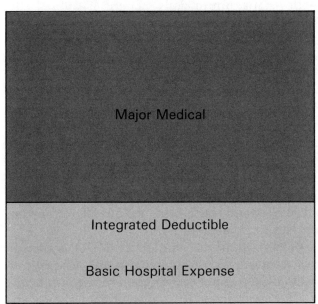

Expenses Not Covered

The only expenses generally not covered under Major Medical plans are those that are not practical or not appropriate. These are usually:

- Expenses for injury or sickness arising out of employment and covered by Workers' Compensation
- Expenses for eye refractions or fitting of glasses or hearing aids or for dental X-rays or other dental care, except as made necessary by accidental injury
- Charges incurred in any U.S. government hospital or other state hospital where charges would not be made if there had not been insurance
- Charges for room and board in excess of those specified in the policy
- Charges incurred for injuries or disease sustained or contracted through war or acts of war or while in the military or naval service

As you can see, Major Medical insurance offers truly umbrella protection. The only exclusions are those that would mean duplicate payment of benefits (Workers' Compensation), or payment where there would be no charges incurred if the policy had not been in force (government hospitals). Also, normal budgetable expenses frequently are not covered.

Insureds Sharing the Costs

For years, the public was educated to think in terms of first-dollar medical protection. An individual goes to the hospital for some common and minor purpose and the total charges amount to $1,000. To pay such charges might be an inconvenience to the average family. But certainly, medical expenses up to $1,000 or a little more would not mean financial disaster. Yet some people expect their insurance to pay most, if not all, of their medical expenses.

Fortunately, the public is now accepting the point of view which holds that minor sickness and accidents should be considered a part of the normal cost of living, the same as repairs to the home and automobile.

This concept is more important today than ever before. And its importance will continue to be magnified as hospital rates increase, and the use of expensive new drugs and equipment increases, as doctors' charges go up and the whole cost of being sick or injured gets higher.

This means, of course, that the first-dollar types of Hospital Expense insurance, with their modest maximum limits, are paying less and less of the total cost of getting well. As a result, the insureds are left with more and more of the bills to pay.

However, under Major Medical protection the insured selects in advance how much of the first-dollar expenses he or she will pay, through the deductible feature.

COMPREHENSIVE MEDICAL EXPENSE INSURANCE

Comprehensive Medical Expense insurance is much like Major Medical insurance, but it includes even broader benefits. It also provides a large maximum benefit.

Significantly, Comprehensive Medical insurance includes a deductible and coinsurance provision, as does Major Medical. The deductible of a comprehensive policy, however, is generally more favorable to the insured than a Major Medical deductible. For example, it is not uncommon for a Comprehensive Medical policy to include a deductible amount of only $100.

However, most Comprehensive Medical insurance is sold on a group basis by which the insurance company can—through the employer—exert more control on potential losses.

DENTAL-CARE AND VISION-CARE COVERAGE

Dental insurance has steadily increased in popularity in recent years, although it is seldom found in individual policies, except coverage for accidental dental injuries. Dental coverage generally is available in group insurance and is offered through dental service corporations, Blue Cross-Blue Shield prepayment plans and others.

With group dental insurance, deductible and coinsurance features usually apply. Frequently, the deductible does not apply, however, to rou-

tine cleaning and oral examinations. A maximum dental benefit, such as $1,000 or $2,000, generally is specified for a calendar year. Benefits normally are payable for cleanings, fillings, extractions, inlays, bridgework and dentures, as well as oral surgery, root canal therapy, and orthodontia. A separate coinsurance requirement, such as 50 percent–50 percent, usually applies to orthodontia and other specified procedures.

Vision-care coverage also frequently is offered with group health insurance. These benefits usually pay for reasonable and customary charges incurred during eye examinations by ophthalmologists and optometrists. Expenses for the fitting or cost of contact lenses or eyeglasses is often excluded.

HOSPITAL INDEMNITY POLICIES

These policies usually provide a daily indemnity of a specified amount based on the number of days the insured is a patient in a hospital.

For example, if the flat benefit in a policy stipulates $80 a day for hospital room and board and the hospital charges $75, the policy will pay the daily amount of $80. Or if the hospital charges $120 a day, the policy would still pay only $80. With most policies, however, a hospital room and board benefit will be paid on an actual expense-incurred, or reimbursement basis, up to a specified maximum. In that case, suppose a policy's maximum daily benefit is $90. If the room and board expense incurred is $140 a day, the policy will pay $90 a day. If the expense incurred is $85 a day, the insured will be reimbursed at the rate of $85 per day. General nursing care is included.

Such insurance has been available for many years, but has been promoted more heavily in recent years due largely to skyrocketing health-care costs. Many companies can offer high benefit plans at reasonable premiums, because underwriting and administration are greatly simplified and claim costs are not affected by increases in medical costs.

Benefits may run as high as $4,500 a month based on a daily hospital confinement benefit of $150 and some are even higher. Maximum benefit periods generally range from about six months to several years or for a lifetime. Benefits are payable directly to the insureds and may be used for any purpose.

Hospital Indemnity policies usually are exempt from most state laws which apply to specific kinds of insurance contracts.

CONTROLLING COSTS

With health-care costs on the rise, more attention is being paid to cost containment. Group medical-expense insurance has innovated several features that help employer group plans minimize expenses. Some of these features also are being adopted by companies in their individual medical-expenses policies.

Second Opinions
Before a policy will pay benefits for surgery, the patient must obtain a second opinion from a different physician. This helps minimize unnecessary surgery.

Preadmission Reviews
In this case, the policy requires that an unaffiliated panel of medical reviewers give advance approval to elective, nonemergency admission to the hospital.

Concurrent Review
Here, a medical review panel examines a patient's medical progress while still hospital-confined to be sure that the level of care and length of stay is not excessive.

Outpatient Surgery
Many routine medical procedures are adequately handled on an outpatient basis. To the extent possible and advisable, policies frequently offer economic incentives to patients who go to hospitals, free-standing surgery centers or clinics for surgery. This saves substantial sums in hospital care and encourages faster recovery.

Wellness
An increasing number of employers are taking the view that if positive actions are taken on a routine basis, employees will be healthier and health-care costs will diminish. To this end, they are sponsoring stop-smoking programs, blood-pressure screenings, weight-loss programs, safe-driving programs, meditation and relaxation clinics and special help for employees with alcohol, drug or mental health problems.

It is clear that the major forms of medical-expense coverage help alleviate the exposure to financial disaster most of us face if medical calamity strikes. At the same time, the health insurance industry is taking active steps to reduce the incidence of health-care usage and to improve the health of the population.

Chapter 5
Other Health Insurance Contracts

The insurance industry constantly is monitoring the needs of the insuring public. As consumers and government express concern about different types of health-care needs, the industry responds by creating policies to address those concerns.

ACCIDENTAL DEATH AND DISMEMBERMENT (AD&D)

Accidental Death and Dismemberment insurance is coverage that provides a benefit for accidental death or for the loss of one or more bodily members, such as hands or feet, or for loss of the sight of one or both eyes caused by accidental bodily injury. The loss of a member may be defined in a policy as actual severance or the loss of use of a hand, foot or eye. Separate benefits for hospital, surgical and other expenses generally are not included, although such policies may pay a medical reimbursement benefit for accidental injuries up to a stated limit.

Exclusions

Common exclusions in AD&D insurance generally include suicide, disease, bacterial infections except pyogenic infections (producing pus) caused by an accidental cut or wound, mental infirmity, war, or flying in any aircraft as a pilot or crew member. Other restrictions may be included, depending on the individual policy.

Principal Sum

The amount payable as a death benefit is known as the *principal sum*. That is the amount of insurance purchased—such as $25,000, $50,000, $100,000 or more. Some policies pay double, triple or even quadruple the principal sum if the insured dies under specified circumstances. A double payment is referred to as double indemnity. If three times the principal sum is payable, it is called triple indemnity.

As mentioned previously, the dismemberment benefit pays specified amounts if the insured loses one or more limbs, or the sight of one or both eyes, as the result of an accident. The benefit of a single dismemberment is usually expressed as a percentage (commonly 50 percent) of the principal sum. In an AD&D policy, the principal sum and the double dismemberment benefit usually are identical.

The company generally will pay the principal sum if the insured is continuously disabled within a specified number of days from the date of injury (e.g., 90 days) and dies within a specified period of time from the date of injury.

Capital Sum

Some health insurance policies provide benefits in the event the insured suffers accidental dismemberment or specific losses. Loss of use, in and of itself, is not generally considered to be dismemberment. The amount paid for the accidental loss of sight or accidental dismemberment is commonly referred to as the *capital sum*. Try not to confuse the terms, principal sum and capital sum. Capital sum does not cover loss of life by accidental bodily injury, but principal sum does.

Suppose Pat O. has an AD&D policy that pays $50,000 for accidental loss of life, and all of this sum for accidental loss of at least two limbs or the sight of both eyes. So $50,000 is the principal sum. Chris T.'s policy pays $40,000 for accidental death, but $20,000 for accidental loss of sight of one eye or dismemberment of one limb. Therefore, $20,000 is the policy's capital sum.

The specific dismemberment benefits are cash settlements, payable in accordance with a schedule that appears in the policy. This schedule sets out the amounts payable in the event of a single dismemberment (loss of one hand, one foot, sight of one eye) or a double dismemberment (two hands, two feet, both eyes, or one hand and one foot, one hand and one eye, one foot and one eye). These lump sums are often expressed in terms of a percentage of the accidental death benefit.

What Is Accidental?

When is death accidental? This is not a simple question to answer.

Some accident policies state that "accidental death must occur by external, violent and accidental means, independently and exclusively of all other causes." Yet death has been held to be accidental by courts even when its cause was not violent or external. For instance, in one case, a man punctured his lip and died. The company in which he was insured was directed by the court to pay a claim for accidental death because dying from puncturing one's lip is so unusual that it had to be classified as an accident.

Most accident policies contain a provision that *disease shall not directly or indirectly contribute to death*. However, when a person dies as a result of treatment while having a disease, courts have said that disease is not a direct or indirect cause of death unless it is a major contributing factor toward that death.

Example: A man suffering from a serious disease was treated with a drug from which he died. The court held the company liable for his accidental death.

Of course, if death is the direct result of a disease brought on by an accident (e.g., traumatic pneumonia, bacterial infection), there would be no question that the company is fully liable for the accidental death benefits promised.

Accidental Means

Some accidental death policies (especially older ones) stipulate that the principal sum will not be paid unless death is effected solely through *accidental means*. This has come to have the accepted meaning that—

> If in the act which precedes the accident, something unforeseen, unexpected, unusual occurs which produces the injury, then the injury has resulted from accidental means.

In short, under this provision, the cause of the injury must be accidental.

Accidental Bodily Injury

Most accidental death policies today, however, protect against accidental bodily injury which results in the insured's death. Assume Robin M. owns an accident policy which contains this type of provision. Robin accidentally falls while patching the roof of the family's home, and dies. Robin's spouse will be paid the principal sum under the policy because the result of the fall is death.

The Difference

The legal distinction between accidental means and accidental bodily injury is quite technical. Many courts tend to disregard this distinction when cases come before them involving policies with an "accidental means" definition. Most companies now are using the broader accidental bodily injury clause.

Elective Indemnities

Some dismemberment provisions stipulate that if the insured suffers an accidental injury that results in a sprain, dislocation, fracture or amputation of fingers or toes, he or she may elect to receive a lump sum in accordance with the schedule of elective indemnities printed in the policy. This election may be made in lieu of any regular income payments the policy may provide. Such election must be made within a stipulated number of days from the date of the accident (e.g., 30 days).

Nondisabling Injury (Physician's) Benefit

Some accident policies include a nondisabling injury or a physician's expense benefit *for nondisabling injuries*. Under this provision, if the insured suffers accidental bodily injury which does not cause total or partial disability but requires treatment by a physician, the company will reimburse the insured for such treatment up to a stipulated maximum. However, this benefit is not payable if any other benefit is payable under the policy at the same time.

CREDIT ACCIDENT AND HEALTH INSURANCE

Credit Accident and Health insurance is a form of protection for creditors. If an insured debtor becomes totally disabled or is killed accidentally, the insurance company will pick up payments during the period of disability or pay off the loan.

Such insurance may be in the form of either an individual or group policy, although most Credit Accident and Health insurance is written as group insurance. In fact, most such group insurance is issued as an addition to group Credit Life insurance.

Typically, group Credit Accident and Health insurance is provided through commercial banks, savings and loan associations, finance companies, credit unions and retailers. A master policy is issued to the institution sponsoring the plan and commissions for its sale are payable to the licensed insurance agent who places the business. Each insured debtor then receives a certificate of insurance that defines all of the coverage.

Minimum Number of Debtors Required

To qualify for group Credit Accident and Health insurance in most states, creditors must have a minimum number of debtors per year and generally that number is 100. As with group Credit Life insurance, evidence of insurability is not required of those to be insured. Debtors generally must pay part or all of the premiums and a high percentage, such as 75 percent, must want the coverage.

An important point is that debtors cannot be forced to take the coverage from any particular insurance company. They have the right to choose their insurers. Another requirement is that the amount of insurance must not exceed the amount of indebtedness. It should be noted that most states have adopted the model bill sponsored by the National Association of Insurance Commissioners (NAIC), or similar legislation, for the purpose of regulating Credit Life and Accident and Health insurance.

LIMITED AND SPECIAL RISK POLICIES

Limited Risk policies provide coverage for specific kinds of accidents or illnesses. Some policies, for example, cover injuries received only as the result of travel accidents. Policies that pay benefits for medical expenses resulting from a specified disease, such as cancer or heart disease, also are Limited Risk policies. (Some states prohibit the sale of "specified disease" policies.)

One should distinguish, however, between Limited Risk policies and Special Risk policies. The latter covers unusual hazards normally not covered under ordinary Accident and Health insurance.

Suppose a pianist's hands are insured, or a test pilot's life is covered or flying a specific experimental plane. Those would be Special Risk policies. But if you purchase an accident policy at the airport to cover you while a passenger on a commercial airlines flight, that would be a Limited Risk policy.

INDUSTRIAL HEALTH INSURANCE

The major characteristics of Industrial health insurance, when contrasted to other insurance, are twofold: (1) premiums are payable weekly or monthly and (2) premiums are usually collected regularly by agents in the field.

Industrial health insurance provides weekly benefits for disability due to sickness or injury and a designated sum per day for hospital confinement. Modest amounts for surgical operations according to a surgical schedule also may be included. Coverage likewise may include Accidental Death and Dismemberment benefits. Thus, if the insured should lose by severance two hands or two feet, or one hand and one foot, or permanently lose the sight of both eyes, the policy will pay the principal sum in cash.

Disability benefits may be offered for life, but with some policies coverage is limited to age 65 or 70.

Provisions in Industrial health insurance normally include a grace period of four weeks. When a policy lapses, reinstatement is handled more liberally than with commercial insurance, and such policies typically can be reinstated with evidence of insurability and the payment of two weeks' premiums. A required provision is that insureds have a right to return their policies within a specified time and obtain a premium refund.

HEALTH MAINTENANCE ORGANIZATIONS (HMOs)

A Health Maintenance Organization is a special type of organization offering health-care services to its subscribers. HMO members are enrolled on a group basis. They pay a fixed periodic fee in advance for services performed by participating physicians and hospitals. Both preventive medicine and early treatment are stressed through prepaid routine physical examinations and diagnostic screening. Complete hospital and outpatient care services for sickness and injury also are provided.

The Health Maintenance Organization Act of 1973, which provided some federal funding, spurred the HMO movement forward. To qualify for federally funded grants, contracts and loan guarantees, HMOs must offer a comprehensive range of health-care benefits, such as physicians' services, outpatient and inpatient hospital care, and emergency health services, with special emphasis on preventive health care.

A principal objective of HMOs is to reduce the number of unnecessary hospital admissions, duplication of services and administrative costs.

By federal law, employers with 25 or more employees who provide health-care benefits for their workers must offer enrollment in an HMO as an alternative to traditional forms of insurance *if requested*—unless no such cooperative plan is located nearby. Physicians working in HMOs may work as salaried staff members in a clinic setting, or provide individual care in their own offices for HMO members, or perform in a group practice for straight salary or payment on a per capita basis.

Independent HMOs may be self-contained and self-funded based on dues or contributions from their subscribers, or they may contract for excess insurance or administrative services provided by insurance companies. In fact, some HMOs are sponsored by insurance companies.

A patient that is an HMO subscriber is locked into that specific HMO for all medical services. Any costs for health care provided—except in emergencies—outside of the HMO are 100% the responsibility of the patient.

PREFERRED PROVIDER ORGANIZATIONS (PPOs)

In a PPO, specific doctors and hospitals are "preferred" because they discount their charges for medical services. These usually are employer-sponsored plans, and any savings are passed on to the employer as lower health-care costs and to the patient as lower out-of-pocket costs.

A PPO is similar to an HMO, but there are differences. While an insured must go to the PPO for health care—as with an HMO—there is a much wider variety of providers to choose from. Also, if a member goes outside the PPO for services, a reduced portion is paid. The insured pays no more than about one-third of the cost.

MEDICARE

A federally sponsored program (Fig 5-1) Medicare provides medical benefits for the *aged* and for qualified persons who are *disabled*. There are two principal parts to the program, namely:

- *Medicare Part A*—Basic hospital insurance which provides specified in-hospital and related benefits. It is financed primarily by tax funds provided through the Social Security program.
- *Medicare Part B*—A voluntary medical insurance plan which pays benefits for charges made by physicians and surgeons and for other health services. It is financed by contributions of those who participate, as well as by tax revenues. (See Figure 5-1.)

Medicare Part A

This plan provides automatic medical-expense benefits for persons age 65 and over who qualify for Social Security or railroad retirement benefits. Most all other elderly individuals who are not covered by Social Security may elect to participate voluntarily on a monthly premium basis. Disabled individuals who receive benefits under either Social Security or the Railroad Retirement Service for at least 24 months also are eligible even if younger than age 65. In addition, survivors and dependents may qualify.

Medicare Part A can help pay for up to 90 days of medically necessary inpatient hospital care in each benefit period. When a covered person is hospitalized, Medicare Part A pays most charges, subject to a deductible, incurred by the insured in a room with two or more beds. The benefit period begins on the day of admittance to a hospital or extended-care facility and ends after the insured has been released for 60 consecutive days. Skilled nursing home care is paid in full during each benefit period, except for a stipulated deductible amount from the 21st to the 100th day of care. No benefits are payable after the 100th day. Benefits for home health-care, hospice care and psychiatric hospital care are also provided.

Following hospitalization, Medicare Part A also provides benefits for up to 100 visits per year

FIGURE 5-1			
			MEDICARE PAYS:
PART A MEDICARE	INPATIENT	First 60 days.	All charges except the Medicare Part A Deductible which is presently $_____†.
		Confined from 61 to 90 days.	All allowable charges subject to a deductible of $_____† per day.
		Confined from 91 days and beyond, during a benefit period.	Nothing unless Lifetime Reserve* is used. If used, charges will be paid subject to a deductible of $_____† per day.
	SKILLED NURSING FACILITY	For the first 20 days.	All allowable charges.
		From 21 to 100 days.	All charges subject to a deductible of $_____† per day.
	PART B	In-hospital physician, surgeon & operating physician & outpatient physician charges.	80% of Part B allowable charges subject to an annual deductible of $_____.

*Each day of continuous hospital confinement over 90 days will deduct a day from your "Lifetime Reserve"—a one-time bank of 60 days. Once your 60 days are used up, Medicare benefits will end after 90 days for any one period of continuous confinement.

†Deductibles change each January 1.

by a certified home health-care agency, all paid in full if approved as medically necessary.

Deductible Provisions

It should be noted that there are four deductibles with Medicare Part A. One is a flat deductible amount when an insured is first hospitalized, the amount being subject to change periodically. A second smaller deductible amount is charged per day from the 61st to the 90th day in a hospital. The third and fourth are also per-day deductibles, applied to qualified nursing home care from days 21–100 and against the Lifetime Reserve, discussed below.

All charges from the 91st day on, unless the individual uses his or her Medicare Lifetime Reserve of an additional 60 days, must be paid by the insured. The additional 60 days may be used only once, during which time all covered charges will be paid in full except for a stipulated deductible amount per day.

Medicare Part B

Medicare Part B is a voluntary plan which provides supplementary medical protection in addition to that available under Part A. Under Part B, the individual pays a monthly premium, a deductible amount of covered medical expenses each year, and coinsurance of 20 percent of all remaining covered expenses. Thus, Medicare Part B pays 80 percent of *approved charges*, which may be less than the charges submitted.

Up to specified limits, Medicare Part B pays for professional medical services, such as physicians' services for surgery, anesthesia, outpatient hospital care, physicians' home and office calls, home or office physical therapy, and for certain services performed by dental surgeons, podiatrists and others. Benefits also are provided for health-care aids, either rented or purchased, including medical equipment used at home if prescribed by a physician, ambulance service, artificial eyes and limbs, braces, surgical dressings, casts and splints. In addition, outpatient hospital services also are covered, including diagnostic and therapeutic services as well as X-rays and laboratory services and physical therapy when administered by a qualified provider.

Also covered are 100% of allowable charges for home health visits by part-time nurses' aids, medical social workers and therapists from a certified home health-care agency—if approved as medically necessary.

Medicare Coverage and Enrollment Periods

Insurance agents should be familiar with the *coverage* and *enrollment* periods in connection with Medicare and be able to distinguish between the two. The coverage period is the time during which the participant is entitled to all benefits.

The enrollment period may refer to either of two time spans. It may be the *initial enrollment period*, which is a seven-month period beginning on the first day of the third month before the individual's 65th birthday. Or, it may be the *general enrollment period* each year extending from January 1 to March 31.

MEDICARE SUPPLEMENTS

Medicare Supplement (or "Medigap") policies offered by insurers normally pay part of all of the deductible and coinsurance amounts that Medicare recipients are required to pay.

An increasing number of states are establishing minimum benefit requirements for Medicare Supplement policies. Comparatively few major commercial insurance companies offer individual policies with Medicare Supplement coverage, which generally is available from Blue Cross-Blue Shield and from various mass marketing and direct mail insurance companies. Group health insurance, including Major Medical coverage, however, often may be continued as a supplement to Medicare for employees and retirees age 65 and older. (See also Fig. 5–2.)

MEDICAID

Not to be confused with Medicare, the Medicaid program provides matching federal funds to states for their medical public assistance plans to help *needy persons* regardless of age. Officially, Medicaid is Title XIX of the Social Security Act. It was added by the Social Security Amendments of 1965 for the purpose of supplementing Medicare for eligible needy persons. If family income is below a specified level, Medicaid benefits generally are available.

A part of the Medicaid benefits, for example, may be used to pay the deductible and coinsurance amount of Medicare for an eligible insured.

Medicaid payments are made in the same manner as Medicare payments—that is, checks are sent directly to the provider of medical service or equipment.

In review of the various kinds of health-care coverages we purposely did not go into detail about many of the provisions found in health insurance, since these are discussed later in the text.

Figure 5-2

Medicare supplement insurance can be sold in only ten standard plans. This chart shows the benefits included in each plan. Every company that sells Medicare supplement insurance must make available Plan A.* Some plans may not be available in certain states.

A	B	C	D	E	F	G	H	I	J
Basic Benefits	Basic Benefits	Basic Benefits	Basic Benefits	Basic Benefits	Basic Benefits	Basic Benefits	Basic Benefits	Basic Benefits	Basic Benefits
		Skilled Nursing Co-insurance	Skilled Nursing Co-insurance	Skilled Nursing Co-insurance	Skilled Nursing Co-insurance	Skilled Nursing Co-insurance	Skilled Nursing Co-insurance	Skilled Nursing Co-insurance	Skilled Nursing Co-insurance
	Part A Deductible	Part A Deductible	Part A Deductible	Part A Deductible	Part A Deductible	Part A Deductible	Part A Deductible	Part A Deductible	Part A Deductible
		Part B Deductible			Part B Deductible				Part B Deductible
				Part B Excess (100%)	Part B Excess (80%)		Part B Excess (100%)	Part B Excess (100)%
		Foreign Travel Emergency	Foreign Travel Emergency	Foreign Travel Emergency	Foreign Travel Emergency	Foreign Travel Emergency	Foreign Travel Emergency	Foreign Travel Emergency	Foreign Travel Emergency
			At-Home Recovery			At-Home Recovery		At-Home Recovery	At-Home Recovery
							Basic Drugs ($1,250 Limit)	Basic Drugs ($1,250 Limit)	Extended Drugs ($3,000 Limit)
				Preventive Care					Preventive Care

*Plan A includes the following: Coverage of Part A co-insurance plus coverage for 365 additional days after Medicare benefits end; coverage of Part B co-insurance; first three pints of blood.

Source: NAIC

Chapter 6
Policy Provisions

People generally have difficulty in understanding some of the provisions in their health insurance policies. Thus, agents like yourself have the continuing challenge of explaining many of the provisions to your prospects and clients to assure their comprehension. This responsibility rests on your shoulders.

As you go through the pages ahead, apply yourself to the task of obtaining a clear grasp of the many technical points involved. Particularly, work out for yourself language and analogies that will permit you to get across to your prospects and clients precisely what each health insurance contract you sell will do. And incidentally—but far from unimportant—this will help you make more sales because your prospects will see their need for the insurance you sell. In short, clear-cut explanations of health insurance policy provisions can be, for you, springboards to sales.

THE HEALTH INSURANCE POLICY

The policies you sell are your stock in trade. They contain promises for the insured's security and opportunity for you. Each policy is a fascinating document when properly understood.

Legally, a health insurance policy is a contract between two competent parties—the insurer and the insured. Physically, the policies issued by different companies may vary in size, shape, color, format, etc. However, each contains a similar series of provisions which set forth the obligations of both parties.

And remember this: every word in the policy is there for a very good reason. Some are included because they're required by state law to protect the insured. Others are necessary to avoid misunderstandings which might otherwise arise after the policy is issued and a claim arises.

We have already examined some of the key words, phrases, clauses and provisions which appear in health contracts. Now, let us examine the format of a typical policy and see where the above occur in relation to one another and other policy language.

A health policy contains two general types of information, that which (1) applies to all policies of that form and (2) describes particular points about the individual insured. For illustration, let's take a typical disability policy. While the arrangement, language, benefits, etc., will differ in most policies, this analysis will help you understand the construction of all health contracts.

FACE OF POLICY

Page one of the health policy is referred to as the *face of the policy* and usually represents the highlights of the contract. It quickly summarizes what appears in more detail inside. Among the items generally found on the face of the policy are:

1. Type of Contract: Whether the policy is for a single term, cancelable by the company at any time, cancelable at the option of the company, guaranteed renewable, or noncancelable and guaranteed renewable, is clearly set out in large type on the face of the policy.
   Example:
   "NONCANCELABLE AND
   GUARANTEED RENEWABLE TO AGE
   65"
2. Type of Coverage: The type of coverage is also set out on the face page.
   Example:
   DISABILITY INSURANCE POLICY
3. Name of Insured: This is typed in and clearly identifies the insured.
4. Policy Date: This identifies the date of policy issue.
5. Policy Number: Each contract carries its own individual number. This is largely for home office record-keeping purposes, but also is valuable when inquires of claims are made.
6. Policy Term: This important item identifies the period of time for which it is intended that the policy shall run.
7. Monthly Indemnity: Here the company stipulates the amount of disability income

it will pay the insured and how often such payments will be made. Whether the contract pays in the event of disability from either illness or injury, or for accident alone is made clear. Also brought out is the length of the waiting or elimination period for which the insured must be disabled before becoming eligible for benefits. Under many contracts, this waiting period is different for accident as against sickness (e.g., 0 accident; 30 days sickness).

8. Maximum Duration of Monthly Income Benefits in Event of Accidental Disability: The duration for which benefits will be paid to the insured in this event is stipulated (e.g., one year, 104 weeks, lifetime).
9. Maximum Duration of Monthly Income Benefits in Event of Disability Through Illness: This is carefully spelled out in loss of time contracts whenever it is covered. The duration differs in various contracts (e.g., one year, 104 weeks, five years, to age 65).
10. Definition of Disability: Closely tied in with the duration of benefits is the interpretation given by the company to disability. As pointed out previously, many contracts use the own-occupation definition up to a stated time (e.g., one year, two years, five years), but then swing over to an *any* occupation for gain or profit definition. Companies that take an income replacement approach define here what percentage of income must be lost due to a disability in order for benefits to be paid. Some companies move the definition clause inside their policies instead of placing them on the face page.
11. Principal Sum: This states the amount (if any) the company will pay if the insured is killed accidentally.
12. Premium Payable: This part of the contract states the amount of premium payable and the interval at which it shall be paid in the future. Some contracts also identify the premium due dates.

These are the major items usually found on the face of a health insurance policy. Two other vital clauses that also often appear on that page are the *insuring clause* and the *consideration clause.*

THE INSURING CLAUSE

The insuring clause is one of the most important features in the policy. It sets forth the conditions under which the company provides the coverage outlined in the contract.

As we have already seen, a health insurance policy is a contract of *indemnity.* Unless the insured suffers some loss defined in the policy, there can be no recovery. The insured is not insured against sickness or accident as such. No matter how severe an illness or injury may be, if it results only in pain or inconvenience, there is no liability on the part of the company.

A typical insuring clause in a disability insurance policy reads:

"The Company insures the Insured against total disability due to accident or sickness, to the extent and in the manner provided on this and the following pages of this Policy."

Listed with the insuring agreement in most states is the insured's right to examine the policy. If the policy is returned to the insurer or agent within 10 days *of delivery of the policy,* for any reason, the full premium is refunded and the contract is considered to have never been in force.

CONSIDERATION CLAUSE

Both parties to a contract must give something—consideration—in order for a contract to be formed. For an insurance contract, the applicant pays a premium and gives written application as consideration. The insurer gives the promise to pay the stated benefits as its consideration. Thus, the insurance contract is formed.

A typical consideration clause reads:

"This contract is made on the basis of the application, a copy of which is attached to and made part of this policy, and in consideration of the payment of premiums as specified in the policy. Subject to the provision regarding a grace period, payment of the full first premium maintains the policy in force for the term specified commencing on the date of issue."

Note that there are two important parts of the consideration:

1. A *written application* which must be attached to the policy and becomes a part thereof.
2. *Payment of the initial premium,* be that monthly, quarterly, semiannually or annually. This premium is the money consideration paid by the insured for the benefits promised in the policy.

Until *both* acts are completed, the consideration requirements have not been met. Thus, if an application is submitted without a premium, there can be no contract. The applicant then is merely inquiring whether the company will insure him or her. If the company agrees, and issues a policy, the individual must be in good health and must meet any other requirements stipulated by the company, before the policy which the company is *offering* can be delivered and accepted.

On the other hand, if the applicant submits a premium with a written application, *he or she makes an offer* to the company. In other words, the applicant says:

"Here is my application and my money. Will you issue me a policy?"

The company may accept the *offer* by issuing a policy or it may *alter the offer* by amending the application in some way. If it does the latter, in essence it says:

"We can't accept your offer. However, we offer you the following terms. Will you accept our offer?"

If the applicant accepts the company's offer, he or she must acknowledge by signing an amendment that becomes part of the policy.

Since the application is photographed and made a part of the policy, every statement made by the applicant—either to the agent or to the medical examiner—can be verified. In the absence of fraud such statements are considered to be *representations* and not *warranties.*

This simply means that the statements made by the applicant must be *material to the risk* or made with fraudulent intent before they can defeat the company's liability under the policy.

Statements made with respect to matters which are not material to the risk need only be substantially true and not literally true, as would be the case if they were warranties. For example, if the applicant states that he thinks his father died at 85, whereas he died at 80, he has made a representation. The inaccuracy of his statement will not permit the company to avoid its liability since it is not material to the risk.

All health insurance contracts contain a provision (discussed later) that stipulates a time period beyond which the company cannot contest its liability except for fraud. Most contracts set this *contestable period* at two years, although the law permits three years.

BENEFIT PROVISIONS

Immediately following the insuring clause, most policies list the benefits payable. These tell whether the policy provides benefits for accidental death only, or hospital and surgical expense, or disability income, etc.

Many companies—taking a leaf from the casualty and property insurance field—have issued schedule policies which list all the available coverages. This permits the writing of different benefit levels and different combinations of benefits within the same policy. The company merely indicates which coverages are involved in each particular policy. If a coverage is not to be included, the words *Not Covered* are usually set opposite it.

In reviewing the benefit provisions of your company's health policies, pay particular attention to the definition given to each coverage. For a disability policy, note carefully such things as:

1. How long are benefits payable? Is there a probationary period? Is there an elimination (waiting) period? Does it apply to both accident and sickness? If so, how many days does it run?
2. Which definition of total disability is used? Does it require that the disability prevent the insured from performing:
    a. *"every duty pertaining to his or her occupation"*? Or,
    b. *"any occupation or employment in which the insured is fit to engage in for wage of profit"*? Or,
    c. *"every duty of his or her own occupation for X years, and inability to engage in any occupation for wages or profit, thereafter"*? Or,
    d. *"a reduction of at least 20 percent earned income from all sources of employment"*?
3. Is partial disability covered? If so, how is it defined? Must total disability precede it? Are residual benefits available?
4. Does the policy require that the insured be house confined before benefits are payable?
5. What about the premiums if the insured becomes disabled? Are they waived? If so, when and under what conditions?
6. How about renewability of the contract? What benefit does the insured have in this regard? Is the contract cancelable, guaranteed renewable, or noncancelable and guaranteed renewable?

If benefits such as hospital room and board, surgical, etc., are included, check them carefully. Make sure you understand under what conditions they'll be paid and up to what limit. If a family policy is involved, check into when dependents cease to be covered. You will find many new sales automatically spinning off from family policies when dependents are no longer insured under the terms of the basic policies.

Being aware of exactly what benefits will be paid under what conditions and for what period of time, under each policy you sell, is a must if you are to serve your prospects and clients properly and successfully. People like to deal with a person who knows the business. Intelligent answers to questions build confidence in an agent. They make recommendations more acceptable. Your prospects will accept your judgement when you show them that you know what you are doing and what you are saying.

It is seldom necessary or advisable to display your full knowledge, for you are primarily a salesperson, and only secondarily a technician. Talking too much can lose a sale. But it's good for you to have enough background about the intricate workings of the policies you sell. Then—and only then—when your prospect asks, "Why is this so?" or says, "I don't like this provision!" can you answer satisfactorily and convince the person to buy.

TYPES OF SETTLEMENT

You should be thoroughly familiar with the various types of settlement that are possible under a health insurance claim. Actually, six settlements are possible:

1. Payment in Full: If the insured has a justified claim which does not exceed the maximums, the full amount of claim will be paid.
2. Adjusted Payment to Conform Limits: If the insured's claim exceeds the limits set under the policy, it will be adjusted so that the payment conforms to those limits.
3. Prorating: If the policy contains either a *relations to earnings* or an *other insurance* provision, the claim may be adjusted downward.
4. Rehabilitation Payments: Some contracts contain a rehabilitation provision which provides for the payment of benefits while the claimant is undergoing rehabilitation. A typical provision reads:

   "In the event you are receiving monthly benefits during the total loss of time resulting from injuries or sickness, the Company will continue to pay such monthly benefits while you are participating in a Company-approved, government-sponsored, or other planned vocational rehabilitation program for a term to be determined by the Company but not to exceed twelve months; notwithstanding the definition of total loss of time contained in this policy."

The philosophy behind this provision is that two advantages can be gained by encouraging disabled claimants to rehabilitate themselves:

   a. The disabled insured can be salvaged from the "living dead."
   b. The company may save money in the long run by helping claimants remove themselves from the disability rolls sooner than they might otherwise.

5. Voluntary Lump-Sum Settlements: Lump-sum settlements are sometimes voluntarily offered by companies to hopelessly disabled insurers. Such settlements, if accepted, will usually save the company the expensive administration costs involved in maintaining records, distributing checks periodically, etc. At the same time, they can help the disabled person and the family defray the heavy medical bills which invariably accompany hopeless disability.
6. Rejection or Denial: Because of the widespread misunderstanding of what health insurance policies offer, it is not uncommon for insureds to submit claims which are not valid under the terms of their contracts. In such cases, the companies have no choice but to reject the claims. However, no company ever takes such action without first weighing very carefully all the merits of such claim. Then, only if it is fully satisfied that it has no obligation under the terms of the contract, will it ever deny that claim.

Some people are completely bewildered when it comes to filling out claim forms. Therefore, you can do them—and yourself— a big favor by helping those insureds complete the paperwork involved with health insurance claims. Each claimant will be grateful for your help. This can and often does pay off in additional business with the family, or referrals to friends.

Study each claim situation in the light of the six settlements just enumerated. Determine for yourself how the company might deal with the claim. If you feel that there is any chance for its being rejected, adjusted or prorated, prepare your insured for that eventuality. Explain fully why you feel this might happen. Then, if and when the claim is submitted, he or she more readily will accept the company's action since you have prepared the person for it. If the company settlement is more liberal than you indicated the person will be pleased. If it's as bad as you anticipated, he or she will be less upset.

However, never fail to tell your insured that final action on any claim is up to the company. Your job is to submit claims, not to settle them. Settlement belongs in the hands of the home office specialists, not the field agents.

EXCLUSIONS

Another section of the health policy specifies any particular types of illness of injury which will not be covered under the policy. The heading of this section varies in different contracts and may be shown as *exclusions, limitations* or *exceptions.* Regardless of which heading is used, this section has only one purpose—to limit the company's responsibility under certain circumstances.

Over the years, the list of exclusions, limitations or exceptions included in health insurance has been reduced gradually. Generally, those that remain are unmeasurable hazards and cannot be included in the regular premium charge. There are others which are contrary to public interest. These are properly excluded.

Benefit Reduction

Certain exclusion provisions reduce benefits instead of completely cutting them off. For example, if the insured is disabled while performing for wage or profit the duties of a more hazardous occupation, then the benefits may be subject to reduction if the policy so stipulates. This is a punitive use of the reduction provision. However, it also has a very constrictive use. It makes it possible for people who arrive at the point in life where benefits used to be cut off completely to remain covered—for reduced benefits—for the rest of their lives. For example, under the Disability Income policy of one company, benefits are paid continuously before age 65. However, for total loss of time beginning after age 65, this provision is made:

> *"Benefits will be paid, at the rate of the Monthly Benefit for each full month, during total loss of time beginning after age sixty-five for as long as twelve months for any one accident of sickness."*

This valuable continuation of *some* protection would be impossible if it were not for the reduction provision.

Endorsements, Exclusion Riders (Waivers)

Special benefit limitations are sometimes added to policies. This may be done at the time the policy is issued or (if the policy permits) after it has been issued. These new limitations may be added by endorsement or by exclusion rider.

Endorsement: An endorsement is made by affixing a rubber stamp impression on the policy or by typing in an appropriate space provided on the policy.

Exclusion Rider (Waiver): More frequently, a limitation is added to a contract through an exclusion rider or waiver. It is attached to and made an integral part of the policy, after being signed by an executive officer of the company. Its purpose is to free the company of liability if certain events occur which lead to medical expense or loss of income. For instance, if the insured has suffered a fractured knee, the company may add an exclusion rider which waives liability in the event the insured has further difficulties with that same knee.

Typical Waiver

Most companies keep their exclusion endorsement or waivers very simple. A typical one reads:

> *"This policy does not cover nor extend to any disability resulting directly or indirectly from...."*

What follows eliminates the impairment or hazard about which the company is concerned.

When a broad waiver is used or when a case is rejected, you can be sure that your company is taking that action because of the facts at its disposal. If it could, it would like nothing better than to issue all contracts on a standard basis. However, your company is responsible for using good business sense in all its transactions. Therefore, it most take appropriate steps to limit the risk when it accepts a person who is not 100 percent okay from an underwriting point of view. Or, if it cannot see accepting the risk even on a modified basis, it has no alternative but to reject it.

Placing Substandard Policies

As any good agent knows, you should not look upon exclusions or ratings negatively. Rather, stress their positive qualities for the insured, for yourself, and for your company. For, indeed, they perform valuable services for each. Think of the following points as did one agent.

"(Client), it used to be that a person who suffered from even the slightest physical impairment (or was exposed to an unusual occupational hazard) would have been ineligible for health insurance.

"However, today, through the use of modified premiums which compensate the company for any additional risk exposure, my company can now offer you exactly the coverage you applied for.

"This policy is issued in light of certain 'ailments suffered by the applicant prior to the policy being issued, or those that are chronic or intermittent in nature.' The duration and extent of these qualified conditions were important considerations in determining whether this policy could even be issued and, if so, at what appropriate premium.

"Considering the information you shared with me (or, with our underwriters, through the physician's report), we were able to provide you with coverage for every type of illness or injury which may occur to you. And, if your condition stabilizes (or improves), the company has said that after xx years, it will reconsider this modification of the premium!"

Here's what another agent did when the applicant's policy was waived for "any illness or injury to eyes." (The applicant had previously been successfully operated on for cataracts.) Upon delivering the waived policy to the applicant, the agent said:

"(Client), when we were together a few weeks ago, I explained that I did not know whether my company would insure you for illness or injury to your eyes because of your recent operation for cataracts. For the time being, my company has seen fit not to protect that part of your anatomy—but this is the only exception. However, we will insure you against the 1,001 things that can go wrong with the rest of your body, for example, your legs, heart, head, arms, etc.—and you would be covered 100 percent for these contingencies."

Whenever you suspect that a substandard rating could be issued on a case, be sure to alert your prospective insured of that possibility. In this fashion, the waiver, if it is attached to the policy, is already half-sold because your client has been preconditioned.

Also, take a leaf from the agent's technique in delivering a substandard policy. Stress that many other things may go wrong with the applicant aside from the limited area which is restricted. After all, by accepting the policy, the person is insured for 90 percent or more of all future disabilities. By not taking it, he or she remains uninsured 100 percent.

THE NAIC

As long ago as 1871, the commissioners of the various states voluntarily formed the National Association of Insurance Commissioners (NAIC) for the mutual exchange of ideas and help. Over the years the Commissioners through the NAIC have accomplished much. They have adopted uniform standards for annual statements and financial strength. They also furnish guides to companies as an aid in drafting contracts for approval.

The NAIC also has worked tirelessly in order to rectify the wide divergency of the contractual provisions among the various insurers and with the objective of attaining more uniformity of such provisions which would be fair to both the insurer and to the insured.

UNIFORM ACCIDENT AND SICKNESS PROVISIONS LAW

In 1950, the National Association of Insurance Commissioners reviewed and adopted a report of its Accident and Health Committee which acknowledged some needed changes. This resulted in the promulgation of what is now known as the Uniform Individual Accident and Sickness Policy Provisions Law.

Under the Uniform Provisions Law there are 23 Uniform Provisions. Twelve are required and must be included in every individual health insurance policy (as contrasted to group). An additional 11 are optional and may be omitted at the company's discretion.

The overall objective of this law, however, is to define the terms of the contract and to clarify the rights and obligations of both the company and the insured. This is done by carefully spelling out the intent in each of the Uniform Provisions. Let us, therefore, take a close look at these provisions to see how clearly this objective has been accomplished.

Required Provision 1—Entire Contract: Changes

This first provision is important to the insured because it guarantees that the contract cannot be altered or changed or modified unless the change is authorized by an officer of the company and notice is attached to the contract.

A copy of the application is generally attached to and made a part of the policy. Other papers which may be attached include riders providing additional benefits and waivers excluding specific impairments.

> **Provision 1—Entire Contract: Changes:**—This policy, including the endorsements and the attached papers, if any, constitutes the entire contract of insurance. No change in this policy shall be valid until approved by an executive officer of the insurer and unless such approval be endorsed hereon or attached hereto. No agent has authority to change this policy or to waive any of its provisions.

Required Provision 2—Time Limit on Certain Defenses

Before the enactment of the Uniform Policy Provisions Law, the accuracy of the applicant's statements could be challenged at any time. If the company issued a policy and subsequently obtained information which indicated that the risk it had assumed was greater than it had been led to believe, it could take action to void the

policy. This unfortunate situation was corrected under required Provision 2 of the Uniform Policy Provisions Law. This reads as follows:

> **Provision 2—Time Limit on Certain Defenses:**—(a) After three years from the date of issue of this policy no misstatements, except fraudulent misstatements, made by the applicant in the application for such policy shall be used to void the policy or to deny a claim for loss incurred or disability (as defined in the policy) commencing after the expiration of such three-year period. (b) No claim for loss incurred or disability (as defined in the policy) commencing after three years from the date of issue of this policy shall be reduced or denied on the ground that a disease or physical condition, not excluded from coverage by name or specific description effective on the date of loss, had existed prior to the effective date of coverage of this policy.

Although allowed three years by law, most companies specify that *"After two years..."* no misstatements, except fraudulent misstatements, shall be used to void the policy or deny claim.

Some policies (e.g., guaranteed renewable policies) substitute for the title *Time Limit on Certain Defenses*, the title, *Incontestable*. When this is done, Part (a) of Provision 2 must read:

> (a) After this policy has been in force for a period of three years during the lifetime of the insured (excluding any period during which the insured is disabled), it shall become incontestable as to the statements contained in the application.

As can be seen, the *Incontestable* language is broader and is very similar to the incontestable clause used in life insurance policies. It makes the policy incontestable for *any* reason, even fraudulent misstatements, after the contestable period has expired. Again, most companies which use the Incontestable provision limit the contestable period to two years instead of the three years permitted by law.

Required Provision 3—Grace Period

Years ago insurance policies expired at noon on the day the premium was due, if not paid. If the insured became disabled that afternoon, he or she received nothing. Now policies must allow extra time beyond the due date in which the insured may pay a premium. The number of days specified in the Uniform Policy Provisions Law is not less than *seven* for weekly premium policies, *ten* for monthly policies, and *31* for all other policies.

Provision 3—Grace Period:—A grace period of _____ days will be granted for the payment of each premium falling due after the first premium, during which grace period the policy shall continue in force.

A policy which contains a cancellation provision may add, at the end of the above provision: subject to the right of the insurer to cancel in accordance with the cancellation provision hereof.

A policy in which the insurer reserves the right to refuse any renewal shall have, at the beginning of the above provision: unless not less than five days prior to the premium due date the insurer has delivered to the insured or has mailed to his last address as shown by the records of the insurer written notice of its intention not to renew the policy beyond the period for which the premium has been accepted.

Required Provision 4—Reinstatement

Although a policy has lapsed for nonpayment of premium, it can be reinstated by the acceptance of an overdue premium by the company or one of its agents, unless a reinstatement application is required and a conditional receipt for the premium given. Then it will be reinstated on approval, or within 45 days without approval except when the applicant has been notified that reinstatement has been refused. The reinstated policy covers accidents occurring only after the reinstatement date, and sickness originating ten days or more after that date. Otherwise the policy is exactly the same as it was before, unless the company has required any modification in order to justify reinstatement.

Provision 4—Reinstatement—If any renewal premium be not paid within the time granted the insured for payment, a subsequent acceptance of premium by the insurer or by any agent duly authorized by the insurer to accept such

premium, without requiring in connection therewith an application for reinstatement, shall reinstate the policy; provided, however, that if the insurer or such agent requires an application for reinstatement and issues a conditional receipt for the premium tendered, the policy will be reinstated upon approval of such application by the insurer or, lacking such approval, upon the forty-fifth day following the date of such conditional receipt unless the insurer has previously notified the insured in writing of its disapproval of such application. The reinstated policy shall cover only loss resulting from such accidental injury as may be sustained after the date of reinstatement and loss due to such sickness as may begin more than ten days after such date. In all other respects the insured and insurer shall have the same rights thereunder as they had under the policy immediately before the due date of the defaulted premium, subject to any provisions endorsed hereon or attached hereto in connection with the reinstatement. Any premium accepted in connection with the reinstatement shall be applied to a period for which premium has not been previously paid, but not to any period more than sixty days prior to the date of reinstatement.

The last sentence of the above may be omitted from policies guaranteed renewable to age 50, or if issued after age 44, guaranteed renewable for at least five years.

Required Provision 5—Notice of Claim

Under this provision, the insured must furnish the company with a notice of claim sufficient to identify the insured, within 20 days, or as soon as reasonably possible. Notice given to an agent is considered sufficient. An additional requirement may be inserted in policies paying benefits for more than two years, which states that the insured should give the company notice of claim every six months, unless he or she is legally incapacitated.

Provision 5—Notice of Claim—Written notice of claim must be given to the insurer within twenty days after occurrence or commencement of any loss covered by the policy, or as soon thereafter as is reasonably possible. Notice given by or in behalf of the insured or the beneficiary to the insurer at _____ (insert the location of such office as the insurer may designate for the purpose), or to any authorized agent of the insurer, with information sufficient to identify the insured, shall be deemed notice to the insurer.

Policies providing loss-of-time benefits payable for at least two years, may insert the following between the first and second sentences of the above provision: Subject to the qualifications set forth below, if the insured suffers loss of time on account of disability for which indemnity may be payable for at least two years, he shall, at least once in every six months after having given notice of claim, give to the insurer notice of continuance of said disability, except in the event of legal incapacity. The period of six months following any filing of proof by the insured or any payment by the insurer on account of such claim or any denial of liability in whole or in part by the insurer shall be excluded in applying this provision. Delay in the giving of such notice shall not impair the insured's right to any indemnity which would otherwise have accrued during the period of six months preceding the date on which such notice is actually given.

Required Provision 6—Claims Forms

Once it has been notified of a claim, the burden is on the company to furnish claim forms promptly within 15 days. If forms are not furnished, then the insured shall be deemed to have complied with all requirements of Provision 7, Proofs of Loss, if he or she submits, within the time limit set in the policy, written Proof of Loss, nature of the cause, and extent of the loss.

Provision 6—Claims Forms:—The insurer, upon receipt of a notice of claim, will furnish to the claimant such forms as are usually furnished by it for filing proofs of loss. If such forms are not furnished within fifteen days after the giving of such notice the claimant shall be deemed to have complied with the requirements of this policy as to proof of loss upon submitting, within the time fixed in the policy for filing proofs of loss, written proof covering the

occurrence, the character and the extent of the loss for which claim is made.

Required Provision 7—Proofs of Loss

This provision sets forth that within 90 days after the termination of the period for which the company is liable, the insured must furnish written proof of loss, if reasonably possible. Except in instances of legal incapacity, proofs of loss must be furnished the company within one year.

Provision 7—Proofs of Loss: Written proof of loss must be furnished to the insurer at its said office in case of claim for loss for which this policy provides any periodic payment contingent upon continuing loss within ninety days after the termination of the period for which the insurer is liable and in case of claims for any other loss within ninety days after the date of such loss. Failure to furnish such proof within the time required shall not invalidate nor reduce any claim if it was not reasonably possible to give such proof within such time, provided such proof is furnished as soon as reasonably possible and in no event, except in the absence of legal capacity, later than one year from the time proof is otherwise required.

Required Provision 8—Time of Payment of Claims

This provision states that as soon as possible as proof of loss is received by the company, benefits are payable. Income benefits are payable at specified intervals not less frequently than monthly.

Provision 8—Time of Payment of Claims:—Indemnities payable under this policy for any loss other than loss for which this policy provides any periodic payment will be paid immediately upon receipt of due written proof of such loss. Subject to due written proof of loss, all accrued indemnities for loss for which this policy provides periodic payment will be paid _____ (insert period for payment which must not be less frequently than monthly), and any balance remaining unpaid upon the termination of liability will be paid immediately upon receipt of due written proof.

Required Provision 9—Payment of Claims

This provision designates to whom benefits will be paid so that settlement of claims can be made promptly by the company without costly legal investigation. Payment for loss of life will be made to the insured's estate if no beneficiary has been named or is alive. Either or both of two optional paragraphs may be added. One is a "facility of payment clause" which enables a company to pay up to $1,000 to any relative by blood or marriage of the insured or beneficiary who the company believes is entitled to receive it. The other clause permits the company to make payment promptly and without red tape directly to a person or hospital rendering service.

> **Provision 9—Payment of Claims:**—Indemnity for loss of life will be payable in accordance with the beneficiary designation and the provisions respecting such payment which may be prescribed herein and effective at the time of payment. If no such designation or provision is then effective, such indemnity shall be payable to the estate of the insured. Any other accrued indemnities unpaid at the insured's death may, at the option of the insurer, be paid either to such beneficiary or to such estate. All other indemnities will be payable to the insured.
>
> **Either or both of the following paragraphs may be included in this provision:**
>
> If any indemnity of this policy shall be payable to the estate of the insured, or to an insured or beneficiary who is a minor or otherwise not competent to give a valid release, the insurer may pay such indemnity, up to an amount not exceeding $_____ (insert an amount which shall not exceed $1,000), to any relative by blood or connection by marriage of the insured or beneficiary who is deemed by the insurer to be equitably entitled thereto. Any payment made by the insurer in good faith pursuant to this provision shall fully discharge the insurer to the extent of such payment.
>
> Subject to any written direction of the insured in the application or otherwise all or a portion of any indemnities provided by this policy on account of hospital, nursing, medical, or surgical services may, at the insurer's option and unless the insured requests otherwise in writing not later than the time of filing proofs of such loss, be paid directly to the hospital or person rendering such services; but it is not required that the service be rendered by a particular hospital or person.

Required Provision 10—Physical Examinations and Autopsy

This provision entitles a company at its own expense to make physical examinations of the insured at reasonable intervals during the period of a claim, and the right to make an autopsy when death benefits are payable, provided it is not forbidden by law.

> **Provision 10—Physical Examinations and Autopsy:**—The insurer at its own expense shall have the right and opportunity to examine the person of the insured when and as often as it may reasonably require during the pendancy of a claim hereunder and to make an autopsy in case of death where it is not forbidden by law.

Required Provision 11—Legal Actions

Under this clause the company has 60 days in which to investigate a claim during which time the insured cannot take legal action.

> **Provision 11—Legal Actions:**—No action at law or in equity shall be brought to recover on this policy prior to the expiration of sixty days after written proof of loss has been furnished in accordance with the requirements of this policy. No such action shall be brought after the expiration of three years after the time written proof of loss is required to be furnished.

Required Provision 12—Change of Beneficiary

This provision states that unless the insured has specifically denied the right to change beneficiary in the application, he or she may change the beneficiary as desired. The insured may also assign the contract, by authorizing the company in writing that he or she wishes it to recognize the prior interest in the policy of someone other than the beneficiary or the insured. Such an assignment becomes effective upon approval in writing by an office of the company.

The company may, if it desires, omit the first part of Provision 12, relating to the irrevocable beneficiary designation.

> **Provision 12—Change of Beneficiary:—** Unless the insured makes an irrevocable designation of beneficiary, the right to change of beneficiary is reserved to the insured and the consent of the beneficiary or beneficiaries shall not be requisite to surrender or assignment of this policy or to any change of beneficiary or beneficiaries, or to any other changes in this policy.

THE OPTIONAL PROVISIONS

The Uniform Policy Provisions Law requires that all of the preceding provisions be included in all health policies. There are 11 additional provisions, any or all of which may be included or omitted. A company may change the wording provided the rewording is not less favorable to the insured. A general knowledge of these provisions is also important for you to have.

Optional Provision 1—Change of Occupation

When this optional provision is contained in a policy, if an insured becomes disabled after changing to a more hazardous occupation, benefits will be on the basis of the more hazardous occupation. Or if he or she changes to a less hazardous occupation, the premium rate will be reduced accordingly and any overpayment will be refunded upon request. This provision never appears in noncancelable contracts, and is not used frequently in other policies.

> **Provision 1—Change of Occupation:—**If the insured be injured or contract sickness after having changed his occupation to one classified by the insurer as more hazardous than that stated in this policy or while doing for compensation anything pertaining to an occupation so classified, the insurer will pay only such portion of the indemnities provided in this policy as the premium paid would have purchased at the rates

and within the limits fixed by the insurer for such more hazardous occupation. If the insured changes his occupation to one classified by the insurer as less hazardous than that stated in this policy, the insurer, upon receipt of proof of such change of occupation, will reduce the premium rate accordingly, and will return the excess pro rata unearned premium from the date of change of occupation or from the policy anniversary date immediately preceding receipt of such proof, whichever is the more recent. In applying this provision, the classification of occupational risk and the premium rates shall be such as have been last filed by the insurer prior to the occurrence of the loss for which the insurer is liable or prior to date of proof of change in occupation with the state official having supervision of insurance in the state where the insured resided at the time this policy was issued; but if such filing was not required, then the classification of occupational risk and the premium rates shall be those last made effective by the insurer in such state prior to the occurrence of the loss prior to the date of proof of change in occupation.

Optional Provision 2—Misstatement of Age

Under this provision, which is often used, the insured is protected when an error is made regarding his or her age. Instead of the policy's being void, benefits are paid in the amount which the premium would have purchased at the correct age. Of course, if coverage would not have been available at the correct age, the insured is entitled to a refund of those premiums.

> **Provision 2—Misstatement of Age:—**If the age of the insured has been misstated, all amounts payable under this policy shall be such as the premium paid would have purchased at the correct age.

Optional Provision 3—Other Insurance in This Insurer

This provision, which is not often used, protects a company against excess insurance by limiting the amount of coverage that will be carried by the company. If an insured already has coverage with the company, which together with this policy, provides benefits in excess of the maximum allowed by the company, only the maximum is payable and excess premiums will be returned to the estate. An alternative wording of this optional provision is permitted which limits the company's liability to the one policy selected by the insured.

Provision 3—Other Insurance in This Insurer:

—If an accident or sickness or accident and sickness policy or policies previously issued by the insurer to the insured by in force concurrently herewith, making the aggregate indemnity for _____ (insert type of coverage or coverages) in excess of $_____ (insert maximum limit of indemnity or indemnities) the excess insurance shall be void and all premiums paid for such excess shall be returned to the insured or to his estate.

Or,

Insurance effective at any one time on the insured under a like policy or policies, in this insurer is limited to one such policy elected by the insured, his beneficiary or his estate, as the case may be, and the insurer will return all premiums paid for all other such policies.

Optional Provision 4—Insurance with Other Insurer

This provides that if an insured has duplicate coverage on an "expense incurred basis" with other companies and a company accepts the risk without being notified of the other coverage, its liability will be a proportionate share of the expenses incurred, and premiums for the unused portion are refunded. This provision, and Provision 5, are not used frequently.

Provision 4—Insurance with Other Insurer:—

If there be other valid coverage, not with this insurer, providing benefits for the same loss on a provision of service basis or on an expense incurred basis and of which this insurer has not been given written notice prior to the occurrence or commencement of loss, the only liability under any expense incurred coverage of this policy shall be for such proportion of the loss as the amount which would otherwise have been payable hereunder plus the total of the like amounts under all such other valid coverages for the same loss of which this insurer had notice bears to the total like amounts under all valid coverages for such loss, and for the return of such portion of the premiums paid as shall exceed the pro-rata portion of the amount so determined. For the purpose of applying this provision when other coverage is on a provision of service basis, the "like amount" of such other coverage shall be taken as the amount which the services rendered would have cost in the absence of such coverage.

If the foregoing policy provision is included in a policy which also contains the next following policy provision there shall be added to the caption of the foregoing provision the phrase "—EXPENSE INCURRED BENEFITS." The insurer may, at its option, include in this provision a definition of "other valid coverage," approved as to form by the commissioner, which definition shall be limited in subject matter to coverage provided by organizations subject to regulation by insurance law or by insurance authorities of this or any other state of the United States or any province of Canada, and by hospital or medical service organizations, and to any other coverage the inclusion of which may be approved by the commissioner.

In the absence of such definition such term shall not include group insurance, automobile, medical payments insurance, or coverage provided by hospital or medical service organizations or by union welfare plans or employer or employee benefit organizations.

For the purpose of applying the foregoing policy provision with respect to any insured, any amount of benefit provided for such insured pursuant to any compulsory benefit statute (including any Workers' Compensation or employers' liability statute) whether provided by a governmental agency or otherwise shall in all cases be deemed to be "other valid coverage" of which the insurer has had notice. In applying for foregoing policy provision no third party liability coverage shall be included as "other valid coverage."

Optional Provision 5—Insurance with Other Insurers

This option is the same as the preceding, except it relates to all benefits *other than expenses incurred.*

Provision 5—Insurance with Other Insurers: —If there be other valid coverage, not with the insurer, providing benefits for the same loss on other than an expense incurred basis and of which this insurer has not been given written notice prior to the occurrence or commencement of loss, the only liability for such benefits under this policy shall be for such proportion of the indemnities otherwise provided hereunder for such loss as the like indemnities of which the insurer had notice (including the indemnities under this policy) bear to the total amount of all like indemnities for such loss, and for the return of such portion of the premium paid as shall exceed the pro rata portion for the indemnities thus determined.

If the foregoing policy provision is included in a policy which also contains the next preceding policy provision there shall be added to the caption of the foregoing provision the phrase "—OTHER BENEFITS." Note: The remaining part of this parenthetical comment is the same as that which follows "Expense Incurred Benefits" in the comment following Provision 4.

Optional Provision 6—Relation of Earnings to Insurance

This is generally known as the "average earnings clause" and may be used only in noncancelable and guaranteed renewable contracts. It protects the company and its insureds against the individual who delays recovery because the disability income is greater than his or her earned income. At the time disability commences, should the total disability income exceed earned income, or average earned income for the preceding two years, whichever is greater, income benefits under the policy will be reduced proportionately. In no case, however, will monthly benefits under *all* policies be reduced to less than $200. Premiums for excess insurance are returned to the insured. This provision is used occasionally.

Provision 6—Relation of Earnings to Insurance:—If the total monthly amount of loss of time benefits promised for the same loss under all valid loss of time coverage upon the insured, whether payable on a weekly or monthly basis, shall exceed the monthly earnings of the insured at the time disability commenced or his average monthly earnings for the period of two years immediately preceding a disability for which claim is made, whichever is greater, the insurer will be liable only for such proportionate amount of such benefits under this policy as the amount of such monthly earnings or such average monthly earnings of the insured bears to the total amount of monthly benefits for the same loss under all such coverage upon the insured at the time such disability commences and for the return of such part of the premiums paid during such two years as shall exceed the pro rata amount of the premiums for the benefits actually paid hereunder; but this shall not operate to reduce the total monthly amount of benefits payable under all such coverage upon the insured below the sum of $200 or the sum of the monthly benefits specified in such coverages, whichever is the lesser, nor shall it operate to reduce benefits other than those payable for loss of time.

The insurer may, at its option, include in this provision a definition of "valid loss of time coverage," approved as to form by the commissioner, which definition shall be limited in subject matter to coverage provided by governmental agencies or by organizations subject to regulation by insurance law or by insurance authorities of this or any other state of the United States or any province of Canada, or to any other coverage the inclusion of which may be approved by the commissioner or any combination of such coverages. In the absence of such definition such term shall not include any coverage provided for such insured pursuant to any compulsory benefit statute (including any Workers' Compensation or employer's liability statute), or benefits provided by union welfare plans or by the employer or employee benefit organizations.

Optional Provision 7—Unpaid Premium

This clause states the right of the company to deduct for a claim any unpaid premium which is due, but is used rarely.

Provision 7—Unpaid Premium:—Upon the payment of a claim under this policy, any premium then due and unpaid or covered by any note or written order may be deducted therefrom.

Optional Provision 8—Cancellation

This provision, which is not prohibited in some states, gives the company the right to cancel at any time with at least five days' notice after the policy has been in force beyond its original term. Excess premiums are refunded. Cancellation does not affect any claim originating before cancellation. This provision is vital in cancelable contracts, but almost is never used in any others.

Provision 8—Cancellation:—The insurer may cancel this policy at any time by written notice delivered to the insured, or mailed to his last address as shown by the records of the insurer, stating when, not less than five days thereafter, such cancellation shall be effective; and after the policy has been continued beyond its original term the insured may cancel this policy at any time by written notice delivered or mailed to the insurer, effective upon receipt or on such later date as may be specified in such notice. In the event of cancellation, the insurer will return promptly the unearned portion of any premium paid. If the insured cancels, the earned premium shall be computed by the use of the short-rate table last filed with the state official having supervision of insurance in the state where the insured resided when the policy was issued. If the insurer cancels, the earned premium shall be computed pro rata. Cancellation shall be without prejudice to any claim originating prior to the effective date of cancellation.

Optional Provision 9—Conformity with State Statutes

Although this is an optional provision, some states require that it be included and it is used frequently in other states. It automatically amends the policy, if necessary, so that it will conform to minimum state requirements.

Provision 9—Conformity with State Statutes:—Any provision of this policy which, on its effective date, is in conflict with the statutes of the state in which the insured resides on such date is hereby amended to conform to minimum requirements of such statutes.

Optional Provision 10—Illegal Occupation

This provision, rarely used, states that the company is not liable if the loss results from any felony or illegal occupation.

Provision 10—Illegal Occupation:—The insurer shall not be liable for any loss to which a contributing cause was the insured's commission of or attempt to commit a felony or to which a contributing cause was the insured's being engaged in an illegal occupation.

Optional Provision 11—Intoxicants and Narcotics

This provision is similar to the preceding clause and also is used rarely. It relieves the company of liability for losses while the insured is under the influence of liquor or narcotics.

Provision 11—Intoxicants and Narcotics:—The insurer shall not be liable for any loss sustained or contracted in consequence of the insured's being intoxicated or under the influence of any narcotic unless administered on the advice of a physician.

ETHICS AND COMPETITION

In analyzing the provisions of your company's contracts, you will find they contain many outstanding features and may have many competitive advantages. It is natural and proper that you become enthusiastic about them. But keep this in mind: Every policy cannot include all the most liberal features. If it did, it would be unsound from an underwriting point of view, or the premium would be too high to be competitive.

In your field activity, you will come up against the health insurance policies of other companies. Perhaps your policies will have desirable features which are lacking in the others. But it is possible that the others may have outstanding features of their own. When you compare policies, be sure your comparisons are complete and accurate. Fairness always pays off. It creates added prestige and respect for you. Your work is a service highly charged with public interest. You serve best when you sell well.

Your duty is to help prospects obtain the kind of protection they need and can afford. Instead of inducing a prospect to drop a good contract he or she already has and to replace it with yours, ethical selling dictates that you add to and build toward what the person needs.

Most people are relatively uninformed about the health insurance they have. Many who purchased policies because of low cost and glowing accounts of benefits are not aware of the exact benefits or limitations of the contracts. They believe what they have purchased through the mail or from an advertisement provides broad coverage. Such insurance is usually very limited in scope, with benefits payable only for accidents occurring under specific circumstances. Many believe they have disability income protection of $300 a month for $50 a year. But what they probably have is an *accident-only* policy which pays $300 a month if total disability results from accidental bodily injury and prevents the insured from doing work of *any kind*. Such contracts are usually worth what they cost. But it is your responsibility to help people understand extremely limited policies and to help them obtain adequate protection.

You can more readily do this if you, yourself, have some understanding of how health insurance premium rates are determined.

DETERMINING HEALTH INSURANCE RATES

In determining the rate for a health insurance contract three factors are involved:

1. Claim cost
2. Cost of doing business
3. Reserve for contingencies

In life insurance premiums a major factor is the age of the applicant. Mortality tables show that the death rate increases each year as people grow older. In health insurance, while the insured's age becomes of increasing importance in later years, the major factor is the *occupational hazard*.

A banker, for example, pays a lower premium for health insurance than a laborer in a pulp and paper factory. The occupational hazards of banking are practically nil. In pulp and paper processing, on the other hand, a worker is exposed to many hazards.

Claim Cost

Over the years much statistical information has been gathered on the number of work-hours lost through sickness and accident in various industries. This information has been compiled into morbidity tables. Assume, for illustrative purposes, that employees in a certain occupation lose on the average ten days of work a year. Remember, that is an average figure. Some will be disabled longer, some less. Then for each $100 of monthly indemnity ($3.33 per day), the portion of the annual premium covering the claim would be $10 \times \$3.33$, which is $33.33. The "loss of adjustment" or direct costs for handling claims and the indirect expenses of operating the claim department must be added to this base to arrive at the "net premium" to be charged.

Expenses and Reserves

To this must also be added the *loading* or *acquisition costs*. These include the agent's commissions, sales equipment, training, medical fees, investment expenses, home office records, supplies, rents and salaries. The third factor, *reserve for contingencies*, is an amount which must be set aside to guarantee that future claims and other payments can be met promptly and fully.

With life insurance, there is only one claim—at death. In health policies, the possibilities of claims are unlimited. Think about it: What is the average number of times we go to the doctor each year? (5.4 times) What is the average number of days lost from work each year due to illness or injury? (5.4) What is the average number of days we experience some limitation of our regular activities as a result of acute or chronic conditions? (14.5) What percent of our disposable income do we spend on personal medical care? (12.5 percent).[1]

Considering the magnitude of the risk exposure, it is incredible that medical and disability policies are priced as reasonably as they are! Let alone available at all!

YOUR REAL COMPETITION

Competing in the health insurance market is the same as in the life insurance field. You will come across prospects who are working with another agent. You will find some of these agents extremely knowledgeable about their own—and your—products. Your strength, your edge, will be your knowledge of your products—and *theirs!* Knowledge is power. The more you have, the more effective and productive you will be.

Your real competition, however, does not come solely from other health insurance agents. It is not a contest between your contract and another good contract. It is not hidden in the clauses or the provisions or the rates of your policies compared with those of other sound policies. Your real competition is for a fair share of the consumer dollar.

There are times, of course, when you cannot make a sale because another agent has. But that is not too serious, because the market is so vast.

You are primarily in competition with pleasures and comforts your prospects can touch or anticipate today. You are competing with your prospects' desire for a modern refrigerator, another television set or new automobile. Your competition is the attractive advertising which offers immediate benefit and satisfactions from tangible goods.

Surveys show that most people know they need more insurance. They intend to buy more—but not just now. Your competition is the put-it-off attitude so common among men and women, the willingness to postpone to some future date what they know they should do, because they have more pleasant ways to spend their money today.

Your business is to make sure that a person's plans and hopes and desires will not be destroyed by a prolonged illness or sudden accident. Yours is a dignified, creative, constructive business. That is the way it is conducted.

[1]1990 Statistical Abstract of The United States

Chapter 7
The Health Insurance Market

LESSON TEXT—Consider Specific Needs . . . Examples Given—The Dentist, the Artist, the Manufacturer's Representative, the Purchasing Agent, the Farmer, the Department Head, the Store Owner—All Typical Real Life Situations Showing Needs for Health Insurance

The concept of *markets* is solidly established in most sales fields. By this is meant the grouping of either prospects or customers into specific categories.

Is there a particular market that is best for you? The important thing is that you work with prospects with whom you feel comfortable. Perhaps you already have a life insurance clientele, which can be part of your ready-made market for health insurance.

Plan to contact new prospects whom you can approach with ease. Talk their language and they'll be more likely to listen attentively to your suggestions. Will your selected market include mostly business executives or professional persons? Career women may be a target market for some agents. Others may prefer to concentrate in the retail field. Giving careful thought to your own market will make you more effective in selling health insurance.

You can profit by using this marketing concept in selling health insurance. Group your prospects according to the health insurance packages you think they'll be most interested in, or by the needs you think they most likely will have. Either way—on a package or on a needs basis—you can catalog the people you call on so as to be more effective in finding them as well as in approaching and selling them.

CONSIDER SPECIFIC NEEDS

However, whether or not you categorize prospects, you may rest assured that each of them needs protection against loss of income and medical expense. Each one's problems are clear cut and well defined. These problems are basic and common to all people who depend on their ability to earn a living. They concern and revolve around a person's need for money with which to meet living costs and other expenses. It is impossible in today's economy to imagine a situation without a specific need for some type of health insurance. Let's study the situation of a few hypothetical prospects to analyze their needs.

EXAMPLES GIVEN

Reading these examples may remind you of someone you know. If so, make sure you call! He or she may be a very good prospect for you—right now!

When the Income Producer Is Disabled, Health Insurance:

Guarantees the mortgage or rent payments will be met...

Pays the grocer, the fuel bill, the utility company...

Provides money for schoolbooks, supplies, lunches, transportation, tuition...

Protects the life insurance...

Furnishes the premiums for automobile, liability or fire insurance...

Meets the installment payment on the car, the television set, the deep-freeze unit...

Guards the savings account, bonds, stocks ...

Insures retirement plans, hopes and dreams ...

Hastens recovery by eliminating worry...

It helps to keep the family together—it is basic protection!

Kirby J. Blake, D.D.S.

Kirby J. Blake, D.D.S., has maintained professional offices in one location for many years. As a dentist, Dr. Blake has built a good reputation, has the latest in equipment and enjoys a large following among business people and members of their families. Dr. Blake drives a late model car, and the family lives in a fine home with their two children. Terry, the elder child, is at-

tending college and hopes to be a dentist, too. Ronnie is a senior in high school and will be starting college next year.

But suppose Dr. Blake develops a serious infection in a hand? It may be a number of months before it is healed completely so that Dr. Blake can treat patients again. Dental work is highly personal, so it is almost impossible to hire a substitute. When the doctor stops working, all income stops too. Yet Dr. Blake cannot close the office, nor leave it unattended by a receptionist. Business expenses continue just as before. And, with a child in college and another one a year away, plus the usual overhead of operating a home, Dr. Blake has heavy living expenses.

Had Dr. Blake been your client before the infection, you would have recommended the purchase of a disability insurance plan that would continue to pay income when disability strikes. You also would have presented a Comprehensive Medical plan to reimburse the doctor for medical and potential hospital bills. Additionally, you would have insisted that Dr. Blake have a Business Overhead Expense policy to provide payments for business expenses which all professional people must meet, even when they are unable to take care of patients.

Sam Y. Wells, Artist

For a young person who completed art school only two years ago, Sam Wells is making very good progress. Within a few days after graduating Sam obtained a job with a commercial art studio which services advertising agencies and several retail accounts. Sam fit in well from the beginning, is well liked, and on a base salary plus commission for work done, and earns a good income. Sam lives at home with his parents, and even while buying a new car, he still saves money out of each paycheck.

On the surface it doesn't appear that Sam has much need for health insurance. But look deeper into Sam's hopes and plans for the future. He does not always want to work for someone else and is saving money in order to buy a studio.

If Sam were unable to work due to an illness or injury, all income would stop. Payments on the car will have to be met. Sam wants to be independent of the family, and doesn't want his parents paying for Sam's doctor or other medical expenses. Yet, if Sam dips into the savings account that is building, all hopes of owning a business will be destroyed.

What Sam Wells needs is a plan to protect savings so that ambitions for the future can be attained. Sam should have a Major Medical policy, and as much disability insurance as his current income will justify, with a guaranteed insurability rider attached.

Leslie Z. Carter, Manufacturers' Representative

Leslie Z. Carter is a manufacturers' representative who sells products produced by a number of manufacturers. Les' territory covers quite an area and requires about 25,000 miles a year of travelling. It is strictly a commission job and Les is every bit self-employed. "The hardest part about my job is driving so much," Les says. But that is a modest statement because Les works hard and keeps to a strict, self-imposed schedule. Les is well known, well liked and well accepted by customers. Les operates at a highly personal level with them: dining with them, playing tennis, socializing with their families, and becoming a friend. Les has a high five-figure income, is single, and lives at a country club. Certainly Les has a well-ordered, secure life.

But something happens. Les is in an automobile accident, and wakes up in a hospital bed with the right leg raised in a cast—a compound fracture. The doctor says it will heal all right, but that it will be several months before Les can drive to see any customers.

So, Leslie Carter writes to all the customers and calls them regularly by telephone. Some repeat orders come in the mail. But Les can't introduce new items and is missing sales. Confined to the room at the club after leaving the hospital, expenses start mounting. "It could have been worse," Les muses, "I might have ended up with a broken back, unable to ever work again."

What Leslie Carter needed was a plan that would have paid an income if Les could work part-time as the result of an illness or injury. While Les needed only minimal medical care, a Hospital Expense or Major Medical policy would have been helpful. It is easy to feel immune to

tragedy when everything is going well. You as an insurance agent have to help your prospects feel the need to protect themselves against unforeseen contingencies.

Kim E. Wilson, Purchasing Agent

Shortly after graduation from college, Kim E. Wilson married and accepted a position in the purchasing department of a manufacturer branching into the consumer field. In the years following, it seemed to Kim that everything showed uninterrupted growth: the company, responsibilities at the plant, income, family. Kim bought a home with a large mortgage, and Kim's spouse and young children are pleased with the neighborhood. They like their new friends, the school and being away from congested city living. Kim is a conscientious, foresighted person, with mortgage life insurance, excellent group medical insurance and enough additional life insurance to provide a monthly income until the children are grown and able to be self-supporting.

Here without question is a happy family unlikely to be disrupted financially too seriously—not even by the possible premature death of the income producer. But Kim has overlooked the more threatening, more destructive event which strikes a more terrible blow and more often than premature death. Kim Wilson's future, the family's happiness and security, their home and their upbringing all depend on Kim's ability to produce income month after month, year after year. There is a big gap in Kim's financial planning. Without a disability insurance program, especially with a Cost of Living Adjustment rider, Kim can't guarantee that the family's future won't be disrupted.

Dale G. Anderson, Farmer

Out in the country on the mailbox in front of a well-kept farm is the name "Dale G. Anderson." By the long low building in the back with its evenly spaced windows you can tell it is a poultry farm. For almost 15 years Dale has been selling chickens and eggs. The land is nearly paid for. In a garden at the side of the house enough vegetables are grown for the family's use. Dale owns some livestock and enough farm equipment to get along without extra help. Dale's two older children attend agricultural college in the nearby city, and the two younger children, ages 13 and 15, help out around the farm. On first thought you might well conclude that here, surely, is an oasis of self-sufficiency.

Farming is one of the most hazardous occupations, with falls on the farm causing more injuries than almost anything else. A disabling illness can prevent a farmer from performing duties for a longer period than the same sickness keeps a city worker away from the desk. It takes more than good land, good equipment and a healthy flock of hens to make a poultry farm profitable. It takes experience and contacts developed over the years. It takes on-the-job management. It takes constant, close supervision of a hundred and one details. Deterioration sets in fast on a farm and must be eternally guarded against. When Dale Anderson is laid up, unable to advise and guide operations on the farm, the black ink on the ledger quickly turns to red. Doctor bills and medical expenses may be extremely heavy, but the farm loss due to lack of management will be even heavier.

Fortunately, Dale has an insurance agent who understands the risks to which Dale is exposed. They have put into place Major Medical, Business Overhead Expense, disability and life insurance plans that will protect Dale for nearly any contingency. Dale feels secure when he sees the sun going down, and is ready to face every new sunrise.

Robbie L. Proctor, Department Head

Robbie Proctor has worked in jobs from sales clerk to department head in a large local department store. Robbie is valued by the store's owners, and is admired by co-workers. Robbie makes an excellent salary and is committed to work. Supplementing the company's pension plan, Robbie has purchased individual investments and insurance in adequate amounts, and the store provides Robbie with Major Medical insurance. To all appearances, it seems that Robbie leads a completely secure life.

Then you learn that Robbie's mother lives in a small town not far away, and Robbie visits her every other week. Mrs. Proctor is a widow but she prefers to live in her own home with her own things around her. And you learn that Robbie pays for her mother's support. The picture changes immediately.

In case of injury or illness, disability insurance can provide Robbie with an income that would be sufficient to take care of both Robbie and Mrs. Proctor. With Cost of Living Adjustment and Guaranteed Insurability riders, Robbie could assure that income will always be adequate, and provide financial security for them both.

Hank O'Brien, Store Owner

Hank O'Brien is an independent business person. As sole proprietor of a small firm, Hank sells indoor-outdoor rugs and installs vinyl floors and counter tops. Hank's income is not as large as you might expect, because the business has been growing only gradually and Hank has been putting money back into it. Hank's monthly take-home pay is large enough, though, to provide the family with a comfortable home plus a few luxuries.

Laying vinyl is a precision job. Mistakes are costly and easily made. For the most part, Hank makes the contacts, quotes on jobs, buys his inventory and waits on customers in the store when time allows. With the aid of two employees, Hank operates a steady, growing business. The need for Business Overhead Expense and disability protection for Hank O'Brien is indisputable. But Hank says, and sincerely believes, that the personal budget cannot be stretched to cover a single additional item.

Why not let the business purchase the protection and pay the premiums, with the income payable to the firm whenever the owner is unable to work? With this income, additional help can be hired to carry on in the owner's absence and the firm can continue to pay at least a part of Hank's income.

This is not an unusual situation, where the business and sole proprietor are one and the same. Frequently the owner will have the business pay the premiums, even though the owner says "I can't afford it."

PROSPECTS ARE ALL AROUND US

These are a few of the typical situations that you will discover all around you. You will find them among your fellow club members, among your neighbors, among the people you come in contact with in your regular daily life. Your grocer, your barber, the druggist, the radio repairman, the plumber—the list is endless. At first glance it may appear to you that the people you know, the people you meet, the people you come in contact with are different. They seem to have their lives so organized that they appear to have no need for income from an outside source in the event that they are unable to work. But scratch the surface a little, look deeper into their lives and you will find that there is an urgent, pressing need for health insurance. The need is there because the problem of replacing lost income and paying medical expenses when disability strikes is universal. It is a major and basic problem for everyone.

Chapter 8
Prospecting

One essential concept is that the process of prospecting is a never-ending one. Your list of prospects is comparable to your bank account. Your daily balance is of vital importance.

THE INVENTORY CONCEPT

There is another way to look at it. Your prospect file is your inventory—the goods on your shelves. Any good merchant knows that the value of inventory is determined by two factors: one, the quality of merchandise and two, the rate of turnover. The merchant has to keep moving it to make a profit. There's no way to use the same merchandise over and over again.

Neither can the health insurance agent maintain the some stock of goods. The agent must constantly replace worn-out merchandise (prospects) with fresh names. And the quality of these names will influence the return on investment.

It is a stimulating thought that you can build your inventory in both quantity and quality, without regard to space limitations or the danger of tying up capital. You can build an inventory which, if turned over frequently enough, can be profitable for months and years ahead.

As a health insurance agent, your objective is not merely to sell a policy. Nor is it your job to create problems.

Life creates problems. Your objective is to help people recognize the problems which already exist and then show how best to solve them. But you must find people with these problems.

How do you go about it? First, let us break down the process of prospecting and explore the following areas of the job:

Who is a good prospect for you? Where can this person be found? How can you reach the person on a prestige basis?

WHO IS A GOOD PROSPECT FOR YOU?

Thousands of new individual health insurance contracts are sold each week. As a result of this, thousands of dollars of new premiums are written.

All of the people who became insureds today were only prospects yesterday. Many of them live around you. They work near you. They pass you on the street daily. Some of them are your own friends. Many of them would have been good prospects for you—in fact, better for you than for any other agent.

Your job, then, is to find out who among these people are prospects. Therefore, it is not merely a matter of collecting names. Names alone are not enough. **A person is only a suspect until you have sufficient information to convert him or her into a prospect.**

There are six good questions to ask yourself which, if answered in the affirmative, will be invaluable in measuring how good a prospect is for you. Is that prospect one who:

1. Has a need?
2. Can pay the premiums?
3. Can meet underwriting requirements?
4. Can be approached on the right basis?
5. Is the *right* type?
6. Is a prospect *now?*

The First Qualifying Question

Is there a need for health insurance? If you have sufficient information about a person, you can decide whether there is such a need. If you can pinpoint the need, you may have a good prospect.

When a person is a salaried employee, dependent upon continuous employment for income, he or she obviously has need for replacement income in the event of accident or sickness.

A professional person who must maintain a private practice in order to live undoubtedly has a need for income to take up the slack when he or she becomes disabled.

When illness or injury could disrupt the smooth functioning of a partnership, there is a need for each partner to have protection against accident and sickness. Can you imagine the economic disruption that occurs when one partner can't work? Income to the disabled partner and income to the partnership become critical issues. Disability buy-outs are increasingly common to prevent financial ruin.

The same thing applies to the other forms of business. A sole proprietor would be devastated. And a corporation would be in turmoil if a key employee became disabled. The disability loss of a stockholder-employee would be even worse, because the business is without one of its prime movers and decision makers. Again, a disability buy-out can keep everyone's finances and pride intact.

It can be established that almost every person who works for a living has a need for health insurance, but knowledge of this specific need is what makes an individual a prospect for you.

The Second Question

Can he or she pay the premium? An obvious basic prospect qualification is that a person must be able to afford the premium. The person who lives carefully and thriftily and earns a good living day in and day our, is usually a better prospect than one whose earnings fluctuate widely. The person will be more interested in your recommendations than will those whose living scale equals or exceeds their income. In addition, the thrifty will hold on to their protection longer and be better future clients for you.

The Third Question

Can the person meet underwriting requirements? Every applicant must qualify for health insurance according to your company's standards. There are varying degrees of insurability, ranging from zero to preferred risks. Health, character, habits, occupation and income are among the factors which influence the type of health insurance a person may obtain.

Early in your career it is well for you to recognize the characteristics which prevent a person from qualifying for health insurance. Your company's classification manual or rate book will quickly point out the highly rated or uninsurable occupations.

The Fourth Question

Can you get the person on the right basis? Even though a person has a demonstrable need, can pay the premiums, and can meet your underwriting standards, you still must be able to meet the prospect under favorable circumstances.

Are you already acquainted? If not, it would be ideal to pave the way with an introduction from a mutual friend or another insured. Does your prospect work in a place where conversation is limited by space or noise? If so, it is wise to try to set up an interview in more advantageous surroundings.

If the prospect is a person whose problems promise to demand a complicated solution, it is essential that you be qualified to give advice. For example, if there is a chance for the development of a business insurance case, you must be thoroughly informed about the application of health insurance to the different forms of business organizations and the tax treatment of both premiums and benefits. If not, even though the need is clear-cut, the person is not just a prospect for your services. Just as a doctor calls in a specialist for consultation about a difficult case, so you would do well to consult with your agency head who will be glad to assist you.

Nest prospecting is as valid in the health insurance market as it is for life insurance. Target marketing to members of a particular association, organization or employer group helps build your reputation in a peer group in advance of your call.

It is evident that several considerations determine whether or not the suspect meets the fourth qualification of a prospect—approachability. To approach your prospect on a favorable basis, it is necessary to—

1. Believe the person is willing to see you.
2. Have a convenient place to talk.
3. Be qualified to discuss the person's problems intelligently.

The Fifth Question

Is the person the right type for you? If you are in the life insurance business or if you have been in the health insurance business any length of time, you will probably know what kind of people are your most likely prospects. You will find them in you insureds' files.

If you analyze your insureds with regard to age, occupation, income, family situation, social status, education and so forth, you will probably find that your buyers fall into a pattern or a group of patterns. For example, you may find that many of them are approximately your age. Their income level is about the some as yours. They live in a similar neighborhood, although are not necessarily neighbors. Their social interests closely parallel yours. They have a similar education. They, too, love their families and their homes.

The people you have already sold may well be the kind of people you will sell in the future. Most of your present good prospects are people you already know and with whom you have something in common.

The Sixth Question

Is the person a prospect now? The question of timing is important in developing prospects. People become prospects because of certain incidents in their lives. A person may have no interest at all in the purchase of insurance on Monday, but on Friday may be eager to buy.

Almost every experienced agent has had the experience of calling on a prospect who seemed to be waiting for the call. The interview moved rapidly to a completed sale. Why? The chances are that something beyond the agent's control has happened to stimulate the prospect into action. If you can isolate the factors which produce these results, it should help you determine not only "Who is a prospect?" but also "When is a prospect?" Let us examine that point.

BETTER PROSPECTS— WHEN SOMETHING HAPPENS!

Something happens to increase responsibilities. When the family increases, so does the need for continuous income. When a person buys a home, financed with a mortgage, he or she has added responsibilities. A person who borrows money or starts a business or purchases a car on time takes on new obligations to meet. All of these people may now be prospects for disability insurance.

Something happens to make it easier to pay premiums. A person with a new promotion and an increase in income finds it easier to pay premiums. An architect is awarded a contract which pays a large fee. An attorney wins an important lawsuit—a person is made a partner in a firm—a college graduate starts on the first job. People receive bonuses—newcomers arrive in town to take over good positions. All these people may now be prospects for disability insurance.

Procrastination is the curse of life. Under its spell people wait for fairer days. When something happens to make it easier to pay premiums, "fairer days" have arrived. Procrastination can be replaced by action.

Something happens to dramatize the need. When a neighbor's sudden heart attack destroys his earning power, the need for income is dramatically brought to the attention of others. An accident to a friend—the grave illness of a relative—bring sudden awareness of the need for income protection.

When people have been scared badly they probably are better prospects because they are ready to act now! So timeliness becomes an asset in prospecting. Look for things that happen which increase responsibilities, make premium paying easier and emphasize the urgency of the need.

There is never a "right time" to buy health insurance, but circumstances can help to convince prospects that *"this* is the right time." *When something happens*, prospects are easier to sell!

WHERE CAN PROSPECTS BE FOUND?

Having drawn the picture of who is a good prospect for you, we now come to the process of finding prospects for health insurance. It does little good to put on paper the description of the ideal prospect unless we are prepared to do something about it. It is not so much a problem of knowing what a prospect should look like but rather one of finding him or her and making a call. It is not enough to *know*. We must also *do*. The secret of successful prospecting is following through.

To impress upon you the scope of prospecting and the necessity for doing it constantly, let's turn to the development of your inventory of prospects. Whether you're new in the business or well established, building lists of prospects is an activity that is more important to your success than anything else you do.

If you are new to the health insurance field, you should probably limit your calls to people whom you know well. This will make it easier for you to secure an interview and to identify specific needs. Existing clients are always the best prospects, and excellent centers of influence as referrers to other well-qualified prospects.

Calling on Friends

You are perhaps saying to yourself, **"I don't propose to try to sell my friends."** If so, the feeling is there because you do not yet have the full picture of all that health insurance can do for a person. Once you have, instead of hesitating to see your friends, you will feel a responsibility toward them that will make you eager to see them. Your willingness to talk to your friends about health insurance is your first real test of strength in the business. For, until you feel strong enough to talk to your friends, you are not likely to be strong enough to talk effectively to others about health insurance.

People prefer to do business with their friends. Do you not, as as matter of course, buy your clothes from a friend who is in that business? Buy your groceries from a friendly merchant who is perhaps your neighbor or who is a member of your church or your lodge? Buy your home through a realtor whom you have known for years? The same rule applies to the purchase of health insurance. You will soon find that many of your friends and acquaintances, instead of hesitating to buy from you, will be glad to do so.

Responsibility Toward Friends

Another point should be remembered. You have a very definite responsibility toward your friends. In many cases, people have delayed buying health insurance until it was too late. When they say: "My friend, Jan, sells insurance," often they're using you as an excuse for not doing anything. Frequently, they *intend* to talk to you about health insurance, but just never get around to it.

However, while your friendship with people may prevent them from doing business with other underwriters, it is the main reason that you have a responsibility to your friends. You *owe* your friends the chance to hear what you have to say. If you fail to offer them protection against the hazards of physical disability, your friends may never be insured. And you will be the first one to hear "Why didn't you tell me?" if anything should happen. If we don't take care of our friends, how can we say we are friends?

When you call upon your friends, keep the interview on a business basis. If you are earnest and sincere and hold uppermost in your mind the spirit of service, your friends will respect you. They will become better friends because you have helped them solve their disability protection problems.

THE FINEST THING YOU CAN DO FOR A FRIEND!

A highly effective talk to use in securing referred leads is to make your source of leads the "hero" in a true-to-life story. The following will illustrate what we mean:

1. *"(Client), I do not know if you have ever given thought to just what a serious accident or illness can do to a person and his or her family. In many cases, the hospital, nurse and medical bills run into thousands of dollars . . . They can literally wreck a person's whole financial life for years to come.*

2. *"Suppose you had given me the name of one of your close friends or business associates to see about disability insurance six or eight months ago . . . and as the result of your placing me in contact with that friend or business associate, he or she had secured a disability plan of the right kind.*
   "Suppose several months later this friend of yours had met with a serious accident, one which involved, not only thousands of dollars in medical, nurse and hospital costs, but also a disability that lasted for years.

3. *"But then because of my having met this person through you, the disability plan your friend had bought from me stepped into the picture to: (a) pay almost all of the medical and hospital bills and (b) pay your friend $400 or more a week income, with the further guarantee that this would continue as long as the disability lasted, even for life!*

4. *"Deep down in your heart, (Client), how would you feel about what you had done for your friend? Would it not make your heart glow every time you thought of what you had done for your friend's family? I am sure it would! For after all, your friend probably would never have had the disability protection but for your having referred me.*

5. *"So you see, (Client), in giving me the names of friends and associates, you may be doing the finest thing any person can do for friends. In case of serious disability, they will never be able to thank you enough."*

NOTE: There are thousands of cases in which "referred lead sources" have played exactly this role. But for their having referred agents to close friends, those friends and their families would never have been able to meet the bills and income losses caused by serious disabilities. Every sensitive person likes to help others. Asking for referred leads on this basis places your request in an entirely different light than simply asking for names on the basis that you hope to sell them something.

Reverse the role. Put yourself in the "source of leads" shoes. Suppose you had sent an agent to a friend and that friend, as a result of your interest, received an adequate monthly income for life because of a serious accident? Wouldn't you feel you had done something truly important for your friend? Most certainly! You would regard it as one of the finest things any person had ever done for a friend. And you would be right!

FIRST PROSPECTING STEP—LIST NAMES

Your first job in prospecting is to make a list of men and women you know.

Accompanying this discussion are 12 ruled pages. At the top of each page is a "memory jogger" that will help you think of names. Your first step is to enter every possible name that comes to your mind, regardless of that person's age or financial condition.

In compiling this reservoir of names, you will of course avoid listing the names of those whom you know could not pass your company's insurability requirements. To help you in this connection your company has underwriting guides for both disability and medical-expense insurance. Your main concern should be to add as many good names as possible, by putting down the names of all those whom you can contact with a reasonable chance of getting interviews.

SECOND STEP—RECORD INFORMATION

When you have completed your list of selected names, fill in the other columns on the ruled pages. In the light of what you know about the people listed, write in the approximate age, approximate income, number of dependents and occupation of each. This not only gives you a picture of how much or how little you know about these people, but also valuable information when you prepare to interview them. If any are insureds of yours, you already have many details about them. This should make them ideal prospects for you.

When you have sold a person insurance, but have not recommended protection against the costs of accident and sickness you have a great deal of unfinished business. There is a definite gap in your client's plan of protection. You can fill this gap by giving your health sales presentation. Do not let your present clients suffer because you have left some business unfinished.

ONGOING PROSPECTING

As we stressed earlier, prospecting must be a continuous process. It is a part of your everyday job. It is something you should do at every opportunity that arises.

INFORMATION TRANSFORMS SUSPECTS INTO PROSPECTS

- Place of residence?
- Age?
- Place of employment?
- Occupation?
- Marital status?
- Number of children?
- Their ages?
- Does prospect own a home?
- Hobbies?
- Income?
- Best time to see?
- In good health?

Sound prospecting is not simply a matter of working harder but working smarter. It is working along well-directed lines. Unfortunately, many agents show excellent sales results for a period of time and then slump. What happens is that they move from prospect to prospect and from sale to sale without uncovering enough new prospects as they go along. Soon they find themselves scraping the bottom of their prospect barrel.

They have forgotten that prospecting is an integral and vital part of the overall sales process. They are unaware that the penalty for neglected prospecting is a deferred penalty.

That point is not always evident. When no selling takes place today, the results are immediate. No sales today! And the agent is very conscious of it. But when no prospecting takes place today, the results are not felt today. It is 30 or 60 or 90 days later that the penalty of no prospecting catches up and income suffers. So it is important to make prospecting a continuous activity, day in and day out, rain or shine.

Prospect After Each Sale

One of the best times to obtain new prospects is right after you have made a sale. You have gained your prospect's confidence. You have demonstrated your services, and obviously, your prospect believes in you. What do you do now? The answer is simple. Capitalize on this favorable

1—I KNOW THESE PEOPLE BECAUSE

They are: Former business associates, former customers and clients, former competitors, former employees, former employers.

NAME	Age	Income	Dependents	Occupation	NAME	Age	Income	Dependents	Occupation
1					23				
2					24				
3					25				
4					26				
5					27				
6					28				
7					29				
8					30				
9					31				
10					32				
11					33				
12					34				
13					35				
14					36				
15					37				
16					38				
17					39				
18					40				
19					41				
20					42				
21					43				
22					44				

2—I KNOW THESE PEOPLE BECAUSE

They are: School or college classmates, fraternity or sorority friends, teachers, relatives of classmates, members of school organizations — athletic, dramatic, debating, musical, language, science.

NAME	Age	Income	Dependents	Occupation	NAME	Age	Income	Dependents	Occupation
1					23				
2					24				
3					25				
4					26				
5					27				
6					28				
7					29				
8					30				
9					31				
10					32				
11					33				
12					34				
13					35				
14					36				
15					37				
16					38				
17					39				
18					40				
19					41				
20					42				
21					43				
22					44				

3—I KNOW THESE PEOPLE BECAUSE

They are: Active in the United Way, Red Cross, Cancer Fund, Heart Fund, Salvation Army, and other civic enterprises.

NAME	Age	Income	Dependents	Occupation	NAME	Age	Income	Dependents	Occupation
1					23				
2					24				
3					25				
4					26				
5					27				
6					28				
7					29				
8					30				
9					31				
10					32				
11					33				
12					34				
13					35				
14					36				
15					37				
16					38				
17					39				
18					40				
19					41				
20					42				
21					43				
22					44				

4—I KNOW THESE PEOPLE BECAUSE

They are: Interested in golf, photography, music, tennis, public speaking, chess, home movies, travel, amateur dramatics, and are members of my hobby club.

NAME	Age	Income	Dependents	Occupation	NAME	Age	Income	Dependents	Occupation
1					23				
2					24				
3					25				
4					26				
5					27				
6					28				
7					29				
8					30				
9					31				
10					32				
11					33				
12					34				
13					35				
14					36				
15					37				
16					38				
17					39				
18					40				
19					41				
20					42				
21					43				
22					44				

5—I KNOW THESE PEOPLE BECAUSE

They are: Interested in my home — real estate broker, landlord, building supply
people, carpenters, plumbers, painters, landscape architects.

NAME	Age	Income	Dependents	Occupation	NAME	Age	Income	Dependents	Occupation
1					23				
2					24				
3					25				
4					26				
5					27				
6					28				
7					29				
8					30				
9					31				
10					32				
11					33				
12					34				
13					35				
14					36				
15					37				
16					38				
17					39				
18					40				
19					41				
20					42				
21					43				
22					44				

6—I KNOW THESE PEOPLE BECAUSE

They are: Neighbors, former neighbors, good friends.

NAME	Age	Income	Dependents	Occupation	NAME	Age	Income	Dependents	Occupation
1					23				
2					24				
3					25				
4					26				
5					27				
6					28				
7					29				
8					30				
9					31				
10					32				
11					33				
12					34				
13					35				
14					36				
15					37				
16					38				
17					39				
18					40				
19					41				
20					42				
21					43				
22					44				

7—I KNOW THESE PEOPLE BECAUSE

They are: Interested in my car — dealer, gas station owner, auto insurance agent, parking lot owners, garage owners.

NAME	Age	Income	Dependents	Occupation	NAME	Age	Income	Dependents	Occupation
1					23				
2					24				
3					25				
4					26				
5					27				
6					28				
7					29				
8					30				
9					31				
10					32				
11					33				
12					34				
13					35				
14					36				
15					37				
16					38				
17					39				
18					40				
19					41				
20					42				
21					43				
22					44				

8—I KNOW THESE PEOPLE BECAUSE

They are: Merchants — grocers, meat dealers, fuel oil dealers, milk company proprietors, laundry owners, cleaners and dyers, tailors, clothing store personnel — anyone with whom I do business.

NAME	Age	Income	Dependents	Occupation	NAME	Age	Income	Dependents	Occupation
1					23				
2					24				
3					25				
4					26				
5					27				
6					28				
7					29				
8					30				
9					31				
10					32				
11					33				
12					34				
13					35				
14					36				
15					37				
16					38				
17					39				
18					40				
19					41				
20					42				
21					43				
22					44				

9—I KNOW THESE PEOPLE BECAUSE

They are: Interested in my children — schoolteachers, parents of playmates, school
principals, swimming instructors, music teachers, dancing teachers.

NAME	Age	Income	Dependents	Occupation	NAME	Age	Income	Dependents	Occupation
1					23				
2					24				
3					25				
4					26				
5					27				
6					28				
7					29				
8					30				
9					31				
10					32				
11					33				
12					34				
13					35				
14					36				
15					37				
16					38				
17					39				
18					40				
19					41				
20					42				
21					43				
22					44				

10—I KNOW THESE PEOPLE BECAUSE

They are: Members of my church or synagogue—active in religious school, social clubs, study groups, religious societies.

NAME	Age	Income	Dependents	Occupation	NAME	Age	Income	Dependents	Occupation
1					23				
2					24				
3					25				
4					26				
5					27				
6					28				
7					29				
8					30				
9					31				
10					32				
11					33				
12					34				
13					35				
14					36				
15					37				
16					38				
17					39				
18					40				
19					41				
20					42				
21					43				
22					44				

*11—*I KNOW THESE PEOPLE BECAUSE

They are: Active in organizations in which members of my family are active —
P.T.A., college alumni association, sorority, fraternity, civic clubs.

NAME	Age	Income	Dependents	Occupation	NAME	Age	Income	Dependents	Occupation
1					23				
2					24				
3					25				
4					26				
5					27				
6					28				
7					29				
8					30				
9					31				
10					32				
11					33				
12					34				
13					35				
14					36				
15					37				
16					38				
17					39				
18					40				
19					41				
20					42				
21					43				
22					44				

12—I KNOW THESE PEOPLE BECAUSE

They are: Active in my organizations—service club, neighborhood club, political club,
charitable group, health or sports club, farm bureau, grange cooperative association.

NAME	Age	Income	Dependents	Occupation	NAME	Age	Income	Dependents	Occupation
1					23				
2					24				
3					25				
4					26				
5					27				
6					28				
7					29				
8					30				
9					31				
10					32				
11					33				
12					34				
13					35				
14					36				
15					37				
16					38				
17					39				
18					40				
19					41				
20					42				
21					43				
22					44				

situation and ask for prospects! If you don't, it will be like leaving your change on the counter.

If you have performed a sound sales job, why not offer to make this protection available to your client's friends and associates? A few minutes spent now with your new client will uncover potential future business. What you say while prospecting should contain the some emphasis on the need for health insurance as your sales talk.

Prospect on Policy Delivery

Another good time to prospect is when you deliver the policy. You might begin by reporting to your policyowner of favorable developments from leads already furnished to you. Then:

"It occurs to me, Mr. Insured, that since I last saw you, you may have thought of someone else among your friends or business associates who could benefit from my services. Whom do you know who has just bought a home? Or who has just been promoted? Or who has just taken on additional responsibilities?"

Prospect After Each Interview

A third favorable prospecting situation often occurs in an interview, when you may have been unable to make a sale. Your nonbuyer may not feel a need for more protection. Or the prospect may be uninsurable. There are sometimes good reasons why an interview does not produce a sale.

The question is: What to do? Again, the answer is obvious. Before you go, spend a few minutes more with that prospect using your proven prospecting techniques. You may have some very profitable results. **Make every interview a productive interview.** For example:

"(Prospect), as we've discussed, health insurance is critical to every adult in this country. That's why [repeat how prospect felt; e.g.: 'you value your group medical and disability plans so highly'].

"Is there anyone you can think of who may want to know more about what is available?"

HOW TO REACH PROSPECTS ON A PRESTIGE BASIS

You now have in your mind the kind of person who is a prospect for you. You now know the wide markets for health insurance. If you have completed every space on the 12 pages of memory joggers, you have 528 potential prospects. This is only a start.

You may think that you have an inexhaustible number of people to see. It may come as a shock to realize that if you call on only ten people a day, your present supply will be used up in approximately 53 days—less than two months!

So, even though you have a large circle of friends and acquaintances, you will want to know more prospects. The time to start meeting more people and gathering more prospects is now. No insurance underwriter has ever complained of having too many prospects.

It is perfectly logical for you to call on your personal contacts to help you in reaching their personal contacts. From information your friends give you about their friends, you can determine whether the latter are suitable prospects for you. If you conclude that they are, then you are in a position to use third-party influence. You borrow the prestige of your friends in introducing yourself and your products to your new prospects.

This kind of prospecting is ofter referred to as "referred lead prospecting" or "center of influence prospecting." In the process of going from one prospect or insured to another, the term "endless chain" is used. Regardless of the terminology, the techniques involved are similar. We shall describe several variations.

AN ORGANIZED PROSPECTING TALK IS ESSENTIAL

Probably no agent would deny the importance of a well-prepared sales talk when approaching a prospect. It is essential that the prospecting talk be as well organized.

Successful prospecting talks should follow a step-by-step sequence. Ideals are marshaled to lead to the desired action—obtaining names of quality prospects. Each idea, each sentence, each word is selected to make a vivid impression on the person to whom they are presented.

Without a definite procedure for obtaining the names of prospects from people willing to help you, you make it difficult for them to help. Through the use of a talk which is brief and direct, you make it easy for them to think of friends who may need your services.

It may be advisable, particularly for the newer agent, to use an illustrated prospecting talk. The story is easier to grasp and to master when you can illustrate your objectives. You are less apt to skip an important point. Moreover, your illustrations hold the attention of your prospect.

An Endless Chain Prospecting Talk

The following prospecting talk is designed to be used, with a slight variation at the conclusion of an interview, whether or not a sale has been made. Note that you are not merely asking for names. You are seeking specific individuals who have a need for health insurance.

"(Client), there's just one thought before I go. I'd like to give you the opportunity to do a good turn for your three closest friends.

"If you learned that one of these friends was laid up in the hospital, you would take time from your business to go see him or her right away, wouldn't you? If there was no money coming in from any source and the family needed money, I'm sure you would feel bad. Isn't that right?

Fortunately, you can make it possible for them to have money when they are sick or hurt, by pointing them out to me now, before the need arises.

"(Client), whom do you know—

1. *"Who has just had a baby?*
2. *"Who has become engaged?*
3. *"Who has just been married or is about to be?*
4. *"Who has just bought a home?*
5. *"Who has recently started or purchased a business?*
6. *"Who is the key person in a business enterprise?*

7. *"Who has just graduated from college or is about to?*
8. *"Who has been promoted or started a new job?*
9. *"Whose medical practice is flourishing?*
10. *"Whose dental practice is growing?*
11. *"Whose law practice is thriving?*
12. *"Whose business is expanding?* *(Etc., etc.)*

"To be specific, (Client), who among your friends and associates could be hurt financially if he or she were laid up for months or years because of an illness or injury?"

Another effective method is to make up a "starter list" of five or six names of persons in advance whom your prospect or client probably knows (neighbors, business associates, etc.) Try to qualify these names as prospects first and this should help the person you are interviewing to think of others.

A Center of Influence Prospecting Talk

If you were to analyze the business written by hundreds of agents, you would find that substantially more than half comes from people they already know and from leads furnished by insureds and friends. Many of these cases stem from calling on prospects furnished by a *center of influence.* It may be an insured, a friend, someone for whom you have performed a service, or merely an influential person who is favorably disposed toward you.

A center of influence is usually described as a man or woman *willing* and *able* to put you in touch with good, new prospects.

Here is a talk for the new field underwriter designed for use with a center of influence:

1. *"(Center), I am in the health insurance business as a field representative for my company.*
2. *"I am here today to seek your friendly cooperation which I hope you are willing to give me.*
3. *"In my training, I learned that my success is going to depend largely upon the type and number of people I call on.*

4. *"As you undoubtedly know, my company specializes in protecting a person's most valuable asset—earning power. We have excellent contracts and my training has equipped me to choose the right one and tailor-make it to fit each individual's own special needs.*

5. *"I realize you are favorably known among the kind of people who would likely be interested in my service. It occurred to me that you might be willing to point out a number of people whom you think I should call on.*

6. *"Who are the three most promising young people you know in this community?" (If the person draws a blank on that question, ask another, designed to stimulate thinking. For example, "Who is the best salesperson who has called on you in the last three months?" or "What young person in this company has an outstanding future?")*

This center of influence talk can be adapted by the experienced underwriter with these minor changes:

1. *"(Center), as you know, I have been in the health insurance business for some time.*

2. *"More and more it becomes evident to me that what success I have enjoyed is due to the friendly cooperation of people like you. These people have made it possible from time to time for me to meet the type of people to whom I've offered my services."*

(Continue with number 4 in the above talk, "As you undoubtedly know, my company specializes. . .")

Note the sequence of ideas in the preceding talks. Study them. Read them and reread them. They can be used profitably if you drill on them and master them. Your objective is to give them naturally in the presence of your center of influence. This kind of prospecting should be made a part of your daily planned sales activities.

One of the powerful by-products of this use of stimulating questions can come when you follow up leads obtained in this way. You can imagine the reception you will get when you say to your referred lead, "I asked (center) to recommend three very promising young people, and you are one of the three."

QUALIFY THE NAMES

A word of caution seems advisable here. It has been true in the past that many agents have been successful in obtaining names, *but merely as names.* They neglected to qualify those names by getting enough information about them to be useful in making a favorable sales approach. Thus they had to walk into a prospect's office without knowing occupation, age, income or even the family situation.

Names alone are in reality only suspects. They remain suspects until you uncover sufficient information about them. The more information obtained about the prospect, the better equipped you will be to conduct the sales interview.

There is a minimum number of facts you should get. If you have the prospect's age, approximate income, occupation and number of dependents, you are at least prepared to make an intelligent approach based on your prospect's estimated needs.

To assist you to obtain that minimum information, here is a helpful device:

A — Age
I — Income
D — Dependents
O — Occupation

After you have obtained a name or group of names from a center of influence, call on A–I–D–O to aid you.

When you are gathering referred leads, get a few names before you start qualifying them. Then, after several people have been suggested to you, go back and ask questions which will make it possible for you to fill in the additional data you need.

There is good reason for following this procedure. If you try to record the name, address and personal information about each person as the name is suggested to you, the person helping you will be diverted and will quickly run out of references.

Finally, do not ask if you can say that the person recommended these people to you. Instead, say,

> *"When I call on these people, may I say that you think well of my services and my company?"*

Another hint that will help your referred lead prospecting is well known to skillful salespeople. There is much more to obtaining potential customers than asking point-blank questions such as, "Do you know anyone in the market for health insurance?" or "Who do you believe would buy a policy?" It is much better to ask leading questions about specific situations. **Prospect for needs not names. By naming specific situations, you will help your friends furnish you with leads. And you are automatically uncovering reasons for making sales calls on these prospects.**

OBTAIN INTRODUCTIONS TO PROSPECTS

Approaching a prospective buyer with the proper introduction gives you valuable prestige. It lays a friendly, yet firm, foundation for your sales presentations.

Frequently the center of influence will offer to introduce you to those recommended. When an introduction is not volunteered, many successful agents discipline themselves to request some type of introduction every time they obtain a referred lead.

Introduction may be by card, by telephone or in person. Regardless of the manner in which the introduction is given your technique is the same. After sufficient information about the prospect has been obtained, you might say,

> *"If you and I were walking down the street together and we met (Prospect), you wouldn't hesitate to introduce us, would you?"*

A request that logical is difficult to refuse.

Following agreement, you can suggest that the person write the prospect's name and your name on his or her business card. Say,

> *"Just write (Prospect's) name on this card. When I present it, I'll say that I asked you for this introduction because he or she is the type of person I want to know...."*

Occasionally, your center will offer to write a brief note. If he or she wants your help in wording it, you might suggest this:

> *"Dear Jim:*
> *"This will introduce Blair Agent who wants to meet you. Blair has an idea which I believe you will find interesting.*
> *"I have done business with Blair and can vouch that Blair will not impose on your courtesy. Why not give Blair a hearing?*
> *   T. R. Policyowner"*

It may be that an introduction by telephone will not be as effective as one in person or in writing. Unless you have good reason to know that your center of influence can control the conversation over the phone, you may never get the chance to interview the new prospect. It is easy for a prospect to say "No" on the phone to a person not skilled in parrying objections.

"All My Friends Have Health Insurance"

In your prospecting activities you will, of course, come up against the person who is trying to evade the issue. He or she may attempt to close the door on you by saying, "Most of my friends have insurance," or "I don't know anyone for you to see." There are a dozen different ways to word the excuse. Here is a clear, concise, quick answer to the excuse for not suggesting prospects to you.

> *"I can appreciate why you say that. But here is a thought which may be new to you. Let me illustrate.... There are three different kinds of prospects.*
> *"First, there are those with no health insurance at all.*
> *"Second, there are those with inadequate health insurance protection.*
> *"The majority of all people fall in these first two groups.*
> *"Third, there are those who have adequate protection. Only a very small percentage fall into this group.*

"In other words, just as with any other person, on the average at least nine out of ten of your friends fall in the first two groups.

"Some will become ill. Some will meet with an accident. Wouldn't you like to feel that you are responsible for their having adequate protection when they need it?

"Tell me, what is the name of your best friend? Who is one of your golfing buddies? Do you have a business associate? Whom do you know who has just bought a home?"
. . . etc.

Note that this answer to an excuse for not furnishing prospects to you is built around the need for health insurance. While answering an excuse, this answer also emphasizes the importance of your service to your insured, to your center of influence, or to anyone else to whom you are speaking.

TAKE PROSPECTING TOURS

Many successful health insurance agents make prospecting tours a part of their regular activities. They visit places and uncover sales situations which they would never have found in their regular field work. They meet people they would have missed otherwise. They find these tours stimulating because they tend to sharpen the skills they use in planned interviews.

Many of these prospects are never called on by health insurance agents. Yet they have problems, too, and are interested in learning how they can have an income when they are sick or hurt and unable to work.

Whenever you have free time between scheduled appointments, make a prospecting tour for fun and profit. It has been estimated that as much as 30 percent of all individual health insurance business written in the United States and Canada is the result of this kind of activity!

USING DIRECT MAIL

Direct mail is not a substitute for personal prospecting. It is a supplement to other effective prospecting methods. In a prospect's mind, it identifies an agency or a company. Used properly, it builds acceptance for you. It provides you with additional favorable interviews and results in a high ratio of interviews to calls.

One typical situation that calls for direct mail occurs when you have leads which cannot be followed up immediately because you have a full schedule. You can warm them up with a direct mail letter. Another important use of letters is to gain entree into select groups such as doctors, attorneys, business executives and other professionals.

One of the major advantages of direct mail is in planning your calls and organizing your work well in advance. Keep in mind, however, that a limited quantity of letters mailed on a steady weekly basis will produce better results than large mailings at infrequent intervals. Direct mail is not a device designed to fill an empty prospecting barrel. It should be used constantly to keep you supplied with a steady flow of names of people to see.

Here is a specimen preapproach letter which can be sent out on your stationery over your signature to a select list of prospects.

"Dear (Prospect):

"One of the biggest problems faced by a successful person these days is loss of income due to sickness or accident. Savings may be eaten away or a burden of heavy debts may be accumulated.

"It is a strange fact that many people protect their homes with fire insurance, their cars with automobile insurance, their family with life insurance, and let their most valuable asset which supports all the rest— their ability to earn income—go unprotected.

"And at every age the chances of a person being sick or hurt before age 65, so that he or she cannot work for an extended period, are much greater than for death.

"My company has designed a special contract which many people in situations similar to yours find of genuine value. In the event of your disability, it will provide much needed income.

"I shall call you within a few days for an

appointment to explain the features of this unusual contract.

> Sincerely yours,
> (signature)"

TELEPHONE FOR APPOINTMENTS

Your letter should be followed up within a week by a telephone call for an appointment. We suggest you study carefully the telephone talk which follows. Remember, the purpose of the phone call is not to sell a policy, but to secure an appointment.

"Good morning, (Prospect), this is Blair Agent. (Pause)

"You may recall that a few days ago I sent you a letter calling your attention to our new health insurance contract designed particularly for people like yourself. (Pause)

"I am sure that after a brief review, you will be able to determine for yourself just how much you can benefit from this concept.

"I am calling to inquire if it will be convenient for you to see me for about 15 minutes tomorrow morning at ten o'clock or would eleven o'clock be better?" (Pause)

Note the definite pattern of this approach. You introduce yourself, you state your business, you request an appointment. It is simple, direct, and businesslike. This exact phraseology is used successfully by many agents who rely on the telephone for many of their appointments.

You will, of course, receive a variety of responses. With a good telephone manner, you will find many prospects going right along with you. You will get a good ratio of appointments.

The "pauses" indicated in the talk are there for a purpose. The first one following the self-introduction permits your name to register and gives you a chance to get a first reaction from the prospect.

The second pause, following the reminder of the letter, gives the prospect a chance to tip his or her hand and you can be guided thereby. The prospect may say, "Oh yes, I remember." Or, if the prospect does not remember receiving the letter, you may answer:

"I'm sorry, (Prospect), the letter probably is on its way. This is an unusual plan designed for people like yourself and if you have about 15 minutes around _____ o'clock tomorrow, I'd like to meet you and show it to you, without any obligation on your part."

Or, the prospect may say: "How much does your health plan cost?" or "I already have health insurance."

Your proper answer then would be:

"Insurance is a technical business, (Prospect). There are many kinds of health insurance policies. We specialize in designing income protection plans which fit exactly an individual's situation. May I see you tomorrow morning, or will tomorrow afternoon be more convenient?"

A TIP ON TELEPHONING

When using the telephone to make appointments, it is essential to know precisely what you are going to say. It is unwise and dangerous to rely on spur-of-the-moment conversation. You may depart from your sole purpose: to make an appointment for an interview.

Many successful agents not only have their telephone approach memorized but also have it word for word over the phone. The manuscript includes answers to anticipated prospect objections on the phone.

PERSONAL OBSERVATION PROSPECTING

Personal observation as a prospecting method is not as easily defined as referred lead or direct mail prospecting. It does, however, deserve considerable attention.

Prospects can be developed by anyone who keeps his or her eyes and ears open. Things are happening to people you know. Situations are being created constantly. Your problem is to learn to look at these situations and to see them in relation to your sales work.

Do not let a thought about a prospect flash across your mind without writing it down. Do not write it on the back of an envelope. Carry a pocket notebook in which you enter names—names—and more names.

Restaurants, social events, street corners, locker rooms of clubs, civic groups, luncheon clubs, school groups, church groups, daily papers—all these and others should provide a never-ending source of productive conversations.

It is almost impossible to hold a conversation with anyone without names being brought into it. And chances are the names are mentioned because something has happened to those people. That "something" could easily make one of them a prospect. When you meet and talk with people, ask yourself the question, "What will happen in this particular situation when this person is unable to work?"

Personal observation too often is overlooked as one of the greatest potential areas for building markets. Keep alert to situations and people around you. Just as successful newspaper reporters develop a "nose for news," so do successful health insurance agents develop a "nose for prospects."

NO ONE BEST METHOD

There are various methods of successful prospecting. All of them have one thing in common. Their objective is to uncover good prospects. Whether you are making a sale, delivering a policy, performing a service, or merely having a conversation, you should constantly seek names of new people with whom you may do business.

In all cases, prospecting techniques emphasize the same need for protection against sickness and injury as do sound sales techniques.

There is no one best method for accomplishing this. The successful prospector employs any sound method which produces good results and achieves a balance among all the methods which work.

QUALITY PROSPECTING

If you would control your income, then control your prospecting. Quality prospecting affects your income more than quantity prospecting.

The kind of people you call on largely determines your success in obtaining an interview and in completing a sale. Quality prospecting not only produces larger sales but also more persistent business.

As any established agent knows, persistency affects income to a very large degree. There is a physical limit to the time an agent can devote to the selling activity. Beyond that point, increased income comes by obtaining policyowners who buy more and hold on to it longer.

In establishing a definition of a quality prospect, keep these questions in mind:

1. Does this person earn a reasonable income in a vocation or industry without severe business fluctuations?
2. Does this person work in a nonhazardous occupation?
3. Are people dependent on him or her for regular income from earnings?
4. Is there an urgent need for health insurance which I should point out without delay?
5. Do I know him or her personally or do I have an introduction on a basis which will earn me a favorable hearing?

If the answer to these questions is "Yes," then you have a quality prospect. Of course, there are some good prospects who do not measure up to all these standards. But, by and large, the majority of your sales should be to people who meet these qualifications.

AN EXCITING ADVENTURE IN
MAKING FRIENDS!

Look upon prospecting as an adventure in making new friends. Then it becomes the most fascinating part of your job. Yes, the most exciting part of the day's work! Learn to approach the next door you are to open in this frame of mind:

- The person behind this door may become the best friend I'll ever have after we get to know each other...he or she may buy the largest policy I'll ever sell...that person may become my best source of new leads.
- What is he or she like? What is his or her spouse like?...How many children to they have? How old are the children? Where do they go to school? What are their names? Which colleges do the parents want them to attend?...
- Where was the prospect born? Where did he or she go to school?...Where was the spouse born?...Where did he or she go to school? What are hobbies and special interests? To which church, clubs, civic organizations and business or professional groups do the people belong? Where do they live? Who are their friends and associates?...
- What do they want out of life? What are the things they want most for their family? What are their plans for the future? Can I turn them into friends?...
- People make life interesting...The richest person in the world is the person with the largest number of friends...There is more real drama in the lives of men and women than in all the library shelves of the world!...I am about to meet and make a new friend! I can't want to meet her or him!...Hurry up and open that door!...

If you can bring this spirit of adventure in making friends into your prospecting work, you will soon find it the most exciting game in the world!

Yes, now and then a person behind some door may be rude but that will happen rarely. And when it does, try to not let it bother you in the least. For fine men and fine women, big-minded men and big-minded women, the kind you want for friends and clients, are most invariably courteous and well mannered. The people who are rude to you only lower themselves. They cannot hurt you. Never forget that.

LET EVERY NEW DOOR be a challenge to turn the person behind the doorknob into a friend. Fears and doubts vanish when you prospect in this frame of mind. And prospecting truly becomes an exciting adventure in making new friends.

Chapter 9
Sales Techniques

LESSON TEXT—Advantages of Planned Selling . . . The Sales Process (Approach, Presentation and Close) . . . Establishing the General Problem . . . Establishing the Specific Problem . . . Presenting the Ideal Solution . . . The Close . . . Techniques of Closing

Winston Churchill, master craftsman with words, said he could make a good two-hour speech extemporaneously but that a good five-minute talk required long preparation. That statement contains excellent advice for every insurance salesperson.

Even though you have the verbal skill of a Churchill, you rarely will have two hours for an interview. In the time allotted you by most prospects, you must make every word count. Under typical selling conditions, it would be foolhardy to rely on the inspiration of the moment.

CANNED SELLING VS. PLANNED SELLING

Organized selling as developed years ago, led to the use of "canned" sales talk. Sales management put words in the mouths of salespeople who otherwise would rely on an uninspired sales vocabulary.

With the growth of modern sales techniques, the canned sales talk came into disrepute. The term has become associated with an artificially recited monologue designed to fit every situation and every prospect. It usually fails to accomplish that objective. But there are also many who erroneously seek to pin the label canned sales talk onto what are actually highly effective and well-planned sales talks. Never make that mistake. Some also seek to avoid the necessity of mastering a planned sales presentation by labeling it a canned sales talk. To do that is a fatal error.

Planned presentations have become basic in the field activity of both the veteran underwriter and the new agent. They are recognized as essential. With an organized sales story, the agent can present a series of ideas to a prospect in logical sequence with appropriate words and economy of time.

Planned presentations are the result of an evolutionary process. Certain techniques have been retained because they worked. Others have been discarded as ineffectual. It would be absurd for today's underwriters not to take advantage of the experience of their predecessors. People learn by experience. But they will learn much faster if they can have the benefit of trials and errors which others have lived through. A Chinese philosopher said, **"The foolish man learns only from his own experience; the wise man learns from the experience of others."**

ADVANTAGES OF PLANNED SELLING

With a planned sales talk your story is better. No thinking person would contend that in an impromptu presentation he or she could give as polished a performance as would be possible with planning and rehearsal. If you were called on to make a speech for a substantial fee, you would prepare it well. You know you would do a better job. It is equally logical to master a planned sales talk which may result in substantial commissions.

With a planned sales talk your choice of words is better. All points in the sales interview require careful wording. Their meaning must not be misunderstood. It would be unfortunate to reach a high spot in your presentation only to falter for the lack of the right phrase. How much wiser to make your choice before you see your prospect.

With a planned sales talk your sequence of ideas is better. A planned sales presentation is a step-by-step process. When you get out of step, your effectiveness suffers. A well-built sequence of questions or statements will have the maximum persuasiveness. It is difficult to construct your best sequence of ideas without prior organization.

With a planned sales talk you stay on the track. The phone rings—the prospect asks a question—leaves the office for the moment. Such interruptions are frequent in a sales interview. With an organized presentation you can pick up the thread of your talk at any point as if no pause had occurred.

With a planned sales talk you have more confidence. You are freed from fumbling and hesitation. Certainty breeds confidence in yourself. This attitude has the collateral value of putting your prospect at ease, creating confidence in you.

With a planned sales talk you have more op-portunity to observe your prospect's reactions. You know exactly what you are going to say next. You do not have to worry about your words. You can listen to what the prospect says.

With a planned sales talk you save the prospect's time—and your own. Planned selling is courtesy selling. Busy prospects appreciate your avoidance of idle chatter. You get to the heart of the matter with fewer words. With a concise presentation, you cover more ground faster and make your work hours more productive.

With a planned sales talk you save wear and tear on your nervous system. To attempt to create a new presentation for each prospect would put a strain on anyone. Energy is expended in any interview. If it is channeled or disciplined, it will produce more effective results at less physical costs to the agent.

With a planned sales talk you automatically anticipate many of your prospect's objections. The majority of objections which a prospect can raise fall into various classifications. A well-planned sales presentation takes these into account. By anticipating what the prospect may say, that agent can forestall many negative responses. Others can be taken in stride. Self-organization prevents being caught off guard.

On the other hand, visualize an acting group about to undertake a play by Shakespeare. The director says, "Here is the script as Shakespeare wrote it. Put it in your own words and change them at each performance if you wish." The result would be chaos!

With an organized sales presentation, you can put your best foot forward in every interview.

Importance of First Impressions

Where does the sale begin? With your very first contact with the prospect. It may be by mail, over a telephone, or face to face. First impressions are lasting impressions. Is your stationery in good taste? Is your telephone manner pleasing? Is your physical appearance attractive? Do you conduct yourself in such a way with the prospect as to inspire immediate confidence with ability and sincerity?

Many leaders in sales management are convinced that the sale begins even before the first contact. It starts with your preparation for the sale, knowledge of the contracts, mastery of the sales presentation, skill in qualifying prospects. Behind all these lies attitude toward the insurance business, toward the job and toward the people you are calling on. Sincerity and conviction are fundamental in making a favorable first impression and laying a firm foundation for a completed sale.

Our purpose is to equip you with the basis of well-planned health insurance sales talks. An understanding of techniques will help you make that good first impression and carry you through to a successful close.

THE SALES PROCESS

The three major parts of the sales process are usually designated as: (a) the approach, (b) the presentation and (c) the close. These broad terms tend to oversimplify the process of selling. They define what a sales talk is; but they do not detail how a successful sales presentation is constructed. It is advisable to know the ingredients of the approach, to recognize the essential contents of an effective presentation, and to become adept in the techniques of powerful closes which will lead naturally to the completion of an application. Here we lift the curtain on the mechanics of making the sales process run its course without a breakdown. As we demonstrate the construction of a smooth, efficient presentation, think of it as an acute angle, open at one end and narrowing toward the close.

The Approach

What is the sole purpose of the approach? To gain an interview on a favorable basis. It is designed to sell the interview—to earn the right to a hearing.

A prospect's first reaction is: Who is this person and what is this about? Your first step is to identify yourself in as favorable a light as possible. How? Simply by giving your name, that of your company and the name of a mutual friend and if you have permission to do so, those with whom you have done business, etc.

Your second step in the approach is to generate enough interest so that your prospect agrees to hear your story. Many approaches fail because the agent starts the sales interview before he or she has earned the right to it.

Practical application of the theory of the approach will be illustrated later in this unit.

The Presentation

When your approach has aroused the prospect's interest to the point where you have his or her attention, move into your presentation. Its purpose is to create a sales situation, to get your prospect to agree that he or she has an urgent need for health insurance, and to win agreement that your plan solves a disturbing problem so that the prospect wants to buy the plan.

In the actual interview, there is no definite break between the steps. One flows naturally and logically into the other without interruption. The interview is dissected here so that each part may be analyzed and its importance to the entire sales process emphasized.

Many successful agents do not know why they do things in a certain way. Ask them and they will say, "Oh, anyone knows why it's done this way." But they often cannot give you the answer. Here you are shown the breakdown of the interview so that you will discover the *why*. This makes it easier to understand the *how* and gain mastery over the planned sales presentation.

A step-by-step presentation outline follows.

THE PRESENTATION

A. Establish the General Problem

OBJECTIVE: To lay a solid base for exposing the individual situation by . . .

Step 1. Pointing out the responsibilities and hopes of people in general

Step 2. Winning agreement that fulfilling these responsibilities and hopes rests on the foundation of earned income

---

People will agree more readily to generalities than to specific personal problems. For example, a person might hesitate to admit that a prolonged disability would wreck his or her home and family. Yet the person will agree that for most people it could cause a financial disaster for years, yes, even a lifetime. The prospect will concede that other people's children might be deprived of their education. This realization must gradually be transferred in the mind to his or her own situation. Most people do not wish to stand alone and admit their personal shortcomings. However, as part of a group, they more willingly admit the financial defects in their own plans.

To lay a solid base for uncovering an individual's needs, first establish a general problem by stressing people's ambitions and responsibilities. Second, win your prospect's agreement that most of these responsibilities and hopes rest on the foundation of earned income.

Having established the general problem, you proceed immediately to your next point, establishing the specific problem as it applies to the prospect.

This sequence, as detailed in Figure 9–1, is the logical one of diagnosis first, then prescription as your objective is to secure the prospect's agreement on his or her own needs. By following it, you do not attempt to offer any solution to the prospect's problem before he or she recognizes and admits that a problem exists. Your prospect must recognize how acute the situation is before he or she is willing to undergo the cure that you recommend.

Your procedure is similar to that followed by a physician. In an examination, you are persuaded to tell where you hurt. Then, depending on the gravity of your case, the doctor makes you realize that you must take care of yourself or suffer the consequences. Because you have confidence in the diagnosis, you are willing to follow the instructions.

As a health insurance underwriter, you uncover a specific weakness in the prospect's financial setup. Then you proceed to the next step of *presenting the ideal solution*. The objective at this point is to win agreement that your plan solves the prospect's needs.

You can approach this part of your sales talk with complete confidence. If you have covered the preceding steps thoroughly, winning agree-

ment on the key points as you go along, a firm foundation for the sale has been laid. You then recommend the best, and for most people the only, solution to the problem of continuing income during sickness or accident.

From this point, you can move directly into the close.

The Close

An able student of our business has said, **"The close is helping a person make the right decision."** Observation of hundreds of agents over a long period of years reveals that many make smooth approaches to skillful presentations. But, when they reach the close, they fumble badly. Some never attempt to fill out the application. Some make a single attempt to close and then give up.

The close is the payoff. Everything else you have done may have been perfect. If you cannot get the prospect's signature on the application, your performance may have been in vain.

Many people feel that closing is the most important aspect of the entire sales procedure and possibly the most difficult. It is certainly the area where many sales are completed or lost. It is the spot at which the benefits are placed in force and the commission is earned or the sale slips through the fingers.

THE ESSENTIAL STEPS OF A SUCCESSFUL SALES PRESENTATION

1. Approach—Disturb, Excite Curiosity: *"I have an idea which may be of help to you."*
2. Fix General Problem: *"...don't you agree that most people..."*
3. Uncover Specific Problem: *"How much income would you have if..."*
4. Present Ideal Solution—Health Insurance: *"Let me illustrate how my plan solves your problem."*
5. Close: *"Please write your name just as you would want it to appear on any claim checks..."*

A skillful close makes it urgent for the prospect to act *now*. It stresses that the plan is not available to everyone, because good health is an important consideration. A smooth close makes it easy for the prospect to buy. It emphasizes the rightness of your contract. It builds constant urgency behind the need for prompt action.

A good closing technique equips you with a series of closing methods designed to obtain the prospect's signature.

PRACTICAL APPLICATION OF THE SALES PATTERN

We have outlined the essentials of a well-planned sales presentation and have established the track on which a successful interview can run. Now let us demonstrate it by building an entire sales talk on the framework of the principles enumerated.

FIGURE 9–1
THE SALES PROCESS

I. The Approach

Step 1: Identify yourself in as favorable a light as possible

Step 2: Generate interest to the point where your prospect agrees to hear your story

II. The Presentation

A. Establish the General Problem
Step 1: Point out the responsibilities and hopes of people in general
Step 2: Win agreement that fulfilling these responsibilities and hopes rests on the foundation of earned income

B. Establish the Specific Problem
Step 1: Turn the discussion to those things that most interest the prospect—self, responsibilities and plans
Step 2: Confirm the importance of the prospect's earned income in fulfilling responsibilities and plans
Step 3: Uncover the person's own critical needs in relation to the responsibilities and plans
Step 4: Win a clear-cut agreement on the seriousness of the needs

C. Present the Ideal Solution
Step 1: Show how your proposed plan guarantees what your prospect agrees is essential
Step 2: Emphasize the unique features and benefits of your policy

III. The Close

Step 1: Stress that good health is an important consideration
Step 2: Make it easy for the prospect to buy
Step 3: Emphasize the rightness of your contract for your prospect's purposes
Step 4: Build urgency behind the need for prompt action
Step 5: Help the prospect fit the plan to his or her budget

I. Making the Approach

The sole purpose of the approach is to *sell the interview, to earn a hearing.* To accomplish that objective, you identify yourself in as favorable a light as possible (Step 1). Then you attempt to generate interest to the point where your prospect agrees to hear your story (Step 2).

Here's an example of how you might approach a referred lead prospect.

Step 1: Identify yourself in as favorable a light as possible

> *"Mr. Prospect, my name is Stacey Agent. I have a card (letter) of introduction from our mutual friend, Jessie Center-of-Influence. Because of the nice things said about you, I wanted to meet you. Jessie gave me this card in the same spirit as if we had met at Jessie's home or office."*

Step 2: Generate interest to the point where prospect agrees to hear your story

> *"I have an idea which I have presented to many successful people in this community. I would like to show it to you. It concerns your income. It will take just a few moments and when I am through, I would like you to tell me frankly what you think of it. Will you do that?"*

Only slight variations in Step 1 are necessary in approaching prospects to whom you have a different introduction or none at all. After stating your name and company affiliation, your next words will depend on the circumstances of your meeting.

> *"A friend of yours, Jenny Brown, suggested I come to see you."*

> *"A friend of yours, (Center of Influence), said you are one of the most promising young people in town."*

> *"I am calling on you in connection with the letter I sent to you (or vice president of my company, general agent, manager, sent to you) a few days ago. You probably recall receiving it, don't you?"*

> *"I am calling in connection with the ap-pointment that we made on the telephone yesterday."*

When you are approaching anyone to whom you do not have an introduction, you have merely to introduce yourself and your company —*"My name is Stacey Agent and I represent the _____ Insurance Company."* Then continue with Step 2 above, which in every instance will have the same phrasing.

II. The Presentation

Having obtained a favorable response to your approach, you are ready to create a sales situation. Your aim is to make an interesting presentation with economy of time and words. Again we follow the sales pattern already set up.

Here is how the general problem could be established.

Step 1. Point out the hopes and responsibilities of people in general

> *"If you and I were to stop a person on the way home tonight and ask, 'Why do you work week after week, month after month, year after year?' the person would probably say he or she works to earn money—to pay bills, support a family, educate the children, provide a home, and so forth. It is not generally thought of in just this way, but there are only two sources of income: either a person at work or dollars at work."*

Step 2. Win agreement that fulfilling these hopes and responsibilities rests on the foundation of earned income.

> *"For most people, it is the dollars they earn which are more important. Almost everything in the world most people hope to do for their families and themselves depends on earned income, doesn't it?"*

This is brief and to the point. Now having established the general problem, proceed immediately to your next principal point—*establishing the specific problem.*

Step 1. Turn the discussion to those things which most interest the prospect—self, family, responsibilities, plans

> *"You're married, aren't you, (Prospect)?*

"You have two children! How old are they?...I assume you are making plans for their education...Do you own or rent your home?...In addition, the responsibilities of housing your family, feeding them, clothing them, protecting them with life insurance, maintaining a car—and a hundred other things—all fall on your shoulders, don't they?"

Questions like these lead directly and naturally into a discussion of your prospect's situation and the need for continuing income.

Step 2. Confirm the importance of the prospect's earned income in fulfilling responsibilities and plans

"Isn't it the dollars you earn which make it possible for you to support your family— pay the rent (meet regular home payments), put food on the table, provide good clothes for your family, give them most of the comforts of life and some of the luxuries? And after all this, most of us have something left over for savings.

"Our security today and our plans for tomorrow depend primarily on our ability to continue to work and earn money. That's certainly true in most cases. I know it is in mine and probably in yours, too, isn't it, (Prospect)?"

Step 3. Uncover the person's critical needs in relation to his or her responsibilities and plans

"What would have happened if on your way home last night you had been hurt seriously and sent to a hospital? A doctor, the expenses of X-rays, drugs, medicines, possibly a nurse, would be necessary. Extra expenses would mount up, in addition to the regular costs of supporting your family and your home.

"What about your income? How long would it go on? Sooner or later it would stop! What about the bills which would continue to mount up? What about all the plans you have made?

"You'd be faced with a serious situation, wouldn't you?"

Step 4. Win clear-cut agreement on the seriousness of the needs

"When this happens, there are only about three ways you can meet your family responsibilities and pay your bills.

"First, you can use up the savings which you have been accumulating.

"Second, you can borrow money. But then you would have to pay it back, plus interest.

"Third, you can fall back on charity. Some people might, but I'm sure you have too much pride to want to do that.

"Do you know any other way of solving this problem?"

Following these steps, you lay a foundation for a sale. Before you call on your prospect, you often will be partially or fully aware of his or her need for health insurance. But do not offer the cure for financial ailments before you bring the situation out into the open. First make sure he or she recognizes the seriousness of the problem and wants to do something about it.

Note the last question in Step 4, *"Do you know any other way of solving this problem?"* It is inserted here deliberately. With it you can uncover early in the interview any existing hospital, surgical or income insurance the person may have. At this point, too, he or she may be more willing to admit the inadequacy of present coverage. In addition you forestall a complacent announcement that he or she has a policy—after you have told your story. (Also, if you find the person has some disability insurance, your presentation may shift to another form of coverage to supplement what the person already has.)

An Additional Technique

There is another strategy occasionally inserted following Step 4 when establishing the specific problem. Many agents believe that at this point in the interview the prospect vividly sees the need for some protection. They suggest that it is timely to ask a question here, such as: *"If I could show you a plan which exactly fits your situation, and solves this problem, how much could you set aside each month?"* If the prospect hesitates to be committed, the agent should reassure the person by saying: *"I did not mean how much you would set aside, but only how much you could set aside so that I can tailor the plan to your situation."* Those who recommend this procedure explain that once the prospect has specified an amount, the agent has largely eliminated the excuse that sometimes arises at the close of the interview, *"I can't afford it."*

Let your judgment guide you. There are prospects who would resent being asked how much they can afford before knowing the details of what you are offering. Also, when you have enough information about your prospect to know that the income is substantial, you may feel that it would be out of order to ask if he or she could afford the plan. Rather than arouse any resentment in such a prospect, you should assume that the person can pay the premium if he or she wants to enough.

Your next step in the well-planned sale is to present the ideal solution. Practice with your rate book will give you a fairly accurate idea of the premiums for different policies at various ages. Make the premium for the recommended plan come close to your estimate of the amount the prospect can afford.

Step 1. Show how your contract guarantees what your prospect agrees is essential

> *"Then, (Prospect), here is a plan to help you solve your problem. Here is how it works in your case.*
>
> *"My company will set aside the equivalent of $225,000 with your name on it."* (use $30,000 for each $200 of monthly income you are illustrating.)
>
> *"When you are unable to work due to sickness, we will pay you 8% interest on that money, which means $1,500 each month beginning with the ____th day you are laid up. This monthly income will be paid to you as long as you are unable to work due to illness, for a maximum of ____ months.* *
>
> *"Or when you are unable to work due to an accident, we will pay you 8 percent interest on $225,000 which is $1,500 each month for as long as you are disabled."*

Step 2. Emphasize the unique features of your company's contract

"In addition, we will pay you ..." (Here, bring out special features of your contract not already mentioned. Explain how they are beneficial to the prospect. These might include extra payments when disability results from travel accident, lump-sum benefits in case of loss of hands or feet or eyesight, or other special policy features.)

> *"You'd like those features in your contract, wouldn't you?"*

By agreeing with you here, your prospect indicates belief that the contract holds a solution to some of his or her problems. You should continue immediately with the close.

III. The Close

There is no sharp breaking point necessary between the body of the interview and the close. The scene does not change. You do not put on a different hat.

Few sales are made on the first closing attempt. Well-trained agents are equipped with a series of different closes. They develop skill in using organized closing procedures. It is not usually desirable to attempt to close twice on the same point. The prospect's pride may force him or her to say "No" even though a change of mind has occurred.

A good closing procedure must be easy to remember during an interview. With this in mind, we have designed a closing procedure with five different points of emphasis. You will find it helpful because the five first letters of each closing attempt combine to spell the word S-A-L-E-S.

This five-point technique of closing and the

A FIVE-POINT CLOSING TECHNIQUE THAT SPELLS S-A-L-E-S

Close "S"–Sound Risk... *"Are you now in good health?"*
Close "A"–Alternate Choice
Close "L"–List Benefits
Close "E"–Example... *"Let me tell you the story about..."*
Close "S"–Suggest Smaller Premium

---

*Vary these words, of course, to fit whatever periods your plan covers.

step-by-step outline of the principles of closing are combined in the following to illustrate five practical closing methods *to obtain action now.*

Close "S"—Sound Risk

People do not like to make immediate decisions. This is particularly true when they feel they will have the opportunity to buy later. To the agent, a postponed sale is frequently a lost sale. What the health insurance agent is especially conscious of is the possibility of uninsurability—that good health is an important consideration to the sale.

Each year, thousands of people cross the line of insurability, never again able to qualify for health insurance. Get this point across to your prospect. Stress that not everyone can qualify for the plan you have outlined. This is your most logical first closing attempt.

Step 1. "S"—Stress that good health is an important consideration

> *"There is just one thing we always like to make very clear. Because the company has thousands and thousands of dollars at stake, they must make sure that you are a sound risk in all respects. Do you have any reason to fear a medical examination, if one is required?"* (At this point move right into the application. Ask one of the health questions such as "Are you now in good health?" Keep going unless you are stopped.)

Close "A"—Alternate Choice

Clothing merchants offer customers a choice between suits. When the prospective buyer prefers one the salesperson concentrates on it and is one step nearer the sale.

These tactics are based on the theory: if offered two alternatives, a person will choose one. If given a choice between something and nothing, he or she may choose nothing. It is better, therefore, to give a choice between two positive acts.

Step 2. "A"—Make it easy for the prospect to buy

> *"Instead of paying you this income of $1,500 a month for (length of time), while you are laid up, unable to work, we can pay you a larger income, say $2,000 a month for (shorter period). Which do you prefer?"*

(When the person answers, start asking the questions on the application. Keep going unless you are stopped.)

Close "L"—List Benefits

You may be interrupted several times when completing the application. By the time a third closing attempt is necessary, your prospect may have lost sight of the needs for protection and the many benefits of your plan. Go back to your proposal and review the provisions of the plan. Use your pen and draw a circle. Divide it into quarters. List one of the major benefits in each quarter. For example, write the sickness income benefits in one quarter, accident income in another, expense benefits in the third, and principal sum benefits in the fourth. (If your proposal has no principal sum, use one of the other benefits for the fourth quarter of the circle.)

By demonstrating benefits in this way, you clearly bring out the advantages of owning the protection.

Step 3. "L"—Emphasize the rightness of your contract for the prospect's purpose

> *"(Prospect), we may have lost sight of exactly what this contract will do when you are unable to work and have no income. Let me illustrate with this simple diagram.*
> *"1. You will receive $1,500 each month for (length of time) while you are unable to work due to sickness.*
> *"2. You will receive $1,500 each month for (length of time) while you are unable to work due to accident.*
> *"3. Should you become disabled in a travel accident, you will receive $3,000 each month during the first three months to help with extra expenses.*
> *"4. And should death result from an accident, your spouse (or mother, father, etc.) will receive $37,500 to help keep your family going. That's important, isn't it?"* (Don't wait for an answer. Continue with the questions on the application. Keep going unless you are stopped.)

Close "E"—Example

Most people believe that their actions are rooted in logical reasoning. They like to think that judgment alone guides their lives. More frequently, emotions compel people to act. They seek reasons to justify what their emotions tell them to do. Many men and women refrain from taking action until their emotions are stirred. To illustrate that point, consider this situation:

> *Behind a certain hospital is an artificial pool, a part of the hospital's air conditioning system. It occurred to many people that the pool might be a hazard if anyone walked in that area at night. But no one made an issue of it.*
>
> *One day a small boy fell in and was nearly drowned. That night the boy's father went from house to house in the community getting a petition signed. He then took the signatures to the hospital administrator. As a result, the pool was immediately fenced in.*

There were many who recognized the hazard but their feelings were not touched. They did nothing. The boy's father was hit hard emotionally. He acted!

The Need For Motivating Stories—There is not much to stir the emotions in the printed words of a health insurance policy. They represent cold, straight logical thinking. But it is what these words promise to deliver in a time of need which makes them come alive. This is the picture which you must paint for the prospect. Motivation is needed to move the prospect to action. He or she must do more than recognize a problem exists. They must be disturbed about it!

Successful agents draw on experiences—their own and those of others—to tell a story that shows health insurance in action. They dramatize the tragedy of inadequate protection against disability. They use *"for example"* in their closing procedure.

Step 4. "E"—Build urgency behind the need for prompt action

> *"(Prospect), we have been discussing the provisions of this plan in terms of dollars of benefits and dollars of premiums. Perhaps we're bogged down in details and have lost sight of the complete picture.*
>
> *"It could be that we have been so concerned with the specific features of this*

> *plan that we have forgotten what happens to a person and a family when income stops. For example—*
>
> *"One of the men in our office has a close friend who is an architect. In spite of frequent opportunities to buy income protection, he always refused. He said he was saving a fair amount of money and was buying good stocks. In time, he claimed, he would have enough income from his stocks to pay any sickness or accident expenses. The agent, not wishing to offend the man, dropped the subject rather than lose a friend.*
>
> *"Coming home from a golf game, the architect was involved in an automobile accident. His back was severely wrenched, a vertebra was fractured. They didn't know if he would ever walk again. He was lucky he wasn't killed. Or, unlucky! After two operations, he was able to sit up in a wheelchair. The time in the hospital, doctor bills, special nurses and extra expenses soon ate up his stocks and bonds and savings. His son had to withdraw from college and go to work. His wife also had to find a job to help with expenses.*
>
> *"(Prospect), that is a heavy price to pay for the protection that architect did not buy.*
>
> *"There is no doubt that if that architect could choose again, he would certainly prefer the easy way of setting aside a few dollars a month for our plan. To be in force when it is needed, insurance must be bought before it is needed!"* (Do not wait for him to comment, but continue with questions on the application. Keep going unless you are stopped.)

Close "S"—Suggest Smaller Premium

When you have made four tries to complete the application, make one more closing attempt. Perhaps the prospect likes the plan but does not want to admit he or she cannot afford the complete coverage. Make it easier by suggesting less coverage for a smaller premium outlay.

Step 5. "S"—Help the prospect fit the plan to his or her budget

> *"Perhaps you would prefer not to take the*

entire plan at once. In that case, why don't we go ahead with one-half the amount now, so you will have that protection? If you can still qualify, you can secure the additional protection later on"(continue completing the application).

TAKE A POSITIVE ATTITUDE

No alarm clock rings when the prospect is ready to buy. He or she seldom invites you to take out your pen and fill in the application.

And no experienced underwriter would ask outright, "Shall I go ahead and write this up?" Such a point-blank question might well shut the door on the sale. Such tactics are neither advisable nor necessary. A well-planned sales talk flows smoothly and naturally into completing the application.

With a carefully selected prospect and a skillful presentation, you have every right to expect the prospect to buy. Your own frame of mind plays a big part in completing the sale. Assume that the prospect is going to buy.

Perhaps the greatest weakness in closing is in not assuming the prospect will buy. The agent who does not have a positive attitude toward a sale, who is afraid of hearing the prospect say "No," postpones filling out the application. This does not make sense.

It is in the last ten yards of a football field where the offensive team usually meets the toughest going. They may have trained for weeks. They may have mastered intricate plays. But if they do not score, they do not win. Practice has been in vain.

When an agent digs for a prospect, qualifies the person, arouses interest and makes a skilled presentation, the sale must be completed to make the preparation pay off. The strong agent *expects to sell* almost every prospect on whom a call is made. Expectancy produces closes if the agent uses all the basic sales points.

KNOW WHEN TO CLOSE

Some football coaches design plays which, if executed perfectly, will score from almost any

place on the field. A good agent does the same. He or she closes quickly the minute an opening presents itself.

There is an occasional prospect almost ready to buy when you walk in. The person may have been warmed up by some other underwriter, or may have been stirred by the experience of a friend. The completion of a sales presentation isn't needed to drive the person to action. Close whenever the prospect indicates that he or she is ready.

There will be signals which say, *"Close now."*

1. The prospect may ask: "Would I have to be examined?" You answer, "Is there any reason you fear medical examination?" and move into the application.
2. He or she may ask: "How much did you say it costs?" Answer, and start to close.
3. He or she may ask: "Do I pay premiums when I'm disabled?" Answer, and start to close.
4. He or she may ask: "Would I have to pay for this all at once?" Answer, and start to close.
5. He or she may ask: "Can I get this without accidental death benefit?" Answer, and start to close.
6. He or she may ask: "What is the maximum monthly income I can have?" Answer, and start to close.
7. He or she may ask: "Can I get a plan which pays for a lesser number years?" Answer, and start to close.

Watch for the flags the prospect flies. They signal, "This is it—close now."

TECHNIQUES OF CLOSING

There are certain recognized techniques in closing which have stood the test of time. Skill in their use will strengthen your ability to close. Each of the five points in the acrostic S-A-L-E-S discussed earlier is based on these standard closing techniques.

Implied Consent—This is just what it sounds like. You feel that your plan is so logical, desirable and necessary that the prospect wants it. You go ahead and complete the papers without actual verbal authorization. This makes it easy for the prospect. The person is not forced to admit out loud that he or she is ready to buy.

Implied consent runs through each of the S–A–L–E–S closes.

Decision on a Minor Point—This is based on the sound theory that a series of small affirmative decisions will inevitably add up to one major decision.

1. *"Would you like to include surgical expense benefits?"*
2. *"Would a 15-day waiting period be a good idea in your case?"*
3. *"To whom would you want death benefits paid?"*
4. *"Would you want extra benefits while you are confined to a hospital?"*
5. *"Don't you agree that this is the finest plan of its kind you have ever seen?"*
6. *"For the same premium, would you prefer a larger income for a shorter period of time?"*

Alternative Choice—Offer a person two suggestions. When one is accepted, the person has made a commitment. The sale is made easier for both prospect and agent.

1. *"Would you prefer to make payments once a year or twice?"*
2. *"in the event of an accident, would you prefer payments to begin on the first day or the eighth day?"*
3. *"Would you prefer premium notices sent to your home or office address?"*
4. *"You may have this sickness income for two or five years. Which would you prefer?"*
5. *"Do you usually pay by cash or check?"*

Action Closes—You start to fill out the application. You ask for more space on the prospect's desk to write on. You put the pen in the prospect's hand.

All of these are physical actions which the prospect must stop if he or she is not going through with the plan. In each step of S–A–L–E–S, we recommend you *keep going unless you are stopped.*

Take-It-Away Closes—When an appliance store advertises *"For a limited time only. . ."* the cus-

tomers arrive early. When a theater hands out a *"Standing Room Only"* sign, the public buys tickets for weeks ahead. People do not want to pass up a good thing. The fear of loss is strong. Much life insurance is purchased just prior to an age change because the premium is about to increase. Many articles of clothing are purchased today because the buyer is afraid they will not be available tomorrow.

As a health insurance agent, you can use the same technique effectively. For example:

"(Prospect), you look like you could qualify for this plan. Why don't we find out? I don't like to promise to bring you a contract which you might not be able to get."

—or—

"Within the next 12 months, several of my clients will probably receive claim checks. You wouldn't want me to pass you up if you needed the money, would you?"

MORE ABOUT MOTIVATING STORIES

The closing technique utilizing motivating stories was discussed at some length under Example in S–A–L–E–S. It deserves additional emphasis.

Your success in using motivating stories depends not only on your skill in telling them but also on your convictions about your product-health insurance. If you believe unreservedly that the plan you are offering satisfies your prospect's needs as nothing else will, you can use a story more effectively. If you have seen health insurance in action, or witnessed the tragedy of its absence, you can motivate more sincerely.

It is not necessary to become overly sentimental in a motivating story. It does not always have to contain a tearful ending. You may make your point sufficiently with photostats of claim checks you have permission to show or with newspaper clippings of accident stories.

There are many sources of stories to tell. Health insurance is a particularly fertile field for them. Most people with claims like to tell their story. You have only to repeat these stories as living testimonials of the benefits you sell. *Remember—people seldom act until they are disturbed—enough.*

Your job will not be to put the pressure on a prospect. The pressure is already on. But in many cases the person does not recognize the problems. To help in this is your job. The whole future of the person and the family depends on the maintenance of his or her earned income month after month. This is real pressure. Your plan is designed to take the pressure off.

USE OF VISUAL AIDS

Two senses are better than one. When you stimulate the eye as well as the ear, your story has a better chance of registering.

Many successful agents build their sales procedure around a series of visual aids. Others introduce visual material into the interview at strategic spots. Some use occasional pencil sketches to illustrate a point. Another method is the use of printed proposal forms completed in front of the prospect.

A combination of these techniques produces maximum results. If you have a printed visual sales piece, you can illustrate each point of your presentation. Then, in outlining the dollar-and-cents benefits of your plan, you can fill in a proposal form.

Completing a proposal form in the presence of your prospect is effective. You hold attention as the plan unfolds before his or her eyes. Like a tailor, you cut and fit the plan to the prospect's individual situation. In addition, visual selling gives you a track to run on. It gives you added confidence when you are with the prospect.

You can mastery over the interview when your sales talk is illustrated. The pictures and words serve you as notes serve a speaker. The ideas and key thoughts come in proper sequence. A visual presentation is easier for the prospect to grasp.

It is a time-saver. It is "courtesy selling." There is little idle conversation. Everything you say is pointed toward your main objective: completing the sale. *As a result, you have time to see more prospects.*

Visual selling is good for the prospect—good for you—good for sales.

POWER PHRASES THAT LEAD TO SALES

"Do you know how long you are going to stay in good health?"

"Postponing the solution doesn't postpone the problem."

"Which will be easier—for you to give up a few luxuries now, or to watch your family give up some necessities later if you become disabled?"

"(Prospect), do you realize that some people are financially better prepared to die than to live?...In other words, life insurance will take care of the family if the income producer dies too soon. But if the person is permanently disabled as the result of accident or sickness, no income has been provided. That is what we mean by financially better prepared to die than to live. That is not a happy situation, is it?"

"(Prospect), health insurance is 'surprise' insurance. A Sunday drive—a crash—surprise! A March wind—a cough—surprise! A pain in the chest—a cardiogram—surprise!

"Life is full of nasty suprises. Health insurance can't eliminate the physical pain, but it can take the financial sting out of the surprise."

"If your employer should tell you on Friday night that it is unable to pay you, you would get along all right next week. Perhaps you would have to stay home over the weekend instead of taking a trip, but there would be no great embarrassment.

"But suppose that on the following Friday night your employer again tells you that it could not pay you. The pinch would be a bit harder. During the second week without pay you would have to do a good deal of worrying.

"Then suppose that on the third Friday night it should again tell you that there would be no pay...and the next Friday night and the next Friday night...until the weeks roll into months and the months roll into years—

"Then you and your family would face a real problem. What wold you do? How would you pay expenses? How would you live? Where would you turn for money?

"That is the problem...the very real problem...that the person who does not have health insurance will come up against when disabled!"

Chapter 10
How to Handle Objections

LESSON TEXT—**Planned Presentations Avoid Difficulties . . . Excuses vs. Objections . . . Tested Methods of Meeting Objections . . . Most Common Excuses . . . Analyzing the Excuses . . . When Your Prospect Says "No"**

Ask experienced agents how they regard objections and when you have analyzed their answers carefully, you can summarize them as follows:

"Oh, we'd be lost without objections. Our toughest prospects usually are the 'dead pans' who won't say a thing. We never know where we stand with that kind of prospect. We do not even know if they are listening to us. But the person who raises objections is much easier to deal with; he or she is really asking questions. It helps us out by telling us what the person wants to know in order to be sold. When one says in a challenging voice, 'Never heard of your company,' the person is really wondering if we have confidence in our company and our product. If we don't have confidence, he or she won't. The prospect is asking us to show how much we believe in what we are recommending. Or the person is frankly saying, 'I want to know more about your company. Tell me about it!' That is your opportunity to give a short sales talk on the strength of your company. If he or she says, 'I'll take a chance, and do without,' the person is telling us where we have been weak in our presentation, so this enables us to go back to our presentation and do a better selling job."

When a prospect starts throwing objections at you, it is usually a sure sign of interest. The person is telling you how to help him or her decide to buy by indicating the points which are not clear.

Have you ever watched a smart collie dog herd sheep through a series of enclosures and into a corral? It does not rush them; it does not stampede them. It keeps them going in the right direction with gentle, steady pressure from behind. When it has guided them into the first enclosure, the well-trained sheep dog noses the gate shut before directing them into the next enclosure. From enclosure to enclosure it moves them, shutting the gate each time, until they are in the corral with the only escape the ramp which leads into a truck or railroad car.

The good salesperson follows the same techniques, wins agreement step by step while moving along, until the result is a completed application. He or she allows no obstacle in the path to halt progress. The good agent gains strength by recognizing objections for what they are. And when they do arise, they are welcome because he or she knows how to use them in closing sales.

PLANNED PRESENTATIONS AVOID DIFFICULTIES

In the well-organized health insurance sale, excuses, stalls and objections present no major problem. You contact your prospect through a mutual friend or other prestige-building reference so that the person has confidence in you and agrees to see you. In your approach you win the prospect's agreement to listen to you, and thus you eliminate the *"I'm too busy"* excuse. You guide your prospect from the general problem to the specific problem. When it has been exposed, you win agreement that the person should take steps to solve it immediately. By this technique one of the most bothersome excuses, often voiced by the prospect at the crucial point of the sale, is usually avoided: *"I can't afford it."* By offering the prospect a sound solution, by stressing the features of your plan, and by making the plan easy to buy, you sidestep the *"no hurry"* excuse.

In this procedure you will recognize the Essential Steps of a Successful Sales Presentation which you have already studied.

Some agents seem to be lucky in finding and selling the easy cases. But rather than luck, it is still in avoiding difficulties. This does not mean, however, that excuses and objections will not come up at the approach, or during the interview, or in the close. The well-trained agent understands these hurdles to complete sales. And

> Well-planned interviews anticipate and avoid stalls, excuses and objections, or answer them before they arise. Sound prospecting habits and mastery of organized sales talks go a long way toward forestalling trouble and eliminating any difficulties in completing sales. By calling your prospect's attention to the urgent needs for insurance and by basing your recommendations on their specific situation, you set up a backdrop against which excuses seem relatively unimportant.

because the agent understands the techniques of handling excuses, he or she maintains a high ratio of sales.

EXCUSES VS. OBJECTIONS

To place excuses and objections in proper perspective it is necessary to realize that there is a distinct difference between the two. Excuses might be called stalls. These are common. They are nothing more than the usual way certain prospects treat all salespeople. Often, disturbing questions or challenging statements are confused with objections, although they are only excuses or stalls. The prospect is looking for an easy way out so a change of plans is not necessary. When the prospect says *"My company has group insurance for me,"* the hope is you will lift the load of worry by agreeing that it is adequate protection. Then he or she will not have to decide on the merits of your plan.

Occasionally prospects who have a feeling of inferiority because they seldom can dominate a situation enjoy their position as a prospect and use excuses and stalls to prolong their new sensation of importance.

A prospect makes negative responses during the approach because he or she does not want to talk about something which should have been taken care of earlier. They are brought up during the interview because you are right and he or she was wrong when these thoughts were pushed to the back of their minds. The prospect voices them during the close just as a game fish fights harder the closer it is pulled to the boat. These stalls and excuses are normal reactions and to be expected.

However, objections are sincere. They must be answered to the prospect's satisfaction.

The prospect does not raise them merely to thwart the agent. They are not brought up simply because the prospect feels he or she must say something negative. The person may honestly believe there is a real reason for not buying now.

The person's budget may be so tight that he or she cannot increase premium outlay without a pay raise. There may be a deeply rooted misunderstanding of the purposes of health insurance. The person may feel obligation to some other underwriter to a degree which prevents doing business with you.

To ignore real objections, to attempt to answer them glibly, or to rush by them is not good sales strategy. You should take particular care that sincere objections are given thorough answers. Help your prospect to eliminate objections. That represents true sales skill. Experience and study will give you this power. And when you possess it, objections will not bother you.

TESTED METHODS OF MEETING OBJECTIONS

There are definite techniques for handling excuses and objections, easily and quickly. If you know these basic principles that have proved useful in handling objections, then you are not at a loss as to what to say or what to do. You have a definite track to run on. The prospect cannot disturb you. Study these tested methods carefully. You will find that the problem of objections will cease to be a troublesome barrier, but will instead become a detour around which you know your way.

Keep in mind two key points: **Always clarify your prospect's question.** Re-phrase it, restate it or ask if you have grasped the main point of what your prospect is saying. You want to be sure you understand, you want the prospect to know you understand and you want to give yourself the opportunity to formulate a response.

Remember This
Whenever a Prospect Objects

He or she is not qualified as an expert in health insurance.

. . . may be the smartest doctor in town—

. . . may be the biggest banker in the state—

. . . may be the most learned professor in the university—

. . . may be the best food store manager, or the best shoe retailer, or the most successful jeweler in your area . . .

But these qualifications do not set him or her up as an expert in health insurance.

Pin that fact close to your mind and keep it there all day long . . . Remember—YOU are the one who is qualified.

Always deal with true objections. Develop the skill of discerning between stalls and objections. Objections must be dealt with, or you will have a short, empty interview. When to deal with a true objection depends on the momentum and progress of your presentation. You want to stay on track as much as you can, but not if your prospect isn't listening to you.

Here are some techniques for handling your prospect's responses, and for helping your prospect move closer to a buying decision.

1. "We'll Come to That Later"

When an objection or question is raised early in the interview, before you have presented your recommendation, one effective method of handling it is to postpone it until later. For example, if your prospect asks, "Does this plan pay me extra when I'm in a hospital?" say, "We'll come to that later," and continue along your sales track. During the interview whenever an excuse or objection threatens to detour your story, tell your prospect you will cover that point later.

When your prospect asks, "Will this plan pay me an income for life if I am totally disabled?" you can say, "We will come to that later, because it is an important part of the plan."

If the question is genuinely important, you can cover it at the appropriate point in your presentation. If it is just a stall, the question often will not be raised again. But when it is a true objection, the prospect may bring it up a second time. Then you must give a completely satisfactory answer or it will block the sale.

2. "Yes, But . . ."

Another successful technique is the '"*Yes, but . . .*" method. The advantage of this method is that you avoid abruptly contradicting your prospect. Instead, you first agree. You disarm the person and put him or her in a favorable state of mind by looking at it from his or her point of view.

When the prospect raises the objection, "I don't like doing business with a stranger," you say,

"Yes, (Prospect), I can understand exactly how you feel, because this is personal insurance just like life insurance. But I talk to many people I don't know. Yet there is not one stranger among my hundreds of policyowners. They are all good friends now."

3. "Glad You Asked That"

Still another way of handling excuses is to tell your prospect, "I'm glad you brought that up." It is effective in turning a question into a sales point. For example, your prospect might ask, "Isn't life insurance more important than health insurance?" Then your answer should be,

"I'm glad you brought that up, because all forms of insurance are important. But don't you agree you should insure the income which pays the premium?"

Or when your prospect says, "My job is too uncertain," you would answer,

"I'm glad you brought that up, (Prospect), because it reminds me of an important point I should mention. If you lose your job but keep your health, you can get another job. But if you lose your health, you lose your job and your income. This plan insures

the most important asset you have, your ability to earn an income."

4. "Let Me Tell You About . . ."

A fourth procedure for meeting excuses is to tell an appropriate story out of your experience. An excuse frequently encountered is, "I have a friend in the business." For example, here is a highly effective way of handling this objection.

"Yes, I expect that a person in your position has several friends in the insurance business. But when you are disabled and unable to work, you will need more than friends. You will need income. Six months ago I called on a dentist and he, too, said he had friends in the business. I convinced him to take the insurance with me since I was right there and on hand. Three months ago he waved goodbye to his wife and child and later that day met with a tragic auto accident. He is still in the hospital and probably will not be able to return to his practice for at least another six months or more. He hasn't any substantial savings. But every month his disability continues, his family will receive an income from the plan he bought through me. Who do you suppose is his real friend in the business today?"

5. "Any Other Questions"

A fifth method is to ask your prospect, "And in addition to that, do you have any other questions?" This system is useful where the prospect offers a series of excuses. Give the person all the time he or she wants to stall. Let them use up all their ammunition without interruption. Then, when he or she finishes, ask again, "And in addition to that, do you have any other questions?" After you have brought all the excuses out into the open, highlight them and answer them all in a group.

For example, the prospect may voice several excuses, "I'm meeting regular mortgage payments and buying a television set. Every month when I think I have everything under control, something always comes up. This month there's a dentist's bill." "And in addition to that, do you have any other objections?" you ask. "Well, I don't want to obligate myself to any other fixed expenses. I'll take a chance." Although the person has indicated by tone that there are no others, you should not assume the store of excuses has been exhausted.

So ask again, "And in addition, Mr. Prospect, do you have any other questions?" When he or she replies negatively, then proceed with your review of the objections, such as, "It's because of your many fixed expenses that you are willing to take this chance then, isn't it?" Next, agree with the point of view before answering the objections in a group. In this situation, you might say,

> *"I can certainly understand what you mean, (Prospect), because that is a very common situation these days. But it is because of those regular expenses that you are working to earn income. Stop and think of what would happen in a serious disability with your income cut off altogether. You would still have your regular living expenses. But also the other bills. You are not the only one taking the chance. Your spouse and children are also taking the chance. Wouldn't it be wiser to economize a little now to guarantee that you will continue to have income to pay for your basic living costs?"*

6. "Would You Mind Explaining . . . ?"

Another method of meeting excuses is the question method. When a prospect raises a point which is difficult to answer because you do not understand it entirely, ask questions to narrow it down to a specific excuse. A prospect may say, "I don't believe in this kind of insurance, because companies don't pay when they should." This could be merely an excuse or it could be a serious objection. But you cannot answer it satisfactorily unless you have the whole story.

Only by asking questions will you find out what the statement is posed on. It may be that an uncle was laid up several weeks with a ruptured appendix and expected an accident policy to pay an income. Many people believe that they have adequate health insurance when all they really have are hospital policies which pay for certain expenses while confined to a hospital. Or

they may have surgical policies which pay specified amounts for certain operations.

When the prospect states, "I have health insurance," use the question method to find out just what is meant. Say, "That's fine, I'm glad to know that you believe in this kind of protection. How much income does your policy pay you when you are sick at home for a prolonged period?"

There are other ways to handle excuses. Some agents have methods which fit their own personality exactly. But often those personalized methods are difficult for others to adopt. Other agents use a combination of the techniques discussed here. Whatever procedure you use, it is important to remember—*do not pause after answering.* Continue toward your main objective: a complete sale. If you hesitate after giving an answer, you are inviting your prospect to bring up another excuse—and the interview soon turns into a battle of wits. If an objection is brought up during the interview and you cannot postpone it with "I'll come to that later," you will, of course, have to meet it then and there. But when you have answered it, pick up the presentation where you left off and continue through all the essential steps of a successful sales presentation.

Health Insurance

What is there to object to . . . ?
  Money for doctor bills?
  Money for hospital bills?
  Money for operations?
  Money to pay for special nurses?
  Money for food and clothing and housing —when you cannot earn a living?
  Tax-free income when you cannot work?
  Ability to afford prompt and proper medical care?
  Freedom from worry and fear of an uncertain, heavy financial burden?
  A reserve fund of hundreds—even thousands of dollars—when disability strikes?
  That your plans for the future will not be destroyed—though you are disabled for months . . . for years?

Excuses and Stalls as Buying Signals

Consider for a moment the man who dresses conservatively. Yet he always has had a secret desire to own a white suit. In a clothing store he sees just what he has in mind. He wants it—but he wonders...will I look foolish in it?...is it too lively for me...too sporty? Because he wants to buy it, he will bring up all the reasons in the world why a white suit looks silly on a man.

And he brings up all those reasons because he wants the clerk to justify the decision he is about to make, which decision is in favor of the white suit.

Wise is the clerk who refuses to get worried or be discouraged by a barrage of objections against white suits...for he or she understands that these excuses and objections are signals that the decision is about to be made.

In the same way, wise is the agent who refuses to become worried and nervous at the barrage of last minute objections advanced by the prospect.

Instead objections should be welcomed because they tell the agent that the prospect is interested and needs help in arriving at a decision. This enables the agent to turn that decision in the right direction.

MOST COMMON EXCUSES

Prospects can voice a great variety of excuses for not buying. When these are studied, it usually turns out that many are the same excuse, but worded differently. They generally can be reduced to just 17, and even some of these overlap in a sense. Here they are listed in the order of the frequency with which they usually will be mentioned.

1. I can't afford it.
2. I have a friend in the business.
3. I've never been sick in my life.
4. I have an accident policy. (I have group insurance. I have hospitalization. I have another policy.)
5. Never heard of your company.
6. I'm too busy—see me later.
7. I'll take a chance—and risk going without.

8. My salary will continue when I'm disabled.
9. I'll talk it over with my spouse.
10. My work isn't hazardous.
11. It costs too much.
12. My job is too uncertain.
13. I want to think it over—leave some literature.
14. I can carry my own insurance.
15. I don't like to do business with strangers.
16. I'd rather put my money in the bank (or in government bonds).
17. My family will help me out when I'm disabled.

Further analysis of prospects' responses reveals something of great significance: all excuses seem to fall under four main headings. When a prospect asserts, "I'm too busy, see me later," he or she is telling you *there's no rush*. When the person states, "It costs too much," he or she is trying to beg off with *there's no money*. When it's, "I've never been sick in my life," they are saying *there's no need*. When they say, "I've never heard of your company," it means *there's no confidence*.

Advantages of Grouping Excuses

Isn't it true that all 17 of the excuses most frequently encountered in the field can be grouped under these four headings: *no rush, no money, no need or no confidence?* If so, it will be of tremendous help to you in conquering and controlling excuses. You will be able to catalog any objection the prospect offers under its proper heading. You will have at your fingertips the key to the barrier that blocks the sale. You can instantly recognize what is in the prospect's mind, expose it and dispose of it by giving the proper concept of sickness and accident protection.

ANALYZING THE EXCUSES

Let us examine these 17 excuses and see how each fits into one of the four classifications: no rush, no money, no need, no confidence. The first one, "I can't afford it," obviously falls under *no money*. The second, "I have a friend in the business" means *no confidence*. The third, "I've

FIGURE 10-3
GROUPING EXCUSES

No Rush	No Money
I'm too busy—see me later. I'll talk it over with my wife (husband). I want to think it over—leave some literature.	Can't afford it. I'll take a chance. It costs too much. My family will help me out when I'm disabled.
No Need	**No Confidence**
I've never been sick in my life. I have an accident policy. My salary will continue. I can carry my own insurance. I'd rather put my money in the bank. My work isn't hazardous.	I have a friend in the business. Never heard of your company. My job is too uncertain. I don't like to do business with strangers.

never been sick in my life," is another way of saying *no need*. The fourth, "I have a policy," also means *no need*. "Never heard of your company," reveals *no confidence*. The next, "I'm too busy— see me later," fits *no rush*. Thus each can be placed in one of four compartments, where your thoughts are marshaled and your answers are waiting.

It is logical for someone at this point to ask, "How would you classify an excuse not listed among these 17? What if the prospect says, for example, 'I'm not interested'?"

That is an excuse with no specific meaning until it is clarified. You can see that it can be placed under *no rush*, *no money*, *no need* or *no confidence*. Naturally, if your prospect said that, you would use the question method to find out just what is meant. "What is it you are not interested in, (Prospect)?" Then, when the person is specific, you can put it in the proper slot where your thoughts are organized. Of course, these 17 do not represent all the excuses you will ever meet. But they do typify the large majority.

From experience and practice will come skill and confidence in handling objections effectively. To help you become completely familiar with methods of dealing with the 17 most com-

mon excuses, effective answers are given here. You may have others you prefer to use. You should study, rehearse and practice them until you have mastered a response for each excuse and are adept in the techniques discussed.

There's No Rush

When Sandy Kirkpatrich stalls with an excuse meaning *there's no rush*, Sandy is admitting no sense of urgency of the situation. Sandy has not considered the problem of time and does not realize that thousands of people who turned off their alarm clock, ate breakfast and went to work this morning will not get out of bed for work tomorrow. When Sandy is numbered among those cold statistics, it will be too late. A prolonged sickness or accident can cut off Sandy's salary, and possibly make Sandy uninsurable. To be in force when it is needed, it must be in force all the time.

"I'm Too Busy—See Me Later"

"Yes, I'd be glad to. How much later would you like me to see you? Two or three months?" ("Three months.") "But can you

guarantee that you will not become sick in the meantime—that you will not be laid up with cancer or heart trouble or arthritis or any other of the 1,800 diseases known to medical science? Can you guarantee that some careless driver won't run into you in the meantime? In my experience, I've found that 'later' may often be 'too late.' I will come back and see you as you suggest. In the meantime, why not put this in effect for the next three months right now and not be sorry?"

"I'll Talk It Over with My Spouse"

"I can understand why some people want to talk with their spouses about something as important as this. I imagine they would be intensely interested because even with you well and earning a good income, there is plenty to do...work...run the house... take care of the children...keep things clean...pay the bills and buy the groceries ...prepare meals. Of course, your spouse would be interested in this plan...because when you are sick or hurt and unable to earn money, your spouse would worry and have to do something about that, too. But it takes more than money to buy this plan. It is bought with good health, also. Let us check your health chart (application) to see if you can qualify before you tell your spouse."

or

"I appreciate how you feel, (Prospect). There are many decisions in a marriage that need to be made jointly. Also, there are many decisions that one spouse will make on behalf of the other. I believe this may be one of those.

"You see, this insurance is a gift. It is something you give to your spouse and children so that they will always have peace of mind. It is something that you do for them, so that all the promises you've made and plans you've formulated won't be destroyed if something happens to your health.

"It is a gift, (Prospect). But it is also a selfish gift. Because it is something you do for yourself. If you were injured or became *seriously ill, you would be the one who would feel the remorse at the loss of your ability to carry your share of the family's load. You would be the one sensing responsibility for a reduced standard of living. And you would be the one powerless to do anything about it. Then.*

"But you can do something about it now. Let's see whether or not you even qualify."

"I Want to Think It Over—Leave Some Literature"

"(Prospect), you have agreed you need this plan. You can afford it. Do you really need time to think it over? If you delay it, you will probably find a thousand other things to do with the premium money. You may have an accident or serious illness. Then what will happen? It's perfectly natural to want to think it over—at first most people do. But they soon realize that the time to do what is right and sound is now! Tomorrow may be too late."

or

"It is natural that you want to think this over. But I have found from experience that when a person hesitates about a plan like this, it is usually for one of three reasons: (1) he or she feels there is something wrong that will prevent qualifying, or (2) the person feels he or she can't afford it, or (3) feels it won't be needed when the person is sick or hurt. Which one of these reasons makes you hesitate?"

There's No Money

Do not take too seriously the excuses falling under the heading "there's no money." Occasionally, you will find it is true. But more often when you have a qualified prospect, then the person who says "I can't afford it," or "It costs too much," is really saying, "You have not made me feel I want it enough to change my spending habits." The person has not grasped the concept that **after first providing for the fundamental need of continuing income he or she has then released other funds for current needs.**

Common among all responsible people is the

desire for security against the emergencies in life. Most people are not aware of this fact: by first setting aside out of paychecks the premium for future security, they can spend what is left with a clear conscience and enjoy spending to fullest extent. By permitting funds otherwise held for emergencies to be spent freely, health insurance increases a person's standard of living rather than competes with it.

"I Can't Afford It"

"I can understand why you say that, Prospect. But the premium amounts to only 2 percent or 3 percent of your salary. Wouldn't it be better for you to take that small a cut now than for you and your family to take a 100 percent cut later?"

or

"I can understand why you feel that way, (Prospect). Most of us have no trouble in spending the money we earn. But suppose last night you noticed that the main supporting column in the basement of your home was about to give way. If it collapsed, everything you have in your home would cave into the basement. You wouldn't wait one minute to call in a repair crew, would you? It wouldn't be a case of affording it, because you couldn't afford not to reinforce that main supporting column. In exactly the same way, you are the main support of your family. The food they eat, the roof over their heads, the clothes they wear, the car they drive, the comforts they enjoy—your fire insurance, automobile insurance—the life insurance you have—all are supported by you. What would happen if you suddenly became sick or were involved in a bad accident? Everything that depends on you would be endangered! Isn't it important to keep that from happening?

"It Costs Too Much"

(Prospect), I can understand why you say that. But let me point out that it isn't this plan which costs—it is living that costs. It isn't this plan which costs—it's the doctor, nurses, hospitals and medicines. When peo-

ple are sick or hurt and can't work, they all need the same thing—continuing income. It takes money to live and to have a doctor and to meet the bills. You can't escape the cost of living. You must have income! And that's what this plan is designed to do: provide continuing income when you can't work."

Go back to the benefits of your plan. Show the prospect the thousands of dollars of potential benefits provided by your plan. Compare a year's income to the year's premium. The contrast will be impressive! Interpret the premium in terms of sales or a day's income, etc.

"I'll Take a Chance"

"I gather from your remark, (Prospect), that you'll take a chance on not being sick or hurt. Let's look at it this way.
"A small wager with your friends may be one thing. But when major bets are involved, the person who can't afford to play for big stakes drops out. Unfortunately, a person can't withdraw from the game of earning a living. So the wise person looks at the odds and insures his or her income."

"My Family Will Help Me Out When I'm Disabled"

"That is fine. You and your family are to be congratulated for your willingness to help one another. But assuming that they are in a position to help, has it occurred to you how difficult it will be to repay them? You will certainly feel morally obligated to pay back what you borrow. How long does it take you to save a month's salary? About a year? Then for every month's salary you borrow, it will take you a year to pay it back. And if you borrow five months' salary, it will take you five years to pay it back. Isn't it better to have a plan like this which pays you a salary when you are disabled and which you won't have to pay back?"

There's No Need

When your prospects tell you they have no need they are actually saying to you that you have not uncovered their needs or fixed their problems in their minds. You have not made them visualize their situations. So retrace their steps and lead them through the presentation again. Make them understand that the average person is disabled several times during life. Make them realize that many illnesses last more than a month. Dramatize the situation with a story. Show them how regular expenses continue while extra costs pile up. Cut off their income. Use a pencil and pad to sketch and illustrate your points.

Most savings plans offer inadequate solutions. Borrowing is not the answer. Relatives, friends or charity provide no satisfactory way out. Your plan of continuing income and supplying money from an outside source is the best way of guarding against the economic disaster which accompanies serious illnesses or injuries.

"I've Never Been Sick or Hurt in My Life"

"You are very fortunate and to be congratulated, because every person is disabled several times during a lifetime. But here is an idea I may not have made clear. This plan cannot be purchased with money alone! An important requirement is you must be in excellent health. This is true of every individual we insure. Yet we are paying hundreds of thousands of dollars every month to people who were in perfect health at the time they signed the application. Many of them had never been laid up by a sickness or accident. And most of them didn't think they would ever be disabled. Today thousands of people who didn't expect to be sick or hurt are receiving money from my company because they are unable to work. Let us see if you can qualify."

"I Have an Accident Policy"

"That is fine as far as it goes. I'm glad to know you believe in this kind of protection. But have you ever looked at it this way? Suppose you had a business building which paid you your entire income. Even if you had plenty of cash in reserve, would you insure only a small portion of that building and let the rest go uninsured? Of course you wouldn't. You would make sure that the
building was adequately covered at all times. You would do that because your home, your better-than-average clothes, your children's schooling, your car and everything you and your family have are dependent on the income from that building. It is the same way with your earned income. Everything you have is dependent on it. Yet you have insured only a small portion of it. Sickness disables several people for every one laid up by accident. Certainly it is more important to protect your earned income adequately than to protect a building. Is there any reason why you cannot qualify for the more complete protection you need?"

(Note: By changing the underlined words to fit the circumstances, the above answer can be adjusted to handle similar excuses such as, "I have group coverage," or "I have hospitalization," or any objection which reveals that the prospect has limited or inadequate income protection.)

"My Salary Will Continue"

"That is fine. You are working for a good company. But how long will your salary continue? That's all right when only a temporary illness makes you stay home for a short time. But have you considered that it costs more to keep a sick person than it does a well person? And what if you are disabled for six months or a year? Experience shows that businesses must stop the pay of an employee who is unable to work after a reasonable time. It's certainly easy to understand that no company can pay you or me very long when we are not producing. That's the beauty of this plan: it pays you needed income when you are unable to work."

"My Work Isn't Hazardous"

"I realized that when I came to see you. That's why I am able to offer you this plan on such a favorable basis. If you were in hazardous work, we would either have to charge a higher premium, or not make this protection available to you at all. But here is an interesting fact which you may not have

noticed. *According to the National Safety Council, almost half of all disabling accidents occur at home. Automobile accidents account for another large number. Recreation, sports and just crossing the street as a pedestrian are responsible for still another large number. Most accidents happen when people are not working. This plan gives you protection whether you are at work or not. It is the perfect solution to your problem if you can qualify for it."*

"I Can Carry My Own Insurance"

"Let me congratulate you. So few people today save any worthwhile amounts. But this plan is designed to protect those savings which you and your family have sacrificed so to accumulate. No doubt you have your nest egg earmarked for some special purpose such as educating the children or for retirement security or for buying something you have always wanted. It is just as important to protect your personal savings as it is for a business person to protect the business surplus. This plan will do exactly that for comparatively few pennies."

"I'd Rather Put My Money in the Bank"

"That is wise. You certainly should save some money that way. But if later this year or next year you are laid up and need money, can your spouse go to the bank and say, 'My family has been putting their savings in your bank. We planned to save $5,000 to see us through any emergency. But our plans have been interrupted. The breadwinner is home in bed now and can't work. We need money. Will you give us the $5,000 we intended to save?' Of course, no bank could do that. All it could let you withdraw are the dollars you had deposited. This plan, on the other hand, will pay you thousands of needed dollars even though you may have acquired it only recently."

No Confidence

This last category of excuses reflects your prospect's lack of confidence in you as an agent, in your company, or in his or her own ability to continue the plan. There are many ways to instill confidence for yourself and your company. Your appearance, your attitude, your selling methods will carry you a long way toward that goal. A referred lead usually starts you on a plateau of prestige. And there are other ways to equip yourself with prestige-building tools. Some agents display a list of their insureds, especially if they have a number of one kind of occupation, and ask the prospect to see if he or she knows any of them. Also, lists of recent claims and photostats of claim checks build confidence in you and your company. Letters from satisfied insureds and claimants accomplish the same purpose. Some home offices furnish this kind of material, and many agents accumulate an impressive array of their own after they have been selling awhile.

Basic Principles of Handling Excuses

- Don't be argumentative
- Don't be impatient
- Don't use superlatives or extreme "exaggerations"
- Listen carefully—let your prospect talk
- Be sympathetic
- Answer briefly and clearly

Basic Methods of Handling Excuses

1. "We'll come to that later . . ."
2. "Yes, . . . but . . ."
3. "I'm glad you brought that up . . ."
4. Use a human interest story.
5. "What other reason do you have in addition to that?"
6. Clarify the objection by asking questions.

Don't pause after answering, but continue with your sales talk or filling out the application until the prospect stops you.

"I Don't Like to Do Business with Strangers"

"That's easy to understand and I'm glad you brought that up. On the other hand, many people don't want their personal affairs such as insurance handled by their

closest friends or relatives. One of the things I like about this business is that I become acquainted with so many people. Many of my clients have become very good friends, especially those who have received checks from my company."

"I Have a Friend in the Business"

"Yes, I realize you must have a number of friends in the insurance business. But I wonder if you have ever thought of it this way? Suppose you don't know how to swim. You are out in the middle of a lake in a boat with a hole in the bottom. The boat is sinking lower and lower. You're in a bad situation. I notice the spot you're in and head my motorboat over to you. You wouldn't shout to me, 'Wait, there's no rush. I have a friend who has a boat.' Of course you wouldn't. And let's not wait any longer to see if you can qualify for this needed protection."

"I Have Not Heard of Your Company"

"I can understand why you say that. There are hundreds of different insurance companies, and though I am in the insurance business, I can't name them all. My company must be licensed and approved by the insurance commissioner in order to be able to do business in this state. The policy I have illustrated to you has been fully approved by the insurance department of this state. You need have no concern about my company paying exactly what this contract says it will. I would not be representing them if I did not have complete confidence in them. My insureds are my friends, and I would not recommend anything to my friends that I did not personally believe in.

My insurance company stands the most rigid investigation."

"My Job Is Too Uncertain"

"I can appreciate your saying that. Most people feel uncertain about some things from time to time. If you lose your health, you will lose your job and your income. That's even more important, isn't it?"

WHEN YOUR PROSPECT SAYS "NO"

When your prospect says "No," he or she is saying . . . Yes, my spouse can leave me and the children at home and go to work . . . Yes, the mortgage holder can foreclose on our home or sell it.

But does the person believe that? Of course not! So carry your head high. Tell people about the importance of continuing income for their spouse, their children and themselves.

Help them think straight. Lead them out of the shadows of confusion into the light of understanding. Do your job diligently and conscientiously.

When a prospect says "No" to health insurance, remind the person that health insurance is always paid for, whether he or she pays for it in premiums, or the person and his or her loved ones pay for it in days and weeks and months without income or enough money to pay the bills.

Viewed in this light, every objection becomes a challenge to help your prospect do what is right. For it can never be repeated too often that in the world today, it takes money to live. And health insurance dollars will, in most cases, represent the only way in which your prospects can keep up financially when serious accident or sickness strikes!

THE MAGIC WORD "ROMANCE"

We have just reviewed the most common excuses all cataloged under four classifications. Now how are you going to remember them? What memorizing formula can we call into use so that you will be able, instantly, to pull from your "mental filing cabinet" good answers to almost any objection your prospect may raise?

Just remember the key word, **Romance**. It is easy to remember because overcoming objections and closing sales compromise the true romance of this business.

R	Keep	no	**R**ush
O	in		**O**
M	mind	no	**M**oney
A	how		**A**
N	it	no	**N**eed
C	is	no	**C**onfidence
E	spelled		**E**

You will note that there are four consonants in the word: R–M–N–C. **Each consonant stands for one of the four categories.** The R stands for excuses prospectives give when they mean there is **no Rush**. The M stands for excuses which mean there is **no Money**. The N stands for the excuses prospects raise when they mean there is **no Need**. And the C stands for all those excuses prospects bring up when they mean there is **no Confidence**.

Now turn back to where the 17 most common excuses are listed under the four classifications, **no Rush, no Money, no Need, no Confidence**. Restudy the answers under each of these headings. While you do this, keep in mind the key word, **Romance**.

Chapter 11
The Application as Sales Tool

LESSON TEXT—Happiest Point in the Sale...
Danger Signals...Sources of Information...
Analyzing the Application...Value of Waivers
for Impairments...Handling the Application...
Obtaining Cash with the Application...Application Checklist

A good comparison can be drawn between the sale of an automobile on the installment plan and the sale of a health insurance contract. The installment contract is comparable to the application. It sets out the conditions under which you purchase the car. It describes how the payments are to be made. It deals with the question of the title of the car. It describes the car, so that there can be no error. It becomes the means through which you secure possession of the car.

In the same way, the application sets forth the plan under which the purchaser is buying medical expense protection or continuing income when disabled to assure the cash to help meet extra bills and provide the funds to keep the home solvent until the person can work again and be self sufficient. It sets forth the terms of the purchase, the amount of the payments, the conditions of the plan and other important provisions.

Without the signed purchase agreement, you can own no car. Without the signed application, the prospect has no protection. As you approach the time to fill in the application and obtain the prospect's signature, you are nearing one of the most exciting points in the entire sales interview. It is a most important link in the work you perform. It joins a person's responsibilities and hopes with the plan which assures that a serious illness or injury will not destroy the individual's financial plan and everything for which he or she has worked so hard.

HAPPIEST POINT IN THE SALE

A keystone in the work of top-level agents is the way they handle the application. For them, completing the application is the happiest part of the whole sales process.

Yet, some agents approach completing the application with misgivings. They look on the application as a necessary evil. Some complete it in a haphazard fashion. They hesitate to ask the applicant for the signature. They do not know how to use it to obtain the full premium at the time the application is taken. Sometimes agents new to the business feel that applications contain many unimportant questions. They feel that completing the application is a distasteful part of the their job. They enjoy prospecting. They get a thrill out of selling. But to them filling out the application is drudgery. They do it only because they have to.

This attitude stems from lack of knowledge and technique. Such agents do not understand the application nor do they know how to handle it. The skilled agent knows the reason for each question on the application and appreciates its importance. For this agent, the application becomes a powerful sales tool. It is useful in closing sales and obtaining initial premium payments.

Our purpose here is to *look behind* the questions in the typical application. To find why they must be answered. To learn simple, effective techniques of handling the application skillfully.

Broadly speaking, underwriting health insurance is the process of evaluating applicants from the moral, financial, physical and occupational points of view. Individuals who are average in these four respects make good insureds for the company and are valuable clients for you. When they fall below average, they do not fit into the pattern on which benefits and rates have been based. Applications are designed to reveal this needed information to home office underwriting departments.

Your future progress requires more than just writing business. Your success rests squarely on writing *good* business. And it largely revolves around the way you submit it to your home office. Complete, accurate applications on quality prospects produce favorable underwriting results.

Inadequate, incomplete applications in illegible writing cause delay. They require you to make embarrassing call-backs, reducing the productivity of your field efforts. Prompt issuance of policies is important to your prospects and to you in establishing a name for businesslike service. So let us look carefully at underwriting in order to understand fully the role of the application in field underwriting and selling.

UNDERWRITING DANGER SIGNALS

In evaluating a risk, there is certain basic information home office health insurance underwriters must know before they can pass intelligently on an application. They need complete information about the applicant. Not only must they know who the person is, but how the person lives.

What is the home like? Who are the person's associates? An individual of questionable character, or one who associates with such people, is a poor risk. An individual with constant marital troubles or with a record of law violations presents moral hazards which a policy is not expected to cover. The individual who is heavily in debt or who avoids financial obligations lacks the stamina and character for health insurance. This raises a question of financial significance: Is the person buying the insurance to "make money" on it?

An applicant's medical history and present mental and physical condition are of fundamental importance to sound underwriting. And from the occupational standpoint, it is necessary to know the applicant's occupation. This information is essential to underwriters on the lookout for danger signals so that exceptional hazards can be avoided and protection provided for good risks at reasonable rates.

SOURCES OF INFORMATION

Companies have a number of sources for information they need. The most important source is the application itself. Usually the application becomes a part of the policy and thus the policy incorporates the applicant's own answers to questions. It often provides information of further value in the representative's personal report on the back of the application. Since the agent sees and talks with the applicants in their business or home environment, the agent is in a good position to give the home office the benefit of personal judgment and recommendations. Many companies generally reserve the right to require a medical examination in any case. The medical examiner then studies the risk from a physical

The Agent's Role

You occupy a most important position in the underwriting process.

You originate the business.

You complete the application.

When you submit an application to your company, you, in effect, recommend the applicant.

Your company's reputation and its services to the public largely depend upon the kind of prospects you submit for approval.

standpoint and prepares a report to the insurance company.

Another source of information to the underwriter is the inspection report This is a factual report made by an independent organization. It covers an individual's age, occupation, income, reputation in the community, credit standing, family and similar information. These reports have a high degree of accuracy. Further sources of information are former employers and any attending physicians' and hospital records reported on the application. Also other companies where the applicant has or has had insurance may be a source of additional information through the Medical Information Bureau (MIB).

With all this data, the home office underwriting department can act intelligently on an application. The more complete and accurate the information the agent can furnish, the more rapidly the business will be processed and issued.

ANALYZING THE APPLICATION

Verbal statements between the agent and the applicant are not binding upon the company. The agent has no authority to alter the application or to waive the answer to any question.

Probably in no other business, where perhaps tens of thousands of dollars are involved, must a company rely more heavily on the representative. You are the important contact, often the only personal contact, a company has with its

insureds. Because you are so essential to efficient operations, all companies set up special instructions for their agents. Printed in a separate manual or contained in the rate book itself, these instructions guide you in conducting activities in conformance with company practices. It is important that you become thoroughly familiar with your company's manual. Much of the information has to do with the selection of risks, with submitting trial applications in doubtful cases and handling applications in normal situations.

All applications are not alike. The broader and more liberal the contract, usually the more detailed the information required in the application. Most applications commonly require certain information essential to sound underwriting. In the following we discuss step by step the elements in a typical application.

Applicant's Name

This, of course, identifies the individual applying for insurance. The insured's name will appear in the policy just as it appears on the application. For that reason, you should *print the name*, making sure that it agrees in every respect with the way the applicant writes his or her signature.

Secure the full name. Do not send in applications with names such as "Mrs. John Brown." Use the full name as, for example, "Mary Alice Brown." There may be many "Mrs. John Browns" in your city. By using the full name of the applicant you avoid delay and time-consuming correspondence.

Date of Birth

Some companies base their health insurance premium rates on the applicant's *nearest* birthday, others on *actual* birthday. Many companies have rates calculated for age groups, such as ages 18 through 45, ages 46 through 50 and 51 through 55. Some companies will issue certain kinds of health insurance at higher ages. Disability insurance usually is not written under age 18 because of the uncertainty of earnings. At the older ages there is the problem of earlier retirement, coupled with the greater frequency of illness and length of disabilities.

Sex of the Applicant

With similarity between some names of men and women, this question is needed for identification purposes. Also there are different problems involved in insuring men and women.

Most policies today draw few distinctions between male and female applications. Many companies have moved to unisex rates for various forms of health insurance. Both working and nonworking applicants are judged on factors discussed earlier, and the sex of the applicant plays a minor role in risk evaluation.

In medical insurance, many policies cover maternity as if it were any other form of illness or injury; and most high quality noncancelable disability contracts treat it the same way.

Marital Status

Indicating whether the applicant is single, married, divorced or widowed gives the underwriting department additional information on which to base its judgment. If all other factors revealed by the application and inspection report are favorable, the applicant's marital status will likely have no use other than identification. But persons with constant marital troubles often present moral hazards. Married men with dependents are known to be better insurance risks than single individuals and generally are entitled to more favorable consideration.

Occupation

The severity of the same injury or sickness varies with different occupations. A scratched hand with a minor infection would not disable most people. But to a doctor, a dentist or a barber it could result in a disability lasting several months. These larger claims must be taken into consideration in establishing the classification which, in turn, is reflected in the rate. In the event the applicant has two occupations, the more hazardous one is used for establishing the correct rate.

It is important for you to distinguish with your prospect between job titles and job duties. Most people describe themselves by titles—manager, director, supervisor, etc. But what it would take for a person to be disabled with an occupational definition of disability is more critical than what the job is called. Explore carefully with your prospects for the details your home office needs to accurately underwrite your applications.

Physical Condition

In determining an applicant's physical condition and acceptability as a risk, several questions are asked about health. These questions usually are divided into three groups:

1. Those to determine if the medical history is acceptable and free from any chronic ailment;
2. Those to determine if the applicant is physically and mentally well now; and
3. Those which make it possible to determine what action other companies may have taken in cases involving the applicant.

Medical History

In the first group are questions asking if the applicant has or ever has had, for example, asthma, hay fever, tuberculosis, lung trouble and so forth. Other chronic ailments of interest to an underwriter include diabetes, arthritis, rheumatism and anemia.

Note that the health insurance underwriter generally needs more information than the life insurance underwriter. Asthma, hay fever, arthritis or rheumatism are ailments which would not necessarily cause premature death. But any one of them could result in an expensive disability and substantial medical expenses. Other illnesses of a chronic or recurring nature of special interest to health insurance underwriters include heart trouble, stomach disorder, nervous or mental trouble, to mention only a few.

Present Health of Applicant

To determine an applicant's present physical condition, an important underwriting consideration is the relationship of height, weight and physical proportions. A heavy person is more susceptible to a sprained ankle, for example, and would not be up on his or her feet as quickly as a normal person. Overweight people are more subject to heart conditions, pneumonia and apoplexy. They are not usually as agile in keeping out of harm's way as lighter-weight people. Generally speaking, overweight is more serious than underweight. Underweight, however, may be a symptom of an existing disease such as anemia or tuberculosis.

After other specific questions have been asked regarding more serious conditions, there is usually a final "catch-all" question inquiring about any illness or injury not already mentioned, and also an outright question to the effect "are you now in good health?"

Other Insurance Company Actions

As a further check on present health, the applicant is usually asked if he or she has ever been declined, postponed or rated for insurance. This insurance history is important to the company because it may disclose some condition not already mentioned. And it is important to the person applying for insurance because a condition previously existing may have cleared up so that insurance can be issued without waiver or extra premium. Complete and accurate information is so important that it merits reemphasis here. **Answers which are inconsistent with information obtained from other sources are especially significant. They raise a red flag of warning to the home office underwriter who quite naturally begins to question the applicant's motive for seeking the insurance.**

Air Travel

Most companies today are lenient in regard to commercial air travel. If the applicant flies other than as a fare-paying passenger on a commercial airline, however, either additional information is required or the policy carries a waiver for non-commercial flying. When additional information is obtained each case is given individual consideration. This varies with companies. The company's action usually is based on the purpose and amount of flying.

Other Health Insurance

It is important to find out how much other health insurance the applicant already has and if he or she is applying for insurance with other companies. When an applicant has other health insurance, careful consideration must be given to needs, insurable value and motives.

For example, a person with more disability insurance than earned income is overinsured! He or she could find it financially advantageous to be disabled and to stay disabled. Such an individual is a speculative risk and for that reason not insurable. It is a known fact that as the amount of indemnity increases, the moral hazard increases. The higher the ratio of disability income to the insured's earned income, the higher the ratio of claims paid to premiums received by the company.

Applications pending in other companies have a direct bearing on the overinsurance hazard. Moreover, an applicant who believes he or she has an uninsurable condition sometimes may make application to several companies simultaneously, hoping that one will approve. So, if more insurance is applied for than appears to be justified, it is important for the company to take this into account in evaluating the risk.

Moral Hazard

Judging an applicant from a moral point of view is more a matter of interpreting psychological indications than physical facts. It is difficult to evaluate a potential moral risk. Reliance must be placed on the individual's reputation and standing in the community. The observations of the people he or she does business with are helpful. Business associates, friends, habits and previous insurance claim record all are important in measuring the moral hazard.

Is the person buying health insurance as protection against an unexpected event, or as an investment? Will he or she be inclined to drag out a disability and malinger? Or will the person return to work as soon as it is reasonably possible?

These are difficult questions for the home office underwriter who has never seen or talked with the applicant. Yet he or she must answer them in order to do a thorough underwriting job.

The majority of people are solid, honest citizens. They buy health insurance for protection. They do not intend to be sick or be hurt.

A $1,000 a month disability claim amounts to $12,000 a year. In ten years one such continuous claim totals $120,000. Claims can run into big figures and rates are calculated to include *just* claims. They cannot be constructed to include unjustified payments to the unscrupulous, or the premiums would be such that no honest person could afford the protection.

Unfavorable information may be revealed to the company through confidential sources which is inconsistent with the information on the application or which has not been noted in the application. Then it becomes especially significant. As a protection to itself, the home office cannot reveal information from confidential sources. Never ask your home office to violate this rule!

The Field Underwriter

It is better from every viewpoint to underwrite business at the time it is sold. This is where you earn your pay as a field underwriter. Think about it: if your sole job was to sell insurance, your official career title would be "salesperson." But doesn't your company call you "agent," "field underwriter," and "representative?" All of these indicate a responsibility on your part for something more than selling. You are expected to help select and identify the risks you are asking the company to underwrite.

You have the obligation to your company to reveal as much information as you can gather about the applicant. Your company relies on you to be thorough and honest. Your reputation is at stake: it won't take too many stretches of the truth before your home office realizes that your applications can't be trusted. From then on, every application you submit will be scrutinized more carefully than would otherwise be warranted.

It is far better to be accurate, complete and helpful to your home office underwriters—

consistently. That reputation will pay you dividends on tough cases!

Beneficiary Designation

All benefits generally are payable to the insured with the exception of accidental death benefits. If there is to be no death benefit in the policy, write "none" or "nil" in the application space provided for naming the beneficiary. If there is, then particular care should be given to whom policy proceeds are to be paid at death. Generally an individual should be named, rather than the insured's estate. And, in most cases, it is desirable to name one or more secondary or contingent beneficiaries.

If a secondary beneficiary is not named, and the primary beneficiary dies before the insured is accidentally killed, the insurance is paid to the estate. When this happens, the proceeds are subject to estate settlement costs, taxes and delay. When paid to a beneficiary, on the other hand, they go direct, without delay or red tape and often tax free.

In naming a beneficiary, both the complete name and relationship should be given. For example, if Fran Faber want the spouse be to beneficiary, be sure to show as "Kelly Lindsay Faber, husband (or wife) of the insured." The policy may not become a claim for many years. When it does, there must be no doubt as to whom the death benefits are payable. In case of doubt, the insurance company simply pays the proceeds into court, and lets the court determine who should receive them. Delay and settlement costs result.

For the prospect with a spouse and children, the contingent beneficiary question should address guardianship and custody arrangements for the children in case of a disaster striking both parents. This inquiry frequently generates a helpful review of that concern, and often opens a discussion of life insurance coverage.

For the contract to be legally acceptable, the beneficiary must have an insurable interest in the insured. A simple test of such interest is: **Will the beneficiary profit by the insured's continuing to live?"** If the answer is *yes*, an insurable interest exists.

Signatures

Applications customarily close with the signature clause. This clause usually signifies that:

1. The applicant's statements are complete and true to the best of his or her knowledge;
2. Verbal agreements between the agent and the applicant are not binding; and
3. The insurance will not take effect until the policy is approved and the first premium has been paid while the applicant is in good health. (A few companies bind an application for disability protection *without* the first premium being paid. The protection given under such contracts is for a short time only. If the premium is not paid within that time, the protection is canceled.)

Be sure to check the signature to see that it agrees in all respects with the name you have printed at the top of the application. Signatures of the applicant and agent also generally are required on disclosure forms to comply with the Fair Credit Reporting Act.

Authorization

A medical permit, or authorization, is often a part of health insurance applications. It generally starts: "To my attending physician," or "To any physician or hospital." It states, in effect, "This authorizes you to furnish the company with any information you have regarding my medical history, physical condition and treatments given me."

The purpose of the authorization is to make it possible for the home office underwriter to obtain information regarding the applicant's physical condition without delay. Hospitals and doctors will not give details about treating a patient without the person's permission. If it is contained in your application have your prospect sign it *in all cases* when he or she signs the application. Even if not needed, it strengthens the company's confidence in the applicant. But if needed, it saves time and avoids inconvenience. Applicants sometimes ignore a company's written request for this authorization, and the case is stalemated until the agent personally contacts the person for a signed medical permit.

VALUE OF WAIVERS FOR IMPAIRMENTS

Insurance companies exist to provide insurance protection. If an individual is insurable at all, companies will devise some way to issue a policy. The large majority of policies are standard and issued as applied for. A few people have an existing impairment which increases the risk, and so are required to pay an extra premium. A few are uninsurable and must be declined. There are others, however, who would not be able to obtain health insurance if waivers were not in use. These waivers, or riders, usually are stated in simple language. For instance: "This policy does not cover or extend to any disability resulting directly or indirectly from...." It is dated and bears the signature of an officer of the company. Some companies also require that it be signed by the applicant.

Waivers are valuable to the applicant, to the agent and to the company. The applicant benefits by obtaining the protection needed. And, even though the contract contains a waiver, the insured still receives full value from the insurance. If the condition clears up, the company may be willing to remove the waiver. Meanwhile, the person has protection from other hazards which he or she should not otherwise obtain. And sometimes an impairment prolongs disability from other causes.

The agent benefits because the prospect becomes an insured. The company benefits because, in providing income protection to a larger portion of the public, it is rendering an important service and spreading the risks.

There are small segments of the public who either must have a broad waiver in their policies, or who can obtain accident-only protection or who are uninsurable. But it must be realized that it is not always possible to issue health insurance *when the impairment is a disease.*

Court decisions sometimes are unpredictable. It might seem that accidents are so far removed from hear conditions that it would be perfectly sound underwriting to issue an accident-only policy to an individual with a heart condition. In a court case, however, an insured with a bad heart and an accident-only contract died while driving a car. Although there was reason to believe that death resulted from heart failure, the court decided that the death resulted from accidental means and the principal sum was payable to the beneficiary.

When a waiver must be used in order to accept a risk, companies make it as simple as possible, eliminating only the claims likely to arise as a result of the impairment. When a broad waiver is used, or when a case is rejected, you may be sure that the company is taking that action only because of the facts at its disposal.

HANDLING THE APPLICATION

Your sales talk should flow smoothly from the close to the application without hesitation. If you pause to reach into your briefcase for an application blank, or if you wait to take out your pen and remove its cap at this point, you may telegraph a warning to your prospect, "Watch out, I'm closing." You can easily avoid both these gestures.

Hints on Handling the Application

- Keep application in sight during the interview.
- Reveal only one application—avoid the suggestion of mass production.
- Use your pen during the interview—so it, too, will be ready for completing the application.
- Start filling in the application by asking your prospect a question about his or her health. It's easy that way.
- Move into the application smoothly—without any abrupt action or change in voice which might signal "I'm closing!"
- Have it folded conveniently—so that you can complete the first questions without exposing the whole application.
- "Write your name here as you usually write it."
- Always ask for the full first premium—make "cash with app" a habit!

And remember—make each sale lead to a new sale—ask for referred leads!

Many experienced agents report it convenient to have an application folded inside each sales visual or proposal at the start of the interview. The application is folded with the health questions on the outside. As the agent begins the interview, he or she puts the application aside, away from the prospect so it will not distract. But it is kept easy to reach when he or she is ready for it, and the prospect has become accustomed to the sight of it.

For the same reason the agent uses a pen during the presentation for figuring and completing the proposal and illustrating sales points. With pen handy and application folded to the questions the agent first asks, the application is unfolded as the questions are completed. To obtain the prospect's signature, many agents prefer to avoid the word "sign." Instead they say, "Just write your name here as you usually write it."

OBTAINING CASH WITH THE APPLICATION

Experienced agents who obtain a high percentage of annual premiums with signed applications frequently explain their success by saying: *"The only way of getting cash with the application is to assume you're going to get it and to ask for it."*

They offer this helpful suggestion: "After all the questions are answered, look the application over for a few moments, and then say, *'Well, this looks right to me, but, of course, the company makes the final decision. The premium is X dollars. Would you prefer to pay for it with cash or by check?'* Then, start filling in the premium receipt at the bottom of the application."

The signed application is the foundation of the health insurance policy. When the prospect signals he or she is ready to buy, start filling in the application. Be accurate and thorough. For delay in completing the application or in filling it out correctly may cause great hardship in event of a sudden disability or medical expense. Get it signed. Then start it on its way.

Should one of your clients fail to receive benefits because of undue delay on your part in getting the protection in force promptly, the responsibility falls on *your* shoulders. The minute your prospect agrees to your plan, it becomes *your* obligation to see that the application is completed fully, and forwarded the same day. This is the "follow-through." Without it, all your efforts are wasted. Promptness in handling requests for additional medical or other information—in doing everything you can to place the protection in force at the earliest possible date—is the mark of successful agents.

When you have a signed application, you are in an ideal position. You can easily ask for the names of others in the family or business or community who may need health insurance. Every completed application should mean new sales for you.

There is no greater thrill than that which comes with the prospect's signature on the dotted line and the check which transforms an acceptable prospect into an insured. Completing the application legibly and accurately is an essential part of this process. Study your compa-

ny's application diligently. Know the reasons for each question. Handle it with respect. Practice and drill yourself on filling it in. Avoid delays by being thorough. You will develop a favorable reputation with your home office underwriter. This will pay you valuable dividends throughout your career.

It is continual practice in the field before your "audience"—prospects—that will give you the force and power that produce sales. And the practice continues for as many years as you are in the business.

A person's highest reward has always come from completing a job! The world is filled with people who start jobs but never finish them. Life's great prizes go to those who complete the jobs they set out to do. In every sense of the word, completing the application, without which there can be no protection, should constitute the high mark of your entire sales process.

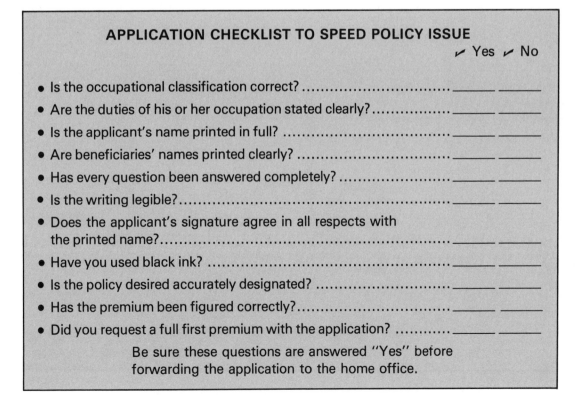

APPLICATION CHECKLIST TO SPEED POLICY ISSUE

✔ Yes ✔ No

- Is the occupational classification correct? ....
- Are the duties of his or her occupation stated clearly? ....
- Is the applicant's name printed in full? ....
- Are beneficiaries' names printed clearly? ....
- Has every question been answered completely? ....
- Is the writing legible? ....
- Does the applicant's signature agree in all respects with the printed name? ....
- Have you used black ink? ....
- Is the policy desired accurately designated? ....
- Has the premium been figured correctly? ....
- Did you request a full first premium with the application? ....

Be sure these questions are answered "Yes" before
forwarding the application to the home office.

Chapter 12
Policy Delivery and Service

LESSON TEXT—Influence of Salespeople on Civilization. . . Unlimited Opportunities. . . Serving the Business. . . Building a Clientele. . . Growing Personally. . . Serving the Public. . . Building Persistent Business. . . Policy Delivery. . . Service through Claims. . . Service through Reviews

---

There are two sides to every job. On one side, we look at it from the viewpoint of utilizing the practical techniques necessary for successful performance.

On the other, we view it in its relation to human progress. . . its place in the great scheme of things, measured not by years but by decades— not by individuals but by generations.

This course has dwelt at length on the principles and techniques of selling. We turn now to the broad vision of your job. Where does it fit in the total picture of human endeavor? As a health insurance underwriter, what role do you play on the stage of life?

Salespeople have made many of time's great contributions to human happiness and to the advancement of civilization.

Without the driving force of salespeople, the work of scientists and inventors, the ennobling thoughts of poets and philosophers, the music of inspiring composers would not today be common possessions of the ordinary person.

On the surface, without deep analysis, a salesperson sometimes questions the importance of the work. In a daily round of business, we often lose sight of the far-reaching results of our services.

Health insurance agents provide an extremely valuable service. When an insured is well and earning good money, a few premium dollars do not seem to make much difference. But when illness strikes and substantial medical expenses accumulate, or when earnings are blacked out by a sudden accident or illness, then the health insurance dollars he or she receives are crucially important!

In your day-to-day activities, it seems that all you sell is a product. In fact, you sell a product, with guarantees, and a service—yours, your agency's and your company's. What you provide has far-reaching implications. Your efforts are multiplied many, many times over. Let that thought inspire you to the vital importance of your work.

This is the challenge to you—to every sales-person!

INFLUENCE OF SALESPEOPLE ON CIVILIZATION

Communication between nations and conti-nents has been and continues to be inspired by salespeople. First known as traders or colonists, they were salespeople nevertheless.

Trade inspired much early American colonization—and trade was also a result.

Selling has always had a profound influence upon transportation. On the demands of traders —salespeople—for speedier transportation of goods, modern railroad, steamship and air lines were founded.

Hires peddled root beer in Philadelphia. Heinz set out each day with a wheelbarrow loaded with horseradish. Wrigley sold chewing gum out of a basket. The faith and zeal of Vail, the salesman, is responsible primarily for the universal use of the telephone today. Television once was almost a scientific myth. Because of salespeople and selling, every American knows what television is and nearly every home has at least one set— many, two or three sets. Computers for business and home use also have to be sold and sales in this area are increasing rapidly.

Selling is not a magic gift bestowed upon a for-tunate few. Selling can be learned. Not only is it a profitable occupation, it is one of the most in-triguing, the most satisfying. It constantly offers fresh challenge to thought, ingenuity and ac-complishment. You would do well to take this counsel to heart: .

"Be proud of your vocation. There is no business in the world that requires more health, brains, character and courage than selling."

Make faith a part of your job: faith in yourself, in your company, in its contracts and services— faith in the future. Beyond that, have faith that those engaged in selling are making a vital con-tribution to our way of life.

Fostering Innovation

Salespeople make us dissatisfied with the old and create a desire for the new. Without their perseverance, there would be little progress, for each new stride is often met with strong opposi-tion. Salespeople are ambassadors of progress. They are the advance agents of civilization. As a result, we enjoy what most of us accept as the benefits of modern living.

Our future technological growth does not de-pend so much on bankers, inventors, engineers, computer programmers and chemists. It depends on the master salespeople who create new de-sires for "things" we can make. This concept is a thrilling challenge to those in sales. And particu-larly to the health insurance salesperson to whom modern conditions direct that challenge.

Our society has changed dramatically. Our in-dependence has increased, while our interdepen-dence on neighbors and family has decreased. We can no longer expect others to care for our de-pendents during long periods of disability. How-ever, with life insurance, we can bridge the economic gap which death makes in a family circle. With health insurance, we can plug the holes in income which long illnesses and serious accidents create. And as the complexity of life increases, the need for this personal insurance protection grows.

Higher Education Brings Better Understanding

More and more people are attending college. A continually greater proportion of our population are high school and college graduates. Inevitably, one result of higher education is a greater com-prehension and appreciation of the economic facts of life. It is easier to communicate the mes-sage of health insurance in an atmosphere of un-derstanding.

Thomas Edison once said, "The most neces-sary task of civilization is to teach men to think." The increasing number of prospects with higher education backgrounds makes possible a wider acceptance of the whole concept of health insurance.

As people go forward in income, in production and in educational achievement, they raise their standard of living. And the more their standard of living climbs, the more determined they are that it not be destroyed by catastrophic medical expenses or by the loss of earning power.

As the salesperson of the business and industrial world is expected to keep the productive wheels moving, so the health insurance agent assumes the responsibility for adequately insuring the financial well-being of our people.

Better salespeople + better products + better educated prospects: this is the formula for assuring economic security on a broad scale. That is your challenge.

UNLIMITED OPPORTUNITIES

You accepted that challenge, in part, when you entered the health insurance field. To meet that challenge, you have spent time: studying, learning, questioning, practicing.

You have learned the story of health insurance—its history and its growth. You have been indoctrinated with the great need for income and medical funds when illness or injury cuts off earned income and runs up a heavy burden of medical bills. You are aware of the reasons this is a good business to be in.

Now there are four parallel tracks you can follow which will lead to unlimited opportunities:

1. Serving the Business.
2. Building a Clientele.
3. Growing Personally.
4. Serving the Public.

As you progress further on this venture of selling health insurance, pause for a moment and take a good look ahead. Consider these tremendous opportunities which lie before you.

SERVING THE BUSINESS

Your first great opportunity is to serve the business in which you make a living. Through good business ethics, you can reflect credit on the entire insurance profession. The opposite is also true, of course.

Use good sales methods. Never resort to subterfuge or misrepresentation. Be fair in competing with other companies and other agents.

Give prompt, efficient service. The public must know that you place its welfare ahead of your own. Good public relations for the entire business will result from your honest efforts to give the public the service it has the right to expect.

Join your local underwriters' association. This is part of a national body representing insurance agents throughout the country. It is the voice of the insurance person. It has been and continues to be of great service to the insureds, the agents and the companies.

Do not be content, however, with being merely a name on the membership list. Take an active part. Volunteer to serve on committees. Get into the spirit of the work. Assume the responsibility of constantly trying to improve the business and you will get back far more than you put in. Not only will you broaden your own activities and make yourself valuable to the business as a whole, you also will meet and work with colleagues, many of whom are important figures in the business. Such contacts will be of inestimable value to you.

Always remember—to the public, you are the company. *You* are, in fact, the health insurance business. *You* are the main contact the public has with an entire institution and industry. It is *you* who can build goodwill for your business!

BUILDING A CLIENTELE

The second broad avenue open to you is that of clientele-building—**the acquisition of a large number of buyers on a permanent basis who look upon you as their health insurance counselor.**

And this permanence means stability of income for you today as well as sources of new business for tomorrow.

Among the fundamentals in clientele-building

is persistency of business. Early in your career, you should recognize its essential nature.

Business with good persistency is business that stays in force. The insured continues to pay premiums. You continue to receive renewal commissions. (An agent with a high lapse rate receives only one-half to one-third the commission earnings he or she would otherwise receive.) And only a health contract in force can render the great service for which it was originally purchased and sold.

GROWING PERSONALLY

No less important than any of the other horizons before you is your own personal growth. Your *financial growth*—your *mental growth*—your *spiritual growth*. There is no limit to any of these except that which you set for yourself.

Financial Growth

You are already acquainted with the unique system of renewal commissions in the insurance business. Through this means, should you maintain the same performance year after year, you would find your income increases annually. **A constant, level production is unlikely. It should increase, so your income picture is even brighter!**

As you become successful in building a clientele, you will find it financially rewarding. You cannot dedicate yourself to serving an expanding group of insureds without automatically making more income.

In addition, you will acquire experience as time goes on. This experience will permit you to see sales possibilities you have previously overlooked. You will be able to handle more complex sales situations. All of these will give you the opportunity to make more money.

Your financial growth is a matter entirely within your control. And the boundaries are limited only by your ambitions.

Mental Growth

Then there is the chance for mental growth. There are many kinds of work which you would not find stimulating. You would feel no mental challenge. Not so in the health insurance business. In fact, you must not fail to grow mentally as your future depends on it.

Continue to study. The business changes rapidly and usually for the benefit of the insuring public. To merit wide public acceptance of yourself and your service, you must keep in constant contact with new developments in the health insurance industry. Know your business and present it accurately to the public. Be a competent, well-trained, educated agent.

Subscribe to trade journals. In this way, you keep well informed on current happenings in the business. You know what is going on in other companies as well as your own. It is always important to be aware of new workable ideas. Trade journals speed your progress.

Attend meetings for the same reason. Listen to talks by experts. Mingle with other people in the business. It is an old saying that anyone can obtain at least one good new idea at any meeting.

It is wise to read business publications dealing with general trends outside the business. Through publications of this kind, you can be alert to problems confronting your prospects.

Keep abreast of what is going on in your community and in your town. Read your local newspapers. Look for not only the important things but also the small human interest items which play a real part in the lives of all of us.

The contacts you make in varied lines of business will be stimulating to mental growth. You may talk to physicians, clergy, teachers, architects, engineers, writers—every sort of person and workers in a variety of different fields. This is broadening in itself. The mind is enriched by constant contact with hundreds of other minds, and from each contact takes away thoughts and ideas which add to your mental stature. Each person gives you something, tells you something of his or her work, something of the world in which the person lives. This is an opportunity open only to salespeople who take their products to the public. "Inside people" and "one-industry" salespeople never have such a rewarding experience.

Spiritual Growth

In addition to all else, you will feel yourself growing spiritually and gaining confidence. You will become almost a new personality. Your appreciation of culture, of human nature, of the realities of life will be enlarged by the contacts you make and the education you obtain. Your whole attitude toward living will be widened. You will see how other people live, the offices in which they work, the clubs to which they belong—and unconsciously you will mold your own life so that you, too, may live on the same rich plane were really successful people dwell.

You will find yourself fulfilling your own obligations to your family and yourself by owning sufficient amounts of personal health insurance. You will acquire a belief in the value of your product far beyond that of anyone you sell. *You will believe*—because you will see health insurance in action on a broad scale.

Not only will you be protecting yourself and your family because of this belief, but you will find there are collateral values. Your personal enthusiasm for an understanding of health insurance will shine through every interview you have with every prospect. That will led to further sales. And you will have run full circle. Financially—mentally—spiritually—each kind of growth interwoven—interdependent one on the other.

Look Ahead—A Long Way

What is it you want out of life? What do you want to have accomplished five years from now—or ten?

Set up long-range goals for yourself. Is it a new home of which you are dreaming? Do you long for the chance to travel—South America, Hawaii, Europe? Do you intend to give your children a chance for a college degree?

Put down what you need financially to accomplish these and the other things you feel important. What will it take? $5,000? $10,000? $25,000 or more? Put down how much time you have. Determine how willing you are to work for what you want.

Then set up quotas of health insurance sales for yourself. How many sales do you need each year, each month, each week? How big an average premium to bring you the desired income? How many calls are necessary to make the required number of sales?

Vow that you will be the best health insurance

agent it is in your power to be. Keep your goals always in your mind and in your plans. Look ahead—with vision.

SERVING THE PUBLIC

Community relations can have a profound influence on the success or failure of any agent. And there are three aspects of that statement which do not always meet the eye. First, there are the jobs you can do beyond the scope of your business. Work in your church—for the United Way—for the American Cancer Society—or on hospital drives, etc. Any good cause deserves your active participation, naturally within your physical limitations.

And it is important to your success that you be a good citizen. Not just an average citizen, but one of constructive citizenship. Since you are a *merchant of social benefits*, your job must not stop with the sale of insurance. To do a real job, carry your work beyond its purely business sphere.

If you perform these outside activites in a noncommercial spirit, you will inevitably build personal prestige. As a natural result, some business will come to you because you deserve it.

So keep in circulation. Keep searching for places where you can make a civic, charitable or religious contribution. Do something with the people who surround you and success will be easier and faster to achieve.

The second phase of good community relations is that of wide personal contact. The advantages are many.

The more worthwhile activities you engage in enthusiastically, the more people you meet on a favorable basis. Your chances of obtaining business are multiplied by the very number of good contacts you make. Not only will the number be large but the quality of prospects will be high. It is usually the successful man or woman who is active in public-spirited enterprises.

It is inevitable that some of these people will ask you for advice about health insurance. In other instances, you will be able to call on people who will immediately recognize you as an associate in some charitable effort. Entirely new circles of acquaintances and friends will be opened up and for the alert insurance agent, these are stepping stones to future business. Your civic contacts of the right kind will enable you to secure interviews on a favorable basis. But a fair hearing for your sales and service story is all you have a right to expect from anyone.

Given that hearing, it is then your obligation to have a worthwhile message to present. This places a grave responsibility on your shoulders. Most people do not buy health insurance voluntarily. They may intend to but they do not get around to it until an agent presents a plan to them.

So your job is to sell contracts which fit the prospect's needs closely...to sell them to the buyers whose occupation, physical condition and moral standing make them good risks...to sell them at a price the buyers can afford so they will remain in force and fulfill their original purpose. Once you sell them, you then get to fulfill your promise—through service.

BUILDING PERSISTENT BUSINESS

The frequency with which a premium falls due has an effect on the persistency of your business. Annual policies persist the best, with automatic monthly checking plans the next best. Quarterly and semi-annual plans simply do not stay on the books as well.

Another element in persistency is the care with which you select and sell your prospects in the first place. Persistency originates with prospecting.

Remember the definition of a prospect in the unit on prospecting. A person who meets all those qualifications is more likely to keep the policy in force. A contract which fills a need—an ability to pay the premiums—a favorable attitude toward you—these are all contributing factors to good persistency.

Additional foundations for persistent business are laid at the time of the sale. **People usually keep what satisfies them and what they can afford.** If your presentation was made only on the strength of one unusual feature in your contract, your insured may later lose enthusiasm for it. If, on the other hand, your policy was tailor-made to fit your client's situation, the chances of his or her keeping it are excellent.

The kind of prospect you approach and the type of sale you make greatly influence persistency and have a strong effect on your work to build a good clientele.

POLICY DELIVERY

An exceptional opportunity for maintaining good persistency and building a loyal clientele occurs at the time of policy delivery. Is it wise to mail a recently issued policy to a new insured? Or should you deliver it in person and merely hand it to the buyer with a "Thanks a lot for the business"? Or if you did not collect the full first premium with the application, should you mail a bill for the balance due? The answer to all three questions is *No.*

Skillful sales ability calls for more thorough methods.

Your client has purchased a bundle of guarantees, the significance of which will be fully felt only at claim time. The more your client understands about what to expect—what is and isn't covered, how claims are filed and how benefits are paid—the greater satisfaction your client will experience, the greater will be your prestige, the longer your business will stay on the books and the more referrals you will get.

Perceptions are at the heart of communication. What will your client think, or feel, if you handled the policy delivery in any of the ways mentioned above? How much will your clients respect what they've purchased? How much will they respect you? People know when they're treated with respect. And they will reciprocate. Likewise, when they feel they've been treated less than professionally, they will reciprocate.

Most states allow your clients 10 days *from the time of delivery* to return a policy and receive a full refund. Policy delivery is your way of making sure your policies aren't returned: because you're there to reinforce the need—and the solution. You're there to congratulate your client for making a wise decision. You're there to show your client how and what benefits are paid. You're there to do your job—provide service.

So make certain your clients understand what is and is not covered. Use colored pencils to underline important points in the contract. Place check marks beside significant clauses. Most of the latter are for your clients' protection. Make sure they understand them.

The Value

A smart agent recognizes the dollars-and-cents value of proper policy delivery. For example, figure your first-year commission on an average size policy and add to it the renewal commissions for ten years. Then compare that total commission to what you would receive if the policy lapsed after only one or two years.

Then multiply the commissions both ways by ten to see what the total difference would be on ten such policies. This earnings comparison between keeping the policy in force only one or two years and keeping it in force for ten years illustrates dramatically the value of persistency.

A Prospecting Opportunity

The important of asking for prospects at the time of policy delivery cannot be overemphasized. Substantial clienteles have been and can be built by moving from a new insured to a circle of friends and acquaintances, with the help of your client.

> *"(Client), you have taken an important financial step. You have guaranteed the security of your family—your goals, your dreams, everything you've planned for—by acquiring a program that is sound and guaranteed.*
>
> *"You certainly have many friends and business associates who probably have been as careful in their financial planning. Yet we find that many such people are unaware of the benefits you have just acquired. Is there anyone that you work with who you feel should know about this type of plan? I would be happy to share with them the type of information I shared with you. Who comes to mind?"*

The ideal you should strive for is to have a substantial block of permanent insureds who are wedded to you because they like you, because you have sold them appropriate contracts and because you have given them good service.

SERVICE THROUGH CLAIMS

One of the vital factors in clientele-building is the manner in which claims are handled. Your eventual success may be related directly to the quality of your claim service and the way you capitalize on claim payments.

Claims generally consume the major portion of the health insurance premium dollar. They are the very heart of the health insurance business, for without claims, health insurance companies would be nonexistent.

A health insurance policy may be a promise to the insured in return for a stipulated premium to continue a part of income in event of accident or sickness; or to pay certain sums of money for doctor, hospital or medical expenses; or to pay a cash benefit to beneficiaries for accidental death. Until one of those events happens, the policy is only a piece of paper tucked away in a desk drawer.

When illness or injury occurs, the contract comes to life—then the health insurance business demonstrates its benefits in action!

A health insurance contract may pay benefits to an insured many times during a lifetime. No other business offers so many opportunities for rendering valuable service. Claims are the raw material from which public opinion is molded. Their prompt and proper handling determines to large extent the popularity and persistency of health insurance.

You may or may not be involved directly in the submission of claims. It depends on your company's policy. Whether or not you are, anything you can do to simplify and expedite the process will be appreciated by your ill or injured client.

There are certain suggestions which will make claim handling easier for you and also lead to further business through client satisfaction.

Be prompt in your service—The claim procedure is a mystery to your insured but he or she expects quick action on a claim. It will pay you big dividends to see that the person gets it.

See your insured personally—This is important. When a person is disabled and entitled to benefits, you go through a transformation in his or her eyes. You change from an agent who has sold a policy to a warm friend who is responsible for the person having the needed protection. So visit the person and say, **"Don't worry. Just concentrate on getting well. I'll notify my company of your claim and help you complete the reports they request."**

Avoid committing the company to the payment of any specific amount—If it is apparent to you that a claim for a loss is not covered by the policy, explain to the insured tactfully before a claim is filed why he or she may not be entitled to benefits.

Expedite paperwork. As an agent, you represent your company in the eyes of the law. When your insured notifies you of a claim, he or she is considered to have given sufficient notice. Be sure to pass word along promptly to your claim department.

In writing the company, furnish adequate information—Give the insured's name and policy number. State whether the claim results from sickness or accident. And it will build goodwill for you to send your insured a copy of your letter.

Claim forms usually required for disability insurance are:

- Insured's first report of disability
- Attending physician's first report
- Insured's final report
- Physician's final report

Obtain leads at check delivery time—Whether the company mails checks to the insured directly to avoid delay or requires you to deliver them personally, it is of primary importance that the insured receive benefit checks promptly. The point to remember is that more goodwill can be created at claim time with thoughtful promptness than at any other time or with any other kind of service.

Your entire process of servicing insureds when they are entitled to benefits should be designed to build an ever-expanding circle of satisfied customers. You want them willingly to suggest that you tell others about the benefits of health insurance. New prospects, personal recommendations and other help can easily be obtained from in-sureds when you perform prompt service on claims. And better persistency results.

Obtain testimonials—Letters addressed to and personally thanking you for your assistance are invaluable instruments in the sales process. They build high prestige for you. They show the health insurance business *in action* and are far more effective than anything you could say. Other testimonials to the usefulness of health insurance are copies of claim checks and lists of actual medical expenses incurred. Obtain permission to use these. They will prove to be powerful sales allies.

The moral behind all of your claim service might well be: Be good to your insureds and they will be good to you!

> The wise business person insures against hazards that can interrupt the flow of income and ruin the business.
> The thoughtful family member insures against lingering illness or serious accident that can interrupt the flow of earnings and destroy the home.

SERVICE THROUGH REVIEWS

Too often, in clientele-building, the importance of keeping in close contact with insureds is underestimated. Once an insured has been sold, there may be a tendency on an agent's part to concentrate entirely on new people. Or the agent may be in touch with the insured only at the time of claim.

Service is not just selling a policy, delivering it or processing a claim. Service entails answering questions that may arise. Service is keeping clients up-to-date on what they have and what they need. Service is making yourself available to those who have trusted you.

Frequent Contact With Insureds

Keeping in touch with your insureds is the service you promised. And service to your clients can serve your needs as well.

Do not overlook the dollar value of your insured file. People's incomes tend to improve every two or three years. It becomes easier for them to buy more protection. And their needs will probably increase, too. To have it fixed well in their minds when they consider more insurance requires keeping in frequent touch with them even when no claim service is involved.

One of the most profitable sources of future business is insureds. So make insured calls a part of your daily business activity. There are many good reasons for making these calls and while personal contact is most effective, there are times when a phone call or a mailing piece will serve the purpose.

Premium due dates—Many agents recommend that you contact each new insured shortly before the time the first renewal premium is due. This is a critical time in the life of a policy—and a call here may prevent a lapse.

Certainly when you are notified a premium is overdue, you should follow up swiftly and not let any time elapse before contacting your client.

Change in client's situation—One of your insureds may have been promoted to a position which is less hazardous. Or may have made a new connection with less risk than the former occupation. The client will be grateful if you point out that he or she may be entitled to a lower premium rate and that you are willing to take it up with the home office.

Your insured may have bought a new home—or had an addition to the family—or started a new business. Any accident or illness occurring to a friend of a client is a good reason to call, on the grounds that he or she may have been emotionally affected by the event and is ready to increase protection.

Items of interest to insureds—If your client is a professional person or a merchant, you may do a good turn by sending someone to him or her. If you run across a news item which concerns a client's business, you can clip it out and send it to your client. If the person has a hobby, you may send him an item or a bit of information of interest. If the client has sent someone to you for business or social reasons, you can report on your progress as an expression of gratitude.

These and other contacts tend to cement your relationships with the people you have already sold. If it is worthwhile to put contracts in force in the first place, it is worthwhile to conserve them. And it is easier to keep a contract in force than it is to try to reinstate it.

Frequent contact with your insureds is an integral part of client-building.

Review Your Own

You will find it easier to communicate the need for health insurance if you address the subject as it applies to *you!* You cannot be of service to your clients if you are inundated with medical bills or unable to work because you have an illness or injury.

Ask yourself all the same questions you ask a prospect. Write down your answers. Analyze your own responses. Calculate what you need. Then buy it! Until you own all the health insurance you need, you'll never be able to convince your prospects to make the financial sacrifice that's needed to provide security. If you can't or won't do it, how can you expect them to?

Your sincere belief in your products will come through when you own them! You can show your prospects what you own—and how much you pay. What better testimonial than that you own what you sell?!

Chapter 13
Planning for Profitable Activity

Lesson Text—The Power of Good Work Habits
. . . Importance of Records . . . Quality Prospecting Improves Work Habits . . . How to Plan Wisely
. . . Build Your Activities Around Your Needs . . .
Total Your Income Needs . . . Your Minimum Objectives . . . A Simple Record-Keeping System
. . . Your Prospect File . . . Daily Work Folder and
Monthly Summary . . . Your Progress Report . . .
Importance of Evening Calls . . . Plan Your Work,
Work Your Plan . . . Be a Good Boss

You have seen why health insurance has a strong appeal to every individual and particularly those who have responsibilities and who work to earn income. You know that the health insurance agent does not create the need any more than a doctor creates pain. But you also know that protection against heavy medical expenses and loss of income because of disability is a deep-rooted need which most people have whether they recognize it or not.

You have learned that the well-trained and well-equipped health underwriter provides the only way today for solving the basic loss-of-income-through-disability problems which constantly threaten the security of the home and the family life of virtually everyone.

You have studied where prospects are found, how to recognize them, the factors and timing that make them good prospects for you and how to reach them. You recognize the importance of planned interviews. You know how to avoid difficulties during the sale, but you also know the sales value of excuses when they do arise.

There is a great deal of important technical and sales information in the preceding chapters. But now that you are studying to improve your sales effectiveness, there is one particularly significant aspect of your business which must be thoroughly explored—how to control your time and how to organize your business activities for profitable work.

You may have mastered sales presentations and be a skillful closer, adept at handling excuses. You may know your rate manual, your company's contracts and how to meet competition. But if you do not organize your work for efficiency and control your time for profit, you cannot hope to attain upper levels of success.

THE POWER OF GOOD WORK HABITS

Have you ever gone out for sports—swimming, tennis, soccer, golfing, basketball, baseball, football? If you have, you no doubt had a coach who pointed out the importance of learning good habits.

Most people who start practice without guidance begin to form certain habits. The coach recognizes the bad habits and knows you can never become a top-notch athlete as long as you stay with those habits. So the coach shows you what you are doing wrong and how to do it right. At first the coach's way may seem more difficult than your old way. And it is difficult. That is because you now must discard a wrong technique and learn the right technique and make it a habit.

But if you keep practicing, just at the point where you may think you are not cut out for that kind of sport, you suddenly feel you are mastering the correct method. When that happens, improvement follows rapidly. You find the right technique is the easy way and you would not return to your old way for anything! When good work habits become a part of you, they give your efforts momentum that makes the job easier.

Psychologists tell us that 95 percent of everything we do in our regular daily life is the result of habit and that only 5 percent is the result of conscious action. Habits get us up in the morning. They put us to bed at night. They tell us what to eat and how to dress and how to act. Unless we acquire right habits at the beginning, we may automatically form bad habits. These penalize us continuously until we unlearn them and acquire good habits. It is three times more difficult to reverse a wheel turning the wrong way than to start it turning the correct way in the first place.

Good Habits Essential

Each person is the builder of his or her own destiny. As a person plans so will success be measured—and in direct proportion. It is not enough merely to "work hard," especially if that hard work is based on unsound habits. For when you are not well organized, you can work yourself to exhaustion without accomplishing much. You will spend more energy going in all directions at once than you will when your activities are well channeled in the light of your needs and ambitions.

Vague plans—half laid and halfheartedly executed—vacillation, procrastination—are the curse of the agent whose capital is time. But organization—that is the measuring rod of a successful agent.

Almost any worthwhile activity requires organization. If you were employed by a business firm, you would be expected to spend a specific number of hours each day at productive work. Does it not make sense that you, too, should set up a schedule and follow it?

Look at the history of business firms. Their success often can be traced to the organized activity of the founder. That person gave the job everything he or she had. You are the founder of your business. Your success depends on your giving it everything you have. Is it not wise to start off on the most favorable basis?

It is said, "In the beginning, man makes his habits—then, habits make the man!" Sow an act, and you reap a character; sow a character and you reap a destiny.

A good habit is not always called by that name. Sometimes it is referred to as willpower, as ambition, even as luck. But call it what you will, it is a road map that shows you always where you are, where you have been, where you are going. It is the continuing ability to make maximum use of time. And no person has a greater number of hours in the day than you.

Success is earned by making sound plans and acting on them. The more definite the plans, the more certain the follow-through.

Do what every successful business does—whether a sole proprietorship or giant corporation. Organize yourself. Self-organization will make you form the good work habits that are essential to success.

Symptoms of Poor Work Habits

Some agents show capacity for outstanding success during spurts or periods when things are going right. But they fall short of success over an extended period of time. In the long run, they are just average producers, turning in occasional brilliant performances, followed by long, cold spells of days and even weeks without sales.

The dangers in this up-and-down production are many. It takes the fun out of the work and dampens enthusiasm for selling. It is wasteful and expensive. Too much time is spent in the office. Valuable selling time is wasted in calling back on prospects and in chasing over wide geographical areas. Spasmodic selling throws a budget out of kilter. An agent must literally fight his or her way out of a slump. Unless an agent profits by this experience, the up-and-down cycle repeats itself.

Such fitful selling is a symptom of poor organization and haphazard time control. The agent is faced with the difficult task of discarding bad work habits and of acquiring good work habits. It is unlikely that such an agent can furnish adequate records of past performance. And it is almost a sure bet that the agent is unable to give the most fundamental information about previous field activities. It is obvious that this agent does not translate facts about the past into plans for the future.

IMPORTANCE OF RECORDS

A study of agent work habits quickly reveals the value of keeping watchful control over your business activities. Of two agents with equal training and ability, the one who keeps records will outdistance the one who does not by two or three to one.

There was a time in business when the storekeeper had two spindles. On one was kept the bills paid—on the other, the unpaid. He or she kept the money in a cash drawer and only occasionally had to take inventory. But that time is past.

Today, business is more complex. Success is built on accurate records and intelligent planning. To make progress you must know your score—at the end of the first quarter, at the half, and all along the line. The right kinds of records give you the score.

Records show you where to find the dollars you need. They pinpoint your weaknesses. They tell you if you are getting enough interviews in relation to calls, if you are making enough closing attempts, if you need more intensive prospectings.

Records point out strengths. They show you the kind of business you are getting. They highlight your most profitable markets. They tell you where to intensify your activities.

Planning and record keeping go together.

Planning—organizing your work so you know what you are going to do next year, next month, next week, tomorrow—concerns *future* performance. Record keeping, on the other hand, deals with *past* events. You cannot do a good job of planning ahead unless you have good records of the past. In order to plan where to go, you must know where you have been and where you stand now.

The Laws of Quantity and Quality

Most agents enthusiastically believe that field success depends upon the quantity of calls made. Most agents believe that the answer to all production problems is to be found in making an abundant number of calls. And they are partially right in that belief. Only they do not go quite far enough.

Quantity of calls alone will produce some business. But it is only when quality comes into the picture that the agent can raise production to high levels.

The success of outstanding agents rests on the fact that they operate under both the laws of quantity and quality. They do not make fewer calls than poor producers. They make more calls.

And then, because they have formed the habit of working in the most fertile markets, and because they have mastered a technique of interviewing that get results, their production moves to higher levels.

Why plan? Why keep records? Because only by doing so can you hope to secure the benefits that come when you bring the law of quality into your business!

What did you do that was profitable? What was unprofitable?

One measure of a successful agent is the answer when you ask, "How is business?" The more successful the agent is, the more accurately his or her reply will be able to tell you where he or she stands today in relation to objectives, and how much business is going to be written next month or two months from now or during the remainder of the year. Top-level producers have this information at their fingertips and can forecast their sales with amazing accuracy. They know how many people they must see. They know if they see these people, good results will follow.

QUALITY PROSPECTING IMPROVES WORK HABITS

Quality prospecting and sound organization for profitable field activity go together. An agent without a full hopper of live prospects finds it difficult to generate enthusiasm for field work. The most invigorating part of the business—talking to people and helping them solve their problems—becomes uninviting. Almost unconsciously he or she begins to avoid contacting people. The agent spends more and more time in the office playing solitaire with old cards in the file of cold prospects. Because he or she does not contact enough good potential customers, the agent finds prospecting hard work and tends to blame the business for all the difficulties. This lack of good prospects becomes worse the longer it continues. If the agent is pulling out of the slump, it is essential for this agent, with cold deliberation, to eliminate the dead prospects from the file and rejuvenate sales with new live leads.

Such an agent faces the difficult threefold job of unlearning haphazard work habits and making a sound prospecting system a part of daily work routine.

The agent who organizes work around live prospects seldom wastes time in the office or anywhere else. When the prospect hopper is full of names of people who need immediate attention, the problem of time control largely solves itself. And because the majority of selling time is spent with quality prospects, there is no problem in picking up live, hot leads. By concentrating activities around people who need urgent attention, the agent can discard the "china eggs" in the file. With an inventory filled with people to see at once, the agent avoids discouraging slumps. Work is stimulating and profitable.

One successful agent reported that he earned in his fourth month in this business more than double the income he had earned after four years in his former business. The secret of his success lies in his words, "Every night after mapping out my next day's work, I can hardly wait for morning to come so I can see people who need my service." This man early in his career formed good prospecting habits. He has no problem keeping his days filled with profitable work in the field.

Prospects are your raw material in the health insurance business. Every day you work you use up a portion of your inventory of this raw material. You make contacts where no interview is granted; you make presentations where the prospect does not buy. You make sales which remove names from your prospect file. Unless you keep a large enough inventory on hand at all times, you suddenly will find that you are out of prospects. Your business will operate at a loss until you have restocked your files. With an ample supply of good prospects, with proper records of your activities, you should have no trouble organizing your work to save time, effort and money.

How Much Is an Hour Worth?

Successful agents know exactly what their time is worth. They know that their profitable hours are those spent with prospects. They realize that when they take an hour to drive across town for an appointment and another hour to drive back, two hours of valuable time have been spent. They will not prepare sales proposals during the workday. They do not take time out during the day for planning or other office work. They know that time spent in the office is time stolen from field work, which is the most profitable activity they perform. Success is less a question of working harder than of working intelligently and organizing your work for best results.

WHY ORGANIZE?

Because if you have good records you can build sound plans,

Because you can accentuate your right habits and eliminate the wrong habits from your work,

Because you can break down your year's goal into easy daily activities,

And know at all times exactly what you have accomplished in relation to where you want to go.

Have you ever figured out how much one hour of your workday is worth? Do you want to know the dollars-and-cents value of organizing your time? Are you willing to face the facts, to know what it costs you to waste just one work hour a day in your office? Glance at the chart (Figure 13-1) that follows. It is based on an eight-hour day, five and one-half days a week and shows the value of your time in the field.

FIGURE 13-1
YOUR TIME IN THE FIELD

Annual Income	Monthly Income	Daily Income	Income Per Hour	Hour/Day Wasted Per Year Totals
$20,000	$1,667	$ 69.93	$ 8.74	$2,500
30,000	2,500	104.90	13.11	3,750
40,000	3,333	139.86	17.48	5,000
50,000	4,167	174.83	21.85	6,250

If your income is $20,000 a year, for example, then your monthly income amounts to $1,667, your income for each day you work is $69.93, and each hour is worth $8.74 to you. If you waste just one hour each day because you do not have an organized schedule for a full day's field work, you are paying $2,500 a year for your carelessness. Two hours a day wasted costs you $5,000 a year! Surely this is a costly penalty to pay for unplanned action during each day. The price of failure to plan is always greater than the cost of planning.

HOW TO PLAN WISELY

Your first step is to select a planning period each day. It should be a time when you will not be interrupted by telephone calls or visitors. It should not be a part of your workday, detracting from the valuable hours you can spend in the field. Many agents set aside the period following dinner for reviewing the day's work; or if they have evening calls, they use the time directly after they return home. Whatever time you select, use it regularly, day in and day out, for this one purpose. Make your family understand the need for respecting your planning hour.

Your next step is to analyze your day's activities. Did you make a sale? Who is your new insured? What is his or her age? What income bracket is the person in? What family does the person have? How did you locate the person as a prospect? What prestige did you have when you made your approach? What sales plan did you recommend? What clinched the sale and why did he or she buy from you? Think through these questions, probing for your strengths.

Next, turn your thinking to the interviews where no progress resulted. Do you know where the sale was lost? What kind of a prospect did you have? How did you find the prospect? What did you know about the individual before contact was made? Did you see the prospect at the right time? What did you say? How did you answer objections? How would you improve the interview if you had it to do over tomorrow?

Having made sure that your records for the day are complete and totaled, you plan your tomorrow's calls. Appointments, of course, are listed for the time you and your prospect have agreed upon. Many successful agents try to arrange an early appointment, around nine o'clock in the morning, and another about four o'clock in the afternoon or later. Such appointments insure an early start and avoid the temptation to quit early. Select carefully the other prospects you intend to contact, giving preference to those who need immediate attention. Arrange your day by area, so that if you have an appointment in a certain section, you will have other prospects to see while you are there. You save travel time and wear and tear on your car. For example, a fruit grower does not run all over the orchard picking one apple from this tree and one from that. *Plan your calls systematically!*

When you have completed your blueprint of tomorrow's activities, ask yourself why you will

> Step by step, weigh and evaluate your work. Look for strengths you can put to good advantage—for weaknesses you can avoid or correct. View your day objectively to find how, with better organizational plan, you could have contacted one or two more prospects.

call on each name you have listed. What are the person's responsibilities? What is the family situation? Why should he or she buy from you?

Ask yourself, *"What if this person becomes disabled today?"* Picture the family without earned income. What will happen to their home? To plans for educating the children? To the morale of the person?

Big producers sell people in their own minds before calling on them. They say they have to see the sale themselves before they can make it in the prospect's mind.

See the sale made first. If you would buy it, the chances are your prospect will.

Look at the dark side of your prospect's picture. Suppose he or she has not bought. The per-

---

A CONTACT TIME CLOCK

When is the best time to contact different types of prospects? The most favorable time for you to see your prospects varies by occupation. Of course, when an appointment is made, you and your prospect agree on a time. But when you are planning your schedule for the next day and intend to follow up leads without appointments, a time clock showing the best time to contact prospects will be useful. Here are some sound suggestions, based on the experiences of many successful agents.

8:00 a.m. – Contractors, builders, other construction before 9:00.
8:30 a.m. – Dentists between 8:30 and 9:30.
9:00 a.m. – Stockbrokers, bankers, bond salespeople, etc., before 10:00.
9:30 a.m. – Physicians and surgeons between 9:00 and 11:00.
10:30 a.m. – Executives and heads of businesses after 10:30.
            – Merchants, store heads, department heads after 10:30.
11:00 a.m. – From 11:00 to 2:00 is a good time to call on lawyers.
1:00 p.m. – Another time for contacting physicians, surgeons: 1:00-3:00.
2:00 p.m. – Druggists and grocers have slack periods from 1:00 to 3:00.
3:00 p.m. – Bankers, managers, and other business people after 3:00.
3:30 p.m. – Contact printers and publishers after 3:00.
4:00 p.m. – Call on lawyers between 4:00 and 5:00, too.
            – Brokers are free after Stock Exchange closes at 4:00.
            – Chemists and engineers are available between 4:00 and 5:00.
5:00 p.m. – Construction people back in the office around 5:00.
6:00 p.m. – Schoolteachers and professors at home between 6:00 and 7:00.
7:30 p.m. – Between 7:30 and 9:00 or 9:30 at home for the salaried worker in modest income bracket and the better income prospect you are unable to see during the daytime.

There will be variations, depending on local customs. In some sections of the country, it is known that doctors take Wednesday afternoon off, except in emergencies. In other sections, some stores stay open all day Saturday and are closed all day Monday. In still other places the hours of opening and closing follow local habits. But the above list will act as a guide and remind you to time your contacts for best results.

son is hopeless physically and financially. Then visualize him or her as a disabled insured, receiving claim checks from you.

Keep these contrasting pictures in mind as you plan your calls. They will add enthusiasm to your work and sincerity to your purpose.

In this way you move from day to day, planning each day's work the night before. Each week, the week before. Each month, the month before. And each year, the year before. Such regular imaginative planning will become a spur to making calls because your mental attitude is always positive. It will give you a feeling of responsibility toward your sales career. You will acquire that asset necessary for anyone in business for themselves—self-discipline.

Clay Hamlin, formerly one of the world's great insurance agents, said: "The biggest problem is not production. The biggest problem is self. Solve that problem—and the rest is easy!"

Keep Records Simple

A record-keeping system should be both accurate and simple. It must be accurate in order to furnish you with the information you need in your planning. It must be simple because each individual agent has to keep his or her own records. No one else is going to do it. If it is a complicated system, it will require too much time and eventually die of its own weight.

Once an adequate record-keeping system has been set up, it will not take much effort to keep it up to date. Your daily review and completion of records will not take more than 15 to 20 minutes. But keep at it daily so it will be most useful to you and not become a burden. It should be up-to-the-minute so there will be a constant flow of new names coming into your inventory. It should be a track to show you where to go as well as tell you where you have been.

Many home offices, general agents and managers have record-keeping systems which they recommend to their field personnel and expect them to follow. If your company, general agent or manager has one which is integrated into other phases of agency operations, you should follow that system.

Systems may vary in detail, some being more extensive than others. But the principles of maintaining a good business control system are the same. There is certain fundamental information you should have. There is other information which might be nice to have, but which is not as essential and which you should keep only if it does not place an extra burden on your time. Above all, any system you use should be easy to keep up to date. Otherwise human nature may cause you to neglect it.

BUILD YOUR ACTIVITIES AROUND YOUR NEEDS

Do you know where you stand financially and what your financial requirements are? If you do not, you cannot plan intelligently for progress. Here is a quick, easy way to determine your financial requirements.

List your living expenses first. How much do you spend for food? How much for rent or for mortgage payments? What are your real estate taxes, federal income taxes, state income taxes and other miscellaneous taxes? What premiums do you pay for general insurance? How much for clothing, doctors, drugs, allowances for the children? Include in your living expenses your donations to church and charities and also the amount you spend on vacation.

Next total up how much you put into health insurance and life insurance and how much you are paying toward reducing debts. Add to this your periodic bank deposits and any other regular investments and you have your savings and insurance item.

TOTAL YOUR INCOME NEEDS

Then include your business expenses—advertising, cost of operating your automobile, club dues and expenses and other business incidentals—and you have your total cash requirements. (Of course, "business expenses" as they are discussed here include not only tax-deductible business expense items, but also other personal expenses such as your lunches.) With the grand total of these items, you have the amount of money you must receive during a

FIGURE 13–2

MY REQUIREMENTS

My Living Expenses

Food	$_____
Rent or Mortgage	_____
Taxes	_____
General Insurance	_____
Utilities (gas, light, telephone, water)	_____
Clothing	_____
Doctor, drugs	_____
Allowances	_____
Education	_____
Church, charities	_____
Amusements, books, papers, theater	_____
Vacation	_____
Miscellaneous	_____
TOTAL	$_____

My Savings and Insurance

Health Insurance	$_____
Life Insurance	_____
Debt Reduction	_____
Bonds and other investments	_____
TOTAL	$_____

My Business Expenses

Advertising	$_____
Automobile	_____
Lunches	_____
Business Entertainment	_____
Incidentals	_____
TOTAL	$_____

TOTAL REQUIREMENTS .... $_____

DEDUCT RENEWAL INCOME FOR SAME PERIOD .... $_____

BALANCE REQUIRED FROM NEW BUSINESS .... $_____

given period in order for you and your family to maintain a reasonable standard of living. This may be figured either on an annual basis or on a monthly basis, whichever you prefer. If you use monthly figures, they should represent one-twelfth of the once-a-year items such as life insurance premiums, club dues or taxes.

Your next step is to deduct your renewal income for this same period. The balance left over is the amount you need to earn from new business. These are your actual cash requirements and the basis on which your plans should be formulated. You can adjust your work formula later to include your ambitions and hopes.

Having determined your requirements, you next set up your minimum work objectives by translating the income you must have into terms of field activity.

YOUR MINIMUM OBJECTIVES

Imagine if you can a business person attempting to run a company successfully without a thorough knowledge of the business ratios—how often the stock turns over, how much is invested in inventory, what average profit amounts to, the relationship of costs to sales and sales to profits. Such a business owner would have no plan of operation or goal toward which to strive. A knowledge of the relative values of your various activities makes it possible to isolate your weak points and concentrate on improvement.

There are standard ratios for virtually every kind of manufacturing, retailing and service establishment, based on nationwide averages. There are also standards in the health insurance business.

One recognized formula of performance is:

> **10 calls**
>
> **=**
>
> **5 interviews**
>
> **=**
>
> **1 sale**
>
> **=**
>
> **10 new leads—at least**

If this is the formula that fits you, and your requirements are one sale a day, then these are your daily field objectives.

How to Establish Objectives

To arrive at your minimum field work objectives, start with the amount of first-year commissions you will need from new business by listing all your regular expenses and deducting from them the renewals you will receive. Then figure what that means in premium volume. Using your company's commission scale, you can determine the premium volume you must write in order to earn your needed first-year commissions.

Let us say, for example, that your average size sale is $X in annual premiums. By dividing the required premium volume by your average premium, let us assume you find you must sell 120 cases in 12 months. To put it on a weekly basis, divide by 48. This allows four weeks out of the year for illness and vacation and as a general buffer against unforeseen events. That works out, in this case, to two and one-half sales a week as your minimum field objective.

Now to carry it further, let us assume your records show that you close one out of every two interviews—and consider an interview only those calls where you make one or more attempts to close. It is not difficult to figure that you must have five interviews a week. Next, if your records reveal that you must contact eight people in order to obtain five interviews, you need to know how many prospects you should have to assure those eight contacts.

If you practice the "rule of replace"—that for every prospect used up, at least one other must be found—you will have no trouble with this next step. Perhaps you have to have 24 prospects in order to have eight contacts. That figure may not be so high if you ruthlessly weed out the prospects who do not measure up to your standards. And realize that only careful selection of prospects will make eight calls produce five different interviews in which you make at least one closing attempt. At any rate, know how many good new leads you need each week, even though you may have more in your prospect file right now than you can call on in several months.

Of course, these are your *minimum* objectives. Give yourself a higher goal and keep it in mind when setting up your weekly schedule.

FIGURE 13–3

MY MINIMUM FIELD OBJECTIVES

For the Period _____

1. First-Year Commission Income Required from
   New Business (last item from "My Requirements")............................ $_____

2. Premium Volume Required (in annual premiums).................................. $_____

   Annual premium of my average size sale is..................$_____

3. Number of New Sales I Must Make (divide premium
   volume required by average size sale)... _____

   > Note: If you completed "My Requirements" for a
   > full year, divide the Number of New Sales above
   > by 48 to obtain your weekly objectives. If you
   > completed "My Requirements" using monthly fig-
   > ures, divide Number of New Sales by four to ob-
   > tain your weekly objectives. Four weeks out of
   > the year are allowed for vacation, meetings, ill-
   > nesses, etc., and as a buffer against unexpected
   > occurrences upsetting your schedule.

My Objectives for Each Week

1. Weekly Commission Required from New Business.................................. $_____

2. Premium Volume Required from New Business (in annual premiums).... $_____

3. Number of Sales I Must Make Each Week... _____
   My ratio of Sales to Attempts to Close is 1 out of _____

4. Number of Attempts to Close I Must Make Each Week......................... _____
   My ratio of Attempts to Close to Contacts is 1 out of_____

5. Number of New Contacts I Must Make Each Week............................. _____

6. Number of New Hot Leads I Must Obtain Each Week........................... _____

One more point. When an application is rejected or not taken, simply add another sale to your objective for the next week.

It is that easy to follow a sound, businesslike procedure for establishing a practical work schedule which you know will produce desired results because it is based on past experience.

A SIMPLE RECORD-KEEPING SYSTEM

After determining your income requirements and establishing your minimum work objectives, you should blueprint your field work for the week and set up your record-keeping system. The main parts of a simple, complete record-keeping system include:

1. Your prospect and insured file
2. Your daily work folder and monthly summary
3. Your progress report

YOUR PROSPECT FILE

A prospect file serves two very important purposes. First, it provides a place to keep, in an organized manner, the names of your prospects and pertinent information about each of them. Second, it furnishes a system which will bring these names to your attention at the right time.

There are many good, workable record-keeping systems available in the market. Some use computer programs; some use file cards. The type of system you use will be a reflection of what you hope to gain from the system.

For example, most computer systems can be used as marketing tools, to help you identify entire groups of prospects. Once you've entered the data regarding your prospects and clients, you can identify readily such groups as "all names of people who own their own businesses," or "everyone who earns $30,000 or more," and so on. Many of the card systems available give some varieties of marketing information. Whatever system you use, the effectiveness of the system will be in direct relationship to the amount of data you collect, input to the system and draw on for field activity.

Many people find it convenient to have their prospect files available in a box or drawer large enough to contain several hundred 3″ × 5″ prospect cards. Even if you have your prospects on computer at the office, the card file is easily kept in the car and thus readily available. Of course, a portable computer could be used to maintain all your records. Having such a system may be a goal for you to establish.

1. The "Master" Section

Your file should be divided into two main sections: (1) the alphabetical or master section; and (2) the "when-to-see" section.

In the "master" section, you place all your prospects in alphabetical order. Write the names of the people you listed on the "memory jogger" sheets in the chapter on prospecting. There may be some names on those sheets which you have already discarded for one reason or another. Obviously, you would not complete cards for them.

Since you are filing alphabetically, list your prospect's last name first. In addition, list all the information possible on the card. It is wise to establish early the habit of obtaining enough information about people and to record the data immediately.

2. The "When-to-See" Section

The "when-to-see" section is divided into two parts. One is a monthly index; the other is a daily index. If your system is a card file, make 12 tabs for the monthly index—one for each month of the year. For the daily index, make tabs numbered 1 through 31.

Your manager or general agent may have a special way of using this file effectively. You should be guided by these suggestions. If you are on your own, the following system is recommended.

Place your best leads for the current month in the daily index section at the front. Also in this daily section put any cards which have been deferred from past months to the present. As you call on these people, return the cards to the master file. If you plan to call on a prospect again in a subsequent month, write only the name on a 3 × 5 card and place it behind the correct monthly tab. When that month arrives, you are reminded to call on this person and you turn to your alphabetical file for complete information.

Other Uses of "When-to-See" Section

Some agents use the monthly index for reminders of their clients' birthdays and other anniversaries. At the proper time, they send greeting cards as an additional means of keeping in touch with their clients. Other successful agents list names in a birthday book with a page for each month. As the birthday month comes around, the agent obtains the client's exact birthday, address, and any other necessary information from the prospect card.

Another optional use of the card file is the inclusion of an area file. On the tabs in this section, write the various areas where you conduct your business. Behind these, place at the beginning of each month names of people whom you have not yet called on or have not developed into hot leads. Then as an appointment or a service call takes you to the east end, for example, you can pick the cards for that geographical area. Selecting a number to call on, you can concentrate your activities for economy of time and travel.

Records of Your Insureds

A most important part of your filing system will be your insured section. Under alphabetical tabs you will file your policy record cards. These cards are furnished by the home office when a policy is issued. They include all the pertinent information about the policy—policy number, date of issue, kind of policy, amount of premium, how and when payable, benefits, beneficiary if any, and waiting period if any.

DAILY WORK FOLDER AND MONTHLY SUMMARY

A second part of an effective record-keeping system includes your *daily work folder* and your *monthly summary* of results. A handy daily work folder contains a page for listing your calls and results for each day of the week. And it has a section in the back for listing new hot leads obtained during the week.

Following each call, check your results in the proper columns. These columns are divided into the four most important activities of your workday: Contacts, Attempts to Close, Sales and Hot Leads. *Contacts* are defined as face-to-face meetings with a prospect. By recording them, you will know if your field activities are properly balanced.

Attempts to Close measure the number of closing interviews you have had. In the next column under *Sales*, you record the amount of annual premium and its value in first-year commissions. The *Hot Leads* column allows space for the number of good qualified prospects obtained and acts as a constant reminder to follow the rule of replace. In the last column is recorded the amount of cash with application and whether it represents an annual, semiannual or quarterly premium. Under each heading you will want to keep track of your results from daytime calls and night calls.

Your daily work folder should be tallied each day and entered each week on your monthly summary. At the end of the month you will have a picture of your daily activities. You will have a record of the number of new contacts, number of closing interviews, number of sales, number of new leads, annual premium volume sold and first-year commissions you have earned.

With this information, you can compare your field performance with your work objectives and determine the pace you must set to meet your minimum monthly requirements.

YOUR PROGRESS REPORT

There is one trait all successful agents seem to have. It appears with consistency in outstanding producers. Although mentioned briefly before, it merits repetition. Ask any company leader "How is business?" and you will invariably be given a complete and accurate answer. **This agent knows "what ground I've covered, where I stand now, how much further there is to go, and how to get there"—and generally succeeds.**

This characteristic is found in successful salespeople in every line of business. They know how their sales compare with last month and with the same month last year. They know what their income is to date and how it measures up to their yearly objective. They know if they are ahead of or behind schedule. In this way they can determine the pace they must maintain to complete a successful year.

The sample Progress Report that appears on a subsequent page divides each of the six columns from the Monthly Summary into two sections: one for *objectives* and the other for *results*. At the left are the months of year. Space is allowed for quarterly totals and a comparison of results with objectives. Below the second, third and last quarters, there is extra space for year-to-date totals and year-to-date comparison of results with objectives.

Your objectives can be recorded for a full year in advance. Transfer your results to your progress report from your monthly summary at the close of the month. In this way you have complete information instantly available showing where you stand, where you have been and where you must go to reach your minimum objectives.

The health insurance agent does not travel like the driver of an automobile on a well-marked highway. He or she is more like the captain of a ship at sea. The captain must take the position every day. The captain must know where the ship is and how it got there, and then, using the information, chart the course each day or the ship will never reach port.

IMPORTANCE OF EVENING CALLS

There is a rich evening market available to the agent who is willing to work it. Evening calls can be among the most satisfying and productive kinds of activity. To suggest that you make evening calls is expecting no more of you than if you were the owner-operator of any other business. You would often work long hours, arriving before the start of the regular business day and staying after the closing hour, preparing advertising, keeping your books up to date, reviewing inventory, arranging displays. And you would do this willingly, knowing it is the price of progress and success.

Evening contacts are the price tag of success in health insurance, at least during your early years in the business. They open the way to earlier success and to becoming established more quickly in a permanent career. They are usually more productive, with a high ratio of closes to contacts.

When a man and his wife are together in their home, surrounded by possessions which earned income has made possible, it is easy to focus attention on the importance of continuing income. Their work for the day is over. They can relax. Their minds are free to absorb what you have to say. It is pleasant work for you in comfortable surroundings.

You obtain evening appointments simply by asking for them. When you observe that a prospect is preoccupied, or when he or she is too busy to talk with you at the moment, or when the prospect wants to talk it over with the spouse, or when you have conflicting appointments which do not allow enough time for a thorough presentation—that is the time to ask for an evening appointment. Whenever you sense that daytime is not the best time for a favorable interview, try to arrange an evening appointment. Obtain a full schedule of work for two or preferably three nights a week.

When you are new to the business, make evening calls a habit—a regular part of your work schedule. Give them a chance to prove their value. Make them regularly each week and keep records of them over the period of a year. You will find that evening calls are a profitable source of business.

PLAN YOUR WORK, WORK YOUR PLAN

A big job is no more than a series of small jobs which are easy to accomplish one at a time.

FIGURE 13–4

MY MONTHLY SUMMARY

For Month of _____

| DATE | NO. of CALLS | ATTEMPTS to CLOSE | SALES | | | HOT LEADS OBTAINED |
			Annual Premiums	1st Year Comm.	New Premiums Collected (A.,S.A.,Q.)	
1						
2						
3						
4						
5						
6						
7						
8						
9						
10						
11						
12						
13						
14						
15						
16						
17						
18						
19						
20						
21						
22						
23						
24						
25						
26						
27						
28						
29						
30						
31						
TOTALS						

ACTIVITY THIS MONTH:

Number of Calls_____ _____

Number of Contacts_____ _____

Attempts to Close_____ _____

RESULTS THIS MONTH:

Number of Sales_____ _____

Annual Premiums_____$_____

1st Year Commissions ____$_____

New Premiums Collected __$_____

Number Annually _____ _____

Number Semi-Annually_____ _____

Number Quarterly_____ _____

Average Size
    Annual Premium_____$_____

Average 1st Year
    Commission_____$_____

CHECK YOUR RATIOS:

Calls to
    Contacts_____ _____

Contacts to
    Attempts to Close_____ _____

Attempts to Close
    to Sales_____ _____

Contacts + Attempts to close + Sales + Hot leads = CASH

FIGURE 13–5

MY OWN PROGRESS REPORT
(OBJ. = Objectives; RES. = Results)

Month	Number of New Contacts		Number of Attempts to Close		Number of Sales		Number of New Hot Leads		New Premium Volume (Annual)		First Year Commissions	
	OBJ.	RES.	OBJ.	RES.	OBJ.	RES.	OBJ.	RES.	OBJ.	RES.	OBJ.	RES.
January												
February												
March												
1st Quarter Totals												
+ or − 1st Quarter Objective												
April												
May												
June												
2nd Quarter Totals												
+ or − 2nd Quarter Objective												
Year to Date Totals												
+ or − 6 Month Objective												
July												
August												
September												
3rd Quarter Totals												
+ or − 3rd Quarter Objective												
Year to Date Totals												
+ or − 9 Month Objective												
October												
November												
December												
4th Quarter Totals												
+ or − 4th Quarter Objective												
Year to Date Totals												
+ or − 12 Month Objective												

Enter first year commissions and premium volume in the month the case is paid for. Record a sale in the month when the signed application is submitted to your home office for approval.

We have given you a step-by-step procedure to break down your big job into a series of small jobs. (1) First you determine your income requirements and from that move into your minimum field objectives, determining your necessary activity. (2) Your next step is to translate this activity in terms of weekly and daily performance, using a booklet in which you record results regularly. (3) Your daily results are tabulated every evening and the total transferred to your monthly summary each evening. (4) Once a month, totaling your monthly summary, you record the information on your progress report which shows instantly your results in relation to your objectives. As we have pointed out, the only other piece of equipment you need is a file in which you keep your prospect cards and your insured cards.

With these simple work tools, you can keep posted on your progress, and by checking your ratios, determine your efficiency.

BE A GOOD BOSS

For the most part we are all people of activity. We like action. We prefer books of action, plays and shows which are fast moving. We admire people of action. We enjoy sports and games which emphasize speed and physical activity.

Even so, it is sometimes difficult to make ourselves tackle a job which requires physical work. We put it off. We just cannot seem to get going.

How much more difficult it is to get started and keep going on *planning*! Because planning is not physical—it is a mental activity. It required thought, analysis, decisions. It takes real effort to make ourselves sit down and think out situation through—to plan for tomorrow, next week, or next year.

Yet, all worthwhile activity is preceded by planning. No person can lay claim to success unless that person decides *what* is wanted out of life, *when* he or she wants it, and *how* to get it. The business world is full of failures who go through all the motions of hard work—but they try to move in too many directions at once. They have not clearly marked the trail that will lead them to their goals. They do not keep on the clearly defined, well-organized path that is the most direct route to achievement. These people pay a high price for freedom from the work of keeping records. They pay a heavy cost for freedom from planning. For planning is a price of success.

There are no bells to ring or whistles to blow to tell you when to start the day's work. There is no system of discipline from without. So you must take yourself in hand. You must learn to be your own boss.

As you begin your program of self-organization, keep in mind the essential nature of planning your work. Easy jobs are easy to plan. Your selection of clothing each day—your weekend recreation—your garden chores—all take planning. You are scarcely conscious of the mental activity they require. The more complex the job, the more planning necessary—conscious, deliberate planning. The health insurance agent has a complex job demanding careful planning if he or she is to succeed.

Decide what your objectives are—and never lose sight of them. Work for them. The very fact that you have clear-cut goals and that you keep them constantly in mind will help you along. Because it is in working toward your goals—in passing milestones along the way—that you will find true satisfaction. Therein lies the thrill of achievement!

Planning is a daily job—only a few minutes but nevertheless daily. Your resolution to improve your effectiveness by more intelligent activity must be made today, tomorrow, and the next day. If you ignore planning for even one day, you break the habit chain. You allow a bad habit to knock out a good habit. Eventually, you lose sight of your objectives. And you are then faced with the difficult job of starting all over again.

But if you keep at your daily planning, you will find yourself in a position of the athlete whose bad habits were pointed out and corrected by the coach. You will awake one morning to find that the correct way is the easiest way after all. You will have formed the habit of doing every job right. From that day on you will not have to resolve firmly to perform the acts demanded by success. You will have acquired the habit of doing them naturally. You will enjoy doing them because you are headed in the right direction.

FIGURE 13–6

FORM THE HABIT

- Form the study habit . . .
    - Form the habit of persistence . . .
        - Form the habit of punctuality . . .

- Form the habit of day in and day out prospecting.

- Form the habit of calling on preferred leads promptly . . .
    - Form the habit of reading trade papers . . .
        - Form the habit of working a full day every day.

- Form the habit of taking an active part in the work of your trade association . . .
    - Form the habit of positive thinking in every interview.

- Form the habit of perpetual enthusiasm for the services you render . . .
    - Form the habit of entering wholeheartedly into the work of your agency . . .
        - Form the habit of giving unstinted support to agency contests.

- Form the habit of helping the newer agents in your agency . . .

- Form the habit of making enough evening calls to capitalize on that part of your market . . .
    - Form the habit of diversifying your business . . .
        - Form the habit of getting at least three new leads from every call.

- Form the habit of contributing to the well-being of your community and church and other worthwhile activities in your city.

You will be on your way to the goals you seek for your family and yourself.

One of the major advantages of this business is being your own boss. If you were paid by someone, you would report to work at an appointed hour each morning and find your work cut out for you. The price of being in your own business is the necessity of managing yourself. You buy independence and opportunity with good business management habits. You alone are responsible for your success or failure. So be a good boss to yourself. **Make yourself form success habits.**

Chapter 14
Regulation Affecting Selling Activity

LESSON TEXT—State Regulation...Canadian Regulation...Duties of Supervising Bodies... Revocation and Suspension of License...Unfair Competition and Practices...Discrimination... Appeal from License Revocation or Suspension ...Business Ethics

In both the United States and Canada, the insurance business is one of the most highly supervised businesses we have. A brief look at the development of U.S. and Canadian regulation of insurance will quickly indicate how thoroughly each country safeguards the insured's interest against the possibility of unfair contracts or irresponsible companies.

STATE REGULATION

The insurance industry in the United States has been and continues to be regulated largely by the states themselves. This concept was firmly established in 1868 when the historical case of *Paul v. Virginia* was settled by the U.S. Supreme Court. In its decision the Court recognized as necessary and proper the broad pattern of state regulation of the insurance business which had developed.

This approval continued up to 1944 when the same court was faced with a judgment concerning the adequacy of state supervision. In an opinion delivered in the landmark case of *U.S. v. Southeastern Underwriters Association*, it pointed out that the insurance business was subject to a series of federal acts—in many cases in direct conflict with existing state laws—and that it was also subject to judicial decisions under the "commerce clause" of the Constitution.

To resolve the turmoil created by this decision, Congress enacted Public Law 15 (McCarran-Ferguson Act) in 1945. This made it clear that continued regulation of insurance by the states *was* in the public's interest. However, it also made it possible for federal antitrust laws to be applied "to the extent that such business (insurance) is not regulated by state law." This legislation led each state to revise its insurance laws to conform with its requirements.

The threat of federal intervention again arose when the Federal Trade Commission (FTC) sought to impose its control over the advertising and sales literature issued in the health insurance field. However, in 1958, the Supreme Court held that the McCarran-Ferguson Act denied such supervision to this agency. In recent years, further attempts have been made by the FTC to force further federal control, but have not succeeded. So—for the moment at least—the insurance business in the U.S. continues to be regulated by the insurance departments of the various states.

CANADIAN REGULATION

In Canada, long and involved constitutional conflicts have also occurred between federal and provincial governments. Over the years, a dual control has evolved under which the federal government is largely responsible for the solvency of Canadian, British and foreign companies licensed or registered by it. The sphere of the provincial superintendents of insurance extends to the supervision of insurers licensed by them, whether or not they hold federal certificates of registry. They also supervise companies operating under provincial charters exclusively.

The Province of Quebec is the only exception to this pattern of dual control. Under the Canadian Constitution, this province is guaranteed the right to make its own laws, which it does.

DUTIES OF SUPERVISING BODIES

Since the regulatory job performed in both Canada and the United States by all supervising bodies leads to the same end results, we can see that the public is protected against insurance irregularities under either system. Because supervision in the U.S. is still concentrated in the hands of the state insurance departments, perhaps it is easier to observe.

Each state's insurance regulatory body is headed by an insurance official who, with staff members, has jurisdiction over all insurance affairs conducted within that state. This includes all forms of insurance—life, health, casualty, fire, etc. It also includes all transactions carried on by a company organized under the laws of the state, regardless of whether its home office is in

that state (domestic company), a company organized inside the United States but *outside the state (foreign company)*, or a company organized *outside the country (alien company)*. Foreign and alien companies must be authorized to operate in the state. Nonauthorized companies are not duly licensed to transact insurance business in the state.

The functions performed by each insurance department are many and varied. The major ones are:

1. Licensing and supervision of new insurance companies formed within the state;
2. Requiring all companies operating in the state to file a detailed financial statement annually;
3. Examining in detail company books and records, at intervals;
4. Fixing the amount of reserves required under various types of contracts;
5. Fixing standards for evaluating securities and limiting the kind of investments that companies can make;
6. Controlling the kinds of contracts which may be sold. This is done by requiring that no policy can be sold without the approval of the insurance department. Some states go further and give the insurance commissioner, superintendent or director the power to disapprove policies if rates are not in keeping with benefits;
7. Making recommendations to the legislature for improving the state's supervision;
8. Investigating complaints of insureds; and
9. Licensing of representatives (agents, solicitors and brokers).

The licensing of representatives, while listed last, is far from the least important one performed by the insurance department. The public deals with insurance companies primarily through these representatives. Therefore, it is essential that they be qualified to properly carry out their duties.

REVOCATION AND SUSPENSION OF LICENSE

In addition to having the power to issue licenses, the insurance department also has the authority to revoke them for certain causes. Or it may refuse to renew the license of anyone whose conduct it doesn't approve, or who flouts the law. It may suspend an insurance agent's license, or impose penalties and fines for certain infractions of the state insurance laws.

The causes for revocation, suspension or refusal to renew the license of an insurance representative are specific in some instances and broad in others. If investigation discloses any of the following acts by the individual, the insurance department may generally revoke, suspend or refuse to renew a license, after ten days' notice to the licensee and the company or companies represented:

1. Misrepresentation
2. Illegal withholding of premiums
3. Twisting
4. Violating certain state laws
5. Not serving public's or company's interest
6. Rebating, where illegal
7. Defamation of company
8. Unfair competition and practices
9. Discrimination

You should be keenly aware of what each of these violations involves so as to avoid any possibility that you may inadvertently commit one.

Misrepresentation

Misrepresentation is defined by a typical insurance department's regulations as:

". . . the making, issuing, circulation, or causing to be issued, or circulated, any estimate, illustration, circular, or statement of any kind which does not represent the correct policy terms, dividends or share of surplus to be received thereon, or the use of a name or title for any policy or class of policies which does not in fact reflect the true nature thereof."

These regulations go on to state that any of the acts included in the definition of misrepresentation are deemed criminal acts and classed as misdemeanors. Conviction of such violations is punishable by fine of up to stated maximum amounts or imprisonment of not less than 30 days nor more than six months. A convicted violator may be both fined and imprisoned.

Illegal Withholding of Premiums

An agent must be extremely careful in handling any premium monies collected. Actions in this regard are closely supervised by the insurance department. Generally, an agent cannot commingle premiums with personal funds. He or she may even be required to keep them in a separate bank account. Such an account must clearly indicate on the signature card that the agent is merely the trustee of the funds deposited.

Some states do permit the agent to deposit collections in his or her own bank account. However, if this is done, the agent must maintain a bookkeeping system which carefully separates personal funds and the premiums collected.

An agent who violates the fiduciary rules imposed by the insurance department may be accused of *embezzlement*. It may be charged that the agent has fraudulently converted to personal use, or taken, or secreted, withheld, appropriated, or otherwise used or applied funds received as an agent, contrary to the instructions or without the consent of the company or person for or on account of which the agent received these funds.

Twisting

Twisting is the reprehensible practice of inducing or tending to induce an insured through misrepresentations or incomplete comparison to lapse, forfeit, or surrender existing insurance in order to buy new insurance. In most insurance statutes, twisting is defined as:

"Any misrepresentation by an agent for the purpose of inducing or tending to induce a policyholder in any company to lapse, forfeit, or surrender insurance. . ."

In most states, twisting is a misdemeanor and anyone convicted of twisting is usually subject to the same penalties that apply to misrepresentation.

Violating Any State Law

Anyone who is convicted of violating a state law ceases to have the type of integrity and character which insurance department officials desire. Therefore, such a person usually will have his or her license to act as an agent, solicitor or broker revoked or suspended as soon as the state insurance official becomes aware of the violation of state law.

Not Serving Public's or Company's Interest

A licensed representative may not break any laws, yet his or her conduct may be grounds for losing a license. If upon review, the insurance official deems the representative's behavior detrimental to the public or the company, it may revoke, suspend or refuse to renew a license.

Rebating

To avoid unfair competition among agents or companies, most states prohibit *rebating*. Where rebating is permitted, strict rules must be followed to avoid illegal behavior coincident to rebating.

Rebating is typically defined as follows:

"Unless specified in the insurance policy, no agent shall offer, promise, allow, give, set off, or pay—directly or indirectly—any rebate or part of
(1) premiums payable on a policy;
(2) agent's commissions; and
(3) earnings, profits, dividends, or other benefits founded, arising, accruing or to accrue on or from any insurance policy.
"An agent is also prohibited from offering, promising, allowing, or giving—
(1) any special advantage in date of policy or age of issue;
(2) any paid employment or contract for services of any kind; and
(3) any valuable consideration or inducement, to or for insurance on any risk, unless specified in the policy. Likewise, an agent is prohibited from offering, promising, giving, optioning, selling or purchasing any stocks, bonds, securities, property or any other thing of value as an inducement or in connection with insurance unless so specified in the policy."

Violation of any of the acts of rebating is

deemed a misdemeanor. Conviction usually carries a fine or imprisonment, or both.

Some states hold that if an agent advances a premium for an insured, he or she may be suspected of rebating. Offering of credit is prohibited except that the taking of a bona fide obligation with legal interest is permitted. Nor can the agent accept merchandise in payment of a premium.

Defamation of Company

Maligning a company's reputation in an effort to sell a policy in your own in always poor business. It's also against the law and can lead to loss of license as well as other penalties. One state has this to say on the subject:

"It is illegal for any person to make, use, publish, print, distribute or circulate, verbally or otherwise, any statement, pamphlet, circular, article, literature, comparison, or rating of companies containing any false statement, criticism, misleading or incomplete statement, or comparison which tends to injure any insurance company in its reputation or business. Likewise, it is illegal for a person to aid, abet, or encourage any of these acts."

UNFAIR COMPETITION AND PRACTICES

Unfair competition and practices are forbidden in all states. Many states have specific laws which set out those deeds (some of which already have been described) which are considered unethical for persons in the insurance business. Many of these statutes are applicable to the companies as well as the agents. However, the following acts of insurance agents are deemed to be unfair competition and practices:

1. Twisting
2. Defamation of any person in the conduct of insurance business
3. Defamation of the financial condition of a company designed to insure any person engaged in the insurance business
4. Committing any act toward a monopoly of insurance business
5. Rebating

The state insurance official is usually given the authority to order any agent to cease and desist any act or practice in the conduct of business which is not to the best interest of the public. The official may, after a hearing, issue a cease and desist order against such an agent. Violation of the official's order subjects the violator to severe penalties.

DISCRIMINATION

Companies cannot discriminate when policies are being issued to individuals of the same class. If any company or agent is found guilty of such an act, it is punishable by law.

APPEAL FROM LICENSE REVOCATION OR SUSPENSION

Within a stipulated time (usually 30 days), a representative whose license has been revoked or suspended, or whose license the insurance official refuses to renew, may apply for a judicial review of the case. If this is done, the insurance department must show cause why the agent should not be reinstated or receive a license. Before this is done, however, the agent must usually post a satisfactory cost bond. If so, the person may be permitted to continue as an insurance agent until a court decides the case.

BUSINESS ETHICS

An old axiom has it that laws are made to keep the few dishonest people honest. This is particularly true of insurance laws. The vast majority of insurance people are honest. They require no curbs or restrictions to keep them so. Just look around your underwriters association. The majority of men and women who are members are usually high principled people, who would never think of being unethical. In fact, they often go out of their way to assist the insurance department and the insurance officials of their respec-

tive states to enforce the laws. They fully realize that this results in more satisfactory conditions for them as well as making the insurance business better serve the public.

An agent has many duties and responsibilities to his or her company. Among these are:

1. To protect the company's interest in every way
2. To account for all monies received
3. To disclose all facts of which he or she may become aware which have a bearing on the risk or risks involved in any applications submitted
4. To be loyal and to act in good faith
5. To obey instructions
6. To be always alert to duties and never negligent in carrying them out

Agents must recognize the importance of continuing education. Every agent has an obligation to himself or herself, the company, and clients to be as well informed about the contracts as possible. An agent should thoroughly know the business. Constant study to learn and to become familiar with new developments makes it possible to offer new and continuing services to those served.

AGENT GUIDELINES

The professional pledge for a Chartered Life Underwriter (CLU) clearly expresses the standard by which all agents should conduct their business affairs:

"In all my professional relationships, I pledge myself to the following rule of ethical conduct: I shall, in the light of all conditions surrounding those I serve, which I shall make every conscientious effort to ascertain and understand, render that service which, in the same circumstances, I would apply to myself."

Know what your clients want. Recommend only what best fits their needs. Make sure that they understand what they have purchased. And keep in touch with them!

Glossary

The following health insurance terms are defined according to common usage.

Accident—An unintended, unforeseen and unexpected event which causes injury.

Accidental Bodily Injury—Bodily injury resulting from an accident.

Accidental Death Benefit—A payment for loss of life due to an accident which was the direct cause of death.

Accidental Dismemberment—Often defined as "the severance of limbs at or above the wrist or ankle joints, or the entire irrevocable loss of sight." Loss of use, in itself, usually is not considered to be dismemberment.

Accidental Means—An unforeseen, unexpected, unintended cause of an accident.

Accumulation Clause—Provides for a slight increase in policy benefits when policy premiums have been paid. it rewards persistency.

Acquisition Cost—The immediate cost of putting a policy on the books: clerical costs, commissions, medical and inspection fees, etc.

Additional Provisions—Provisions in addition to the insuring and benefit provisions, and to the uniform provisions, which define and limit the coverage. Also called *General Provisions*.

Adjustable Premium—The right of the company to modify premium payments under certain specified conditions.

Administrative Services Only (ASO) Plan—An arrangement under which an insurance carrier or an independent organization will, for a fee, handle the administration of claims, benefits and other administrative functions for a self-insured group.

Adverse Selection—The tendency of persons with poorer than average health expectations to apply for, or continue, insurance more so than do persons with average or better than average health expectations.

Age Limits—Minimum or maximum age limits for the insuring of new applicants or for the renewal of policies.

Agent—An insurance company representative who solicits, negotiates or effects contracts of insurance and services insureds for the company.

Aggregate Amount—The maximum dollar amount that can be collected under any policy, for any disability or period of disability.

Aggregate Limit Clause—Under this clause (used in non-cancelable policies), the company promises to pay up to a total of 15 months, two years, five years or even ten years for an aggregate of all disabilities. When the total payments for all the insured's disability reach the aggregate limit, the policy expires.

Alien Company—A company incorporated outside the United States.

Allocated Benefits—Payments (in some policies) for specified services which are limited to maximum specified amounts.

Application—A signed form on which an individual states facts required by the company and on the basis of the company decides whether or not to issue a policy. The application becomes part of the policy.

Assignment—The signed transfer of the benefits of a policy by an insured jointly under a group policy.

Association Group—A number of trade or professional association members insured jointly under one master health insurance contract.

Authorized Company—A company duly authorized by the insurance department to operate in the state.

Average Earnings Clause—A provision in the policy which permits the company to reduce the monthly income disability benefits payable if the total income benefits under all coverages owned by the insured exceed either current monthly earnings or average monthly earnings during the two-year period immediately preceding the disability. Found only in Guaranteed Renewable and Noncancelable Policies.

Beneficiary—Person(s) designated to receive the accidental death benefit.

Benefit Period—The maximum length of time which benefits will be paid for any one accident, illness or hospital stay.

Benefits—A benefit may be either money or a right of the insured upon the happening of the conditions set out in the policy. Not synonymous with "indemnity." See *Indemnity*.

Binding Receipt—A receipt given by a company upon an applicant's first premium payment. The policy, if approved, becomes effective from the date of receipt.

Blanket Accident Medical Expense—Entitles the insured who suffered a bodily injury to collect up to a maximum established in the policy for all hospital and medical expense incurred, without any limitations on individual types of medical expenses. Hospital confinement is not required.

Blanket Policy—Covers a number of individuals who are exposed to the same hazards, such as members of an athletic team, company officials who are passengers in the same company plane, etc.

Blue Cross—An independent membership association providing protection against the costs of hospital care. Benefit payments are made directly to the hospital. Benefits vary among various Blue Cross associations.

Blue Shield—An independent membership association providing protection against the costs of surgery and other items of medical care. Benefit payments are made directly to the doctor.

Broad Form—Policies which offer broad protection with few limitations (as compared with limited form plans).

Broker—A licensed insurance representative who does not represent a specific company but places business among various companies. In law, a broker is usually regarded as a representative of the insured rather than of the company.

Business Health Insurance—Health coverage issued primarily to indemnify a business for the loss of services of a key person or a partner, or an active close-corporation stockholder; or to buy out the interest of a partner or stockholder in a close corporation, who becomes permanently disabled.

Business Overhead Insurance—A type of short-term disability insurance that reimburses the insured person for specified fixed, monthly expenses normal and customary in the operation of his or her business or office.

Cancelable Contract—A contract of health insurance that may be terminated by the insured or insurer at any time.

Capital Sum—The amount provided for the loss of two members or eyesight. Indemnities for loss of one member or the sight of one eye are usually percentages of the Capital Sum.

Catastrophe Insurance—See *Comprehensive Medical* and *Major Medical*

Certificate of Insurance—A document issued to persons insured under a group master policy and which outlines the coverage provided.

Claim—A request or demand on the insurer for payment of benefits under the policy.

Coinsurance (percentage participation)—A principle under which the company insures only part of the potential loss, the insured paying the other part. For instance, in a Major Medical policy, the company may agree to pay 75 percent of the insured's expenses, the insured to pay the other 25 percent.

Collectively Renewable Contract—Disability insurance policy which may be cancelled by the insurer by class in a certain state. The contract may not be cancelled on an individual basis.

Commercial Policy—A policy in which the company retains the right to cancel or refuse to renew the coverage.

Commissioner—The head of a state insurance department. The public officer charged with the supervision of the insurance business in the state and the administration of insurance laws. Called "Superintendent" in some states.

Comprehensive Medical Insurance—A policy designed to give the protection offered by both a basic and a Major Medical policy. It is characterized by a low deductible amount, coinsurance clause and high maximum benefits.

Compulsory Health Insurance—Plans of insurance, under the supervision of a state or federal government, providing protection for medical, hospital, surgical and disability benefits to all who qualify.

Concealment—Failure of the insured to disclose to the company a fact material to the acceptance of the risk at the time application is made.

Conditional Receipts—Receipts given to applicants when they pay a premium at the time they make application. Such receipts bind the insurance company if the risk is approved as applied for, subject to any other conditions stated on the receipt.

Conditionally Renewable Contract—A contract of health insurance that provides that the insured may renew the contract from period to period or continue the contract to a stated date or an advanced age, subject to the right of the insurer to decline renewal only under conditions defined in the contract.

Confining Sickness—Sickness which confines the insured to the home — which is usually defined to include hospital and sanatorium.

Consideration—One of the elements of a binding contract. Consideration is acceptance by the company of the payment of the premium and the statements made by the prospective insured in the application.

Consideration Clause—That part of an insurance contract that sets forth the amount of initial and renewal premiums and the frequency of future payments.

Contingent Beneficiary—Person or persons named to receive proceeds in case the original beneficiary is not alive. Also referred to as *Secondary Beneficiary.*

Continuous Disability—Most contracts require that the insured's disability be continuous. However, a trial effort to return to work, or work done as medical therapy, usually is not construed as breaking the continuity of disability.

Contributory Plan—A group insurance plan issued to an employer under which both the employer and employees contribute to the cost of the plan. Seventy-five percent of the eligible employees must be insured. (Also see *Noncontributory.*)

Conversion Privilege—The right granted the insured to change coverage from a group policy to an individual policy within a specified period regardless of whether the insured is in good health at that time.

Coordination of Benefits (COB) Provision—This is the provision designed to prevent duplication of group health insurance benefits. It limits benefits from multiple group health insurance policies in a particular case to 100% of the expenses covered and designates the order in which the additional carriers are to pay benefits.

Corridor Deductible—In superimposed Major Medical plans, a deductible amount between the benefits paid by the basic plan and the beginning of the Major Medical benefits.

Cost of Living Adjustment—A rider on a disability insurance policy which provides for increases in benefits if the disability lasts longer than the period stated in the policy (usually 1–2 years). The amount by which the benefit increases is stated in the policy, as a specific percentage or in relation to some stated standard measure.

Covered Expense—See *Eligible Expense*

Cut-Off Provision—Regulates the period during which benefits are payable under Major Medical and Comprehensive Medical Expense insurance.

Deductible—An amount of expense or loss to be paid by the insured before the policy starts paying benefits.

Diagnosis-Related Groupings (DRGs)—A system that reimburses health-care providers fixed amounts for all care given in connection with standard diagnostic categories.

Disability—A physical or mental inability to work.

Disability Insurance—A form of health insurance that provides periodic payments when the insured is unable to work as a result of illness, disease or injury.

Dismemberment—See *Accidental Dismemberment, Double Dismemberment* and *Single Dismemberment*

Dividend—An insured's share in the divisible surplus of a company issuing insurance on a participating basis.

Domestic Company—A company is a domestic company in the state in which it is incorporated or chartered.

Double Dismemberment—Loss of any two members, sight of both eyes or one member and sight of one eye.

Double Indemnity—A provision under which the principal sum in an accident policy (and sometimes the other indemnities) is doubled when accident is due to certain causes.

Dread Disease Insurance—A limited policy providing benefits, subject to a maximum amount, for expenses incurred for the treatment of specific illnesses or diseases (such as cancer).

Duplicate Coverage—A term applied to benefits other than the loss of time where the insured is covered by several policies with one or more companies providing the same type of benefits, and often resulting in overinsurance.

Earned Income—Gross salary, wages, commissions, fees, etc., derived from active employment. This does not include unearned income, such as income from investments, rents, annuities, insurance policies, etc.

Effective Date—The date a policy becomes effective. If the hour is not specified, the effective time is 12:01 A.M. on the appropriate date.

Elective Indemnities—If the insured suffers an accidental injury resulting in a sprain, dislocation, fracture or amputation of fingers or toes, the insured may elect to receive a lump sum, in accordance with the policy schedule, in place of any regular income payments provided.

Eligible Expense—Expenses that are permitted to be included under the broad terms of Major Medical or Comprehensive Medical Expense insurance. Also called *Covered Expense*.

Eligibility Date—The date on which an individual member of a specified group becomes eligible to apply for insurance under a group insurance plan.

Eligibility Period—A specified length of time, frequently 31 days, following the eligibility date during which an individual member of a particular group will remain eligible to apply for insurance under a group insurance policy without evidence of insurability.

Elimination Period—See *Waiting Period*

Emergency Accident Benefit—A hospital benefit payable for outpatient emergency treatment of an injury.

Endorsement—A provision added to a policy, usually by being written on the printed policy page. An endorsement may also be in the form of a rider. No endorsement is valid unless signed by an executive officer of the company and attached to and made a part of the policy.

Enrollment Card—A form to be signed by an employee as notice of his or her desire to participate in a group insurance plan.

Evidence of Insurability—Any statement or proof of a person's physical condition, occupation, etc., affecting the acceptance for insurance.

Excepted Period—See *Waiting Period*

Exceptions—Same as *Exclusions*.

Exclusions—Certain causes and conditions, listed in the policy, which are not covered.

Experience Rating—A review of the previous year's claims experience for a group health insurance contract by the in-

surer in order to establish premiums for the next period or year.

Experience Refund—A provision in most group policies for the return of premium money to the policyowner because of lower than anticipated claims experience.

Facility of Payment—A "facility of payment" clause, permitted under Uniform Provision 9, allows the company to pay up to $1,000 of benefits or proceeds to any relative appearing entitled to it if there is no beneficiary or if the insured or beneficiary is a minor or legally incompetent.

Family Policy—A health insurance policy covering eligible members of one family.

Flat Deductible—An amount of covered expenses payable by the insured before Major Medical benefits are payable.

Foreign Company—A company is a foreign company in any state other than the one in which it is incorporated or chartered.

Franchise—See *Wholesale*

Fraternal Insurance—A cooperative type of insurance provided by the fraternal benefit societies for their members.

General Provisions—See *Additional Provisions*

Grace Period—A period of time after the due date of a premium during which the policy will remain in force without penalty.

Group Insurance—A policy protecting a group of persons, usually employees of a firm.

Guaranteed Continuable—Same as *Guaranteed Renewable*.

Guaranteed Insurability Rider—An optional benefit attached to a disability insurance policy which allows the insured to buy additional amounts of monthly benefits without evidence of insurability.

Guaranteed Renewable Contract—Contracts that the insured has the right to continue in force by the timely payment of premiums for a substantial period of time during which period the insurer has no right to make unilaterally any change in any provision of the contract while the contract is in force, other than a change in premium rate for classes of insureds.

Health Insurance—Insurance against loss through sickness or accidental bodily injury.

Health Maintenance Organization (HMO)—A health-care center which stresses preventive health care, early diagnosis, and treatment on an outpatient basis. Persons generally enroll voluntarily in an HMO by paying a fixed fee periodically.

Hospice—A health-care facility that provides medical care and support services to terminally ill people.

Hospital Benefits—Benefits payable for charges incurred while the insured is confined to, or treated in, a hospital, as defined in the policy.

Hospital Expense Insurance—Benefits subject to a specified daily maximum for a specified period of time while the insured is confined to a hospital, plus a limited allowance up to a specified amount for miscellaneous hospital expenses such as operating room, anesthesia, laboratory fees, etc.

Hospital Indemnity—A form of health insurance that provides a stipulated daily, weekly or monthly indemnity benefit during an insured's hospital confinement. The indemnity is payable on an unallocated basis without regard to the actual hospital expense.

Hospitalization Insurance—Same as *Hospital Expense* insurance.

Identification Clause—If the insured is physically unable to communicate with his or her relatives and friends, the company will notify them and defray necessary expenses (up to a specified amount) to put him or her in their care.

Illegal Holding of Premiums—State laws specify how premium monies collected by an agent are to be handled. Unless these laws are followed, the agent may expose himself or herself to being accused of embezzlement or fraudulently converting funds to personal use.

Impaired Risk—Insured who has a health condition, or is exposed to an occupational hazard, which makes the insured substandard.

Income Replacement Contract—A disability policy that relates benefits to the amount of earnings loss an insured incurs as the result of disability. Benefits are not related to the insured's occupation.

Incontestable Clause—A clause which makes the policy indisputable regarding the statements made by the insured in the application after a specified period of time has elapsed (usually two years). It differs from the provision for Time Limit on Certain Defenses which makes the policy contestable at any time for fraudulent misstatements.

Incubation Period—See *Probationary Period*

Indemnity—The payment of a benefit for a loss insured under a policy. The insured is indemnified for a specific loss, or part thereof.

Individual Insurance—Policies which provide protection to the insured. (As distinct from Group and Blanket Insurance.) Sometimes called *Personal Insurance*.

Industrial Policy—Provides modest benefits and relatively short benefit periods. Premiums are collected on a weekly or monthly basis by an agent who calls at the homes of insureds.

Inpatient—A person who is admitted to a hospital as a resident case (i.e., as a bed patient).

Inside Limits—The upper benefit limits that cannot be exceeded if the charges are to be considered "customary and reasonable."

Insurable Interest—Loss which would be sustained on death or disability of another sufficient to warrant compensation.

Insurability—All conditions pertaining to an individual which affect his or her health, susceptibility to injury, as well as expectancy of life, and go into the makeup of that insurance characteristic called insurability.

Insurance History—A record of personal insurance in force, as well as the story of a person's experience with previous insurers.

Insured—The individual who is covered by the contract of insurance.

Insuring Clause—A clause which defines and describes the scope of the coverage provided as well as the limits of indemnification.

Integrated Deductible—In superimposed Major Medical plans, a deductible amount between the benefits paid by the basic plan and those paid by Major Medical. All or part of the integrated deductible may be absorbed by the basic plan.

Intentional Injury—An injury resulting from an act, the doer of which intended to inflict injury. Self-inflicted injuries are not covered by an Accident policy because they are not an accident.

Key-Executive or Key-Employee Insurance—An individual policy (or group insurance) designed to protect an essential employee(s) of a firm against the loss of income resulting from disability. If desired, it may be written for the benefit of the employer, who usually continues to pay the salary during periods of disability.

Lapse—Termination of a policy upon the insured's failure to pay the premium within the grace period.

Legal Reserve—The minimum reserve which a company must keep to meet future claims and obligations as the reserve is calculated under the state insurance code.

Level Premium—A premium which remains unchanged throughout the life of a policy.

Lifetime Disability Benefit—A payment to help replace income lost by an insured for as long as he or she is totally disabled.

Limited Policies—Those which restrict benefits to specified accidents or diseases, such as Travel Policies, Dread Disease Policies, Ticket Policies, etc.

Loss-of-Income Benefits—Same as *Loss-of-Time* benefits. Benefits paid because the insured is disabled and unable to work.

Major Medical Expense Insurance—Policies designed to help offset the heavy medical expenses resulting from catastrophic or prolonged illnesses or injuries. Generally, they provide benefit payments of 75 percent–80 percent of all types of medical expenses above a certain amount first paid by the insured, and up to the maximum limit of liability and within the time period provided by the policy.

Malingering—Feigning a disability in order to collect insurance benefits.

Master Contract—An insurance contract, as between an employer and an insurance company, covering employees or some other group.

Medicaid—A program to provide medical care for the needy under joint federal-state participation.

Medical Attendance—Treatment or care by a legally qualified physician.

Medical Expense Insurance—Pays benefits for nonsurgical doctors' fees commonly rendered in a hospital. Sometimes payable for home and office calls as well.

Medical Information Bureau (MIB)—A clearinghouse which maintains records received from and releases relevant data to participating insurance companies.

Medicare—A federally sponsored program of health insurance for persons 65 years of age and over. It is administered under provisions of the Social Security Act.

Minimum Premium Plan—An arrangement under which an insurance carrier will handle, for a fee, administration of all claims and insure against large claims for a self-insured group.

Miscellaneous Expenses—Hospital charges other than room and board, i.e., X-rays, drugs, laboratory fees, etc. (in connection with hospital insurance).

Misrepresentation—The act of making, issuing, circulating or causing to be issued or circulated, an estimate, illustration, circular or statement of any kind which does not represent the correct policy terms, dividends or share of surplus, or the name or title for any policy or class of policies, which does not in fact reflect the true nature thereof.

Moral Hazards—Habits, morals or financial practices of an insured which increase the possibility or extent of a loss.

Morbidity Table—Shows the incidence and extent of disability which may be expected from a given large group of persons. This table is used in the computation of rates. It is similar to the use of a mortality table in connection with life insurance.

Multiple Benefits—Under certain conditions, benefits may be doubled, tripled or even quadrupled.

Multiple Employer Group—A plan where the employees of two or more employers not financially related are covered under one master insurance policy.

Mutual Company—One which is owned and controlled by the insureds, and is directly managed by a board of trustees or directors chosen by the insureds.

National Association of Insurance Commissioners (NAIC)—An association of state insurance commissioners active in the discussion of insurance regulatory problems and in the formation and recommendation of model legislation and regulations.

Newspaper Policies—Limited accident policies, usually purchased through a newspaper as a part of a subscription.

Noncancelable and Guaranteed Renewable Contract—A contract which the insured has the right to continue in force by the timely payment of premiums set forth in the contract for a substantial period of time, during which period the insurer has no right to make unilaterally any change in any provision of the contract while the contract is in force.

Nonconfining Sickness—That which prevents the insured from working, but does not confine the insured to a home, hospital or a sanitorium.

Noncontributory—A term applied to employee benefit plans under which the employer bears the full cost of the benefits for the employees. One hundred percent of the eligible employees must be insured.

Nondisabling Injury—One which requires medical care but does not result in a loss of time from work.

Nonduplication Provision—Stipulates that insured shall be ineligible to collect for charges under a group plan if the charges are reimbursed under his or her spouse's group plan.

Nonoccupational Policy—A plan of insurance which insures a person against off-the-job accidents or sicknesses.

Nonparticipating—A plan of insurance when the insured is not entitled to share the divisible surplus of the company.

Nonprorating Policy—One in which the benefits stipulated in the policy will be paid whether or not the insured changes occupations.

Nursing Expense Provision—Provides per diem benefits to the insured if nursing care is required. The nurse must be a private-duty registered nurse (RN).

Nursing Home Provision—Provides benefits if the insured is confined to a nursing home when intensive care in a hospital is no longer needed.

Occupational Hazard—A danger inherent in the insured's line of work.

Occupational Policy—A plan of insurance which insures a person against both off-the-job and on-the-job accidents or sicknesses.

Optional Benefit—An additional benefit offered by the company which may be included in a policy at the applicant's request, usually for an additional premium.

Optionally Renewable Contract—A contract of health insurance in which the insurer reserves the right to terminate the coverage at any anniversary, or, in some cases, at any premium-due date, but does not have the right to terminate coverage between such dates.

Outpatient—One who receives care at a clinic or hospital without being confined to that institution as a resident.

Overhead Insurance—See *Business Overhead Insurance*

Overinsurance—An excessive amount of insurance carried by an insured which might tempt the individual to prolong the period of disability, remain in a hospital longer than necessary, etc.

Partial Disability—An illness or injury that prevents an insured from performing one or more, but not all, occupational duties.

Participating—A plan of insurance under which the insured receives shares of the divisible surplus of the company. Such shares are commonly called "dividends."

Participation Limit—The total amount of disability insurance that can be written by all carriers on one given earned income.

Permanent Disability—A disability that will last forever, or for an indefinite and undetermined period of time.

Personal Insurance—Same as *Individual Insurance*.

Physical Hazard—That type of hazard which arises from the physical characteristics of an individual (e.g., impediments of hearing or sight). It may exist because of a current condition, past medical history or physical condition present at birth.

Policy—That instrument, including endorsements and attached papers, constituting the entire contract of insurance.

Policy Fee—A small flat sum charged by some companies in addition to the premium.

Policy Term—The term of policy, usually the period for which the premium is paid.

Preexisting Condition—An injury occurring, sickness contracted or physical condition which existed prior to the issuance of a health policy.

Preferred Provider Organization (PPO)—An arrangement whereby a third-party payor contracts with a group of medical-care providers who furnish services at lower than usual fees in return for prompt payment and a certain volume of patients.

Premium—The periodic payment required to keep a policy in force.

Prepaid Group Practice Plan—A plan under which specified health-care services are rendered by participating physicians to an enrolled group of persons with a fixed periodic payment in advance made by or on behalf of each person or family. If a health insurance carrier is involved, it is a contract to pay in advance for the full range of health services to which the insureds are entitled under terms of the health insurance contract. Such a plan is one form of Health Maintenance Organization (HMO).

Presumptive Disability—Specific physical condition(s) for which total disability is presumed (such as loss of sight or hearing).

Principal Sum—The amount payable for accidental loss of life.

Probationary Period—A specified number of days after the date of the issuance of the policy, during which coverage is not afforded for sickness. Sickness protection does not become effective until after the end of such probationary period. Also called *Incubation Period*.

Professional Standards Review Organization (PSRO)—An organization in which physicians assume responsibility for reviewing the propriety and quality of health-care services provided under Medicare and Medicaid.

Prorating—The reduction in the amount of benefits payable because the insured has changed to a more hazardous occupation since the issuance of the policy, or because benefits payable by all the insurance exceed current or average earnings over the preceding two years.

Qualified Impairment Insurance—Substandard or special class insurance that restricts benefits for the insured's particular condition.

Quarantine Indemnity—A benefit payable while the insured is involuntarily quarantined because of exposure to a contagious disease.

Reasonable and Customary Charge—A charge for a health-care service that is consistent with the going rate or charge in a given geographical area for an identical or other similar service.

Rebating—Returning part of the commission or giving anything of value to the insured as an inducement for buying the policy. Rebating is cause for license revocation in most states and illegal in others. In some states, rebating is an offense by both agent and person receiving the rebate. Where rebating is permitted, specific rules must be followed; otherwise the activity is illegal.

Recurring Disability Clause—A provision that specifies a period of time during which the recurrence of a condition is considered a continuation of a prior period of disability or hospital confinement, thereby eliminating a new deductible period. If the insured resumes his or her occupation for a period of time, a new indemnity limit is created.

Reduction of Benefits—Automatic reduction in coverage under certain specified conditions, e.g., the monthly benefits may be reduced by 50 percent while the insured ceases to be fully and gainfully employed away from home, or after the insured has reached age 60, 65, etc.

Rehabilitation Benefit—A provision that continues benefits or other financial assistance while a totally disabled insured is retrained or attempts to resume productive employment.

Reinstatement—Putting a lapsed policy back in force by producing satisfactory evidence of insurability and past-due premiums required.

Reinsurance—The acceptance by one or more insurers, called reinsurers, of a portion of the risk underwritten by another insurer who has contracted for the entire coverage.

Relation of Earnings to Insurance—If at the time disability commences the total benefits payable under all coverages owned by the insured exceed the average earnings of the insured over the preceding two years, the benefits will be reduced pro rata to such amount.

Renewal—Continuance of coverage under a policy beyond its original term.

Replacement—The act of replacing one policy with another. May be handled legally by an agent only under certain conditions and providing a state's requirements are met in this regard.

Representation—Statements made by an applicant on the application that he or she represents as being substantially true to the best of his or her knowledge and belief, but which are not warranted as exact in every detail.

Reserve—A fund held by the company to help fulfill future claims.

Residual Disability Benefits—Benefits are payable in proportion to a partial loss of earnings as a result of disability, as opposed to the insured receiving benefits based on a full loss of income due to the inability to work full time.

Riders—Strictly speaking, a rider adds something to the policy. However, it is loosely used to refer to any supplemental agreement attached to and made a part of the policy, whether the conditions of the policy are expanded, and additional coverages added, or a coverage or condition is waived.

Risk—Technically, the degree or percentage of chance that a given contingency will occur—"the odds." The term is loosely used (a) to designate an insured; (b) to designate a peril insured against.

Schedule—A list of specified amounts payable, usually for surgical operations, dismemberment, fractures, etc.

Schedule Type Policy—Includes a listing and a complete text of the provisions of each of several benefits, most of which are optional, and some of which may be omitted at the election of the applicant.

Self-Insurance—A program of providing group health-care benefits financed solely by a company or other organization instead of buying coverage from commercial carriers.

Service Insurance—A type of insurance or prepayment plan that pays benefits in medical or hospital services rather than in dollars. Best known examples of such coverage are the Blue plans.

Single Dismemberment—Loss of one hand, or one foot, or sight of one eye.

Social Security Freeze—A long-term disability policy provision which establishes that the offset from benefits paid by Social Security will not be changed, regardless of subsequent changes in the Social Security law.

Solicitor—One who acts for an agent in soliciting risks, but who has no authority to bind those risks. May seek prospects and collect premiums on behalf of the agent.

Sound Health Clause—A clause sometimes included in a policy which states that the policy will not take effect on delivery unless the applicant is alive and in good health.

Special Class—An applicant who cannot qualify for a standard policy, but may secure one with a rider waiving the payment for a loss involving certain existing health impairments. The applicant may be required to pay a higher premium, or the policy may be issued with lesser benefits than those requested.

Standard Provisions—Forerunners of the Uniform Provisions. Still found in policies issued some years ago.

Standard Risk—A person who, according to a company's underwriting standards, is entitled to insurance protection without extra rating or special restrictions.

Starter Plan—Disability insurance which allows young professionals or specific students to purchase more disability benefits than their incomes would otherwise justify, in anticipation of substantial earnings increase.

Statutory Disability Insurance—Compulsory disability insurance sponsored by a state which provides specified benefits for nonoccupational disabilities. Presently, only a few states have such insurance programs.

Step-Rate Plan—A disability insurance premium structure that begins low and increases after the first few years.

Substandard—Below the standard (or "average"). Substandard risks in health insurance are usually underwritten by the use of waivers (See *Special Class*).

Supplemental Health Insurance—Policies generally issued to persons age 65 or older to supplement government-sponsored plans, such as Medicare.

Surgical Expense Insurance—A policy that provides benefits to pay for the cost of surgical operations.

Surgical Schedule—A list of cash allowances which are payable for various types of surgery, with the respective maximum amounts payable based upon the severity of the operations. The stipulated maximum usually covers all professional fees involved (e.g., surgeon, anesthesiologist).

Temporary License—Some states permit an agent to operate under a temporary license, usually for six months. After that time, compliance with the state's licensing is required.

Term Contract—A contract of health insurance that makes no provision for renewal. The policy terminates at the end of the policy term.

Term of Policy—The period for which the policy runs, which is usually the period for which a premium has been paid in advance. In some instances, it may be for a year, even though the premium is paid on a semi-annual or other basis.

Third-Party Administration (TPA)—Administration of a group insurance plan by someone other than the insurer or the policyholder.

Ticket Insurance—Accident-only protection which is issued in conjunction with a ticket for transportation on a common carrier.

Total Disability—Disability which prevents the insured from performing any duty of his or her usual occupation or from performing any occupation for remuneration. The actual definition in any case depends upon the wording in the policy.

Travel-Accident Policies—Policies limited to indemnities for accidents while traveling, usually by common carrier.

Twisting—Inducing an insured to drop an existing policy (especially one in another company) in order to take a similar policy from the agent doing the twisting. The act is usually defined in law as inducement "by misrepresentation." Twisting is cause for license revocation in most states and a legal offense in many.

Unallocated Benefit—A reimbursement provision, usually for miscellaneous hospital and medical expenses, which does not specify how much will be paid for each type of treatment, examination, dressing, or the like, but only sets a maximum which will be paid for all such treatment.

Unearned Income—Income generated generally by means other than as one's employment. It includes such things as dividends, interest, rents, etc., unless one's fulltime occupation is to generate this form of income.

Underwriter—The term as generally used applies to any of the following: (a) a company which receives the premiums and accepts responsibility for the fulfillment of the policy contract; (b) the company employee who decides whether or not the company should assume a particular risk, or (c) the agent who sells the policy.

Underwriting—The process by which an insurer determines whether or not, and on what basis, an application for insurance will be accepted.

Uniform Provisions—A set of provisions relating to the "operating conditions" of the policy. The model provisions were adopted by the National Association of Insurance Commissioners, and all states either require their use in every policy issued or authorize their use. The Uniform Provisions replaced the Older Standard Provisions.

Uninsurable Risk—One that is not acceptable for insurance due to an excessive or unacceptable risk.

Waiting Period—The duration of time between the beginning of an insured's disability and the commencement of the period for which benefits are payable. Also called "Elimination Period."

Waiver—An agreement which waives the liability of the company for a certain type (or types) of disabilities or injuries ordinarily covered in the policy.

Waiver of Premium—A provision included in some policies which exempt the insured from the payment of premiums after being disabled for a period of time (e.g., 90 days).

Warranties—Statements made on an application for insurance which are warranted to be true; that is, that they are exact in every detail as opposed to "representations" (See *Representation*). Statements on applications for health insurance are rarely warranties, unless there is fraud involved.

Wholesale (Franchise) Insurance—A system for covering a group of people (usually the employees of one employer or the members of a trade association) under uniform individual policies. Wholesale insurance is used when the number of people is too small for true group insurance.

Workers' Compensation—Benefits paid a worker for injury, disability or disease contracted in the course of employment. Benefits are conditions are set by law, although in most states, the insurance to provide the benefits may be purchased from regular insurance companies. Some few states have monopolistic state compensation funds.